W9-AHO-926

HABERMAS ON HISTORICAL MATERIALISM

*Studies in Phenomenology and
Existential Philosophy*

HABERMAS ON HISTORICAL MATERIALISM

TOM ROCKMORE

INDIANA UNIVERSITY PRESS

Bloomington and Indianapolis

Library of Congress Cataloging-in-Publication Data
Rockmore, Tom
Habermas on historical materialism.
(Studies in phenomenology and existential
philosophy)
Bibliography: p.
Includes index.
1. Habermas, Jürgen—Views on historical materialism.
2. Historical materialism—History—20th century.
I. Title.   II. Series.
B3258.H324R63   1989   335.4'119   88-45449
ISBN 0-253-32709-1
ISBN 0-253-20504-2 (pbk.)
1   2   3   4   5   93   92   91   90   89

CONTENTS

INTRODUCTION

This book concerns Habermas' reading of historical materialism, with special attention to the relation of theory and practice. His interest in Marx and Marxism, which is often mentioned, but little studied, remains one of the main themes of his entire corpus. As a result, there is an insufficient appreciation of Habermas' discussion of historical materialism, which is important in itself, for the comprehension of his theory of communicative action, and for the relation of his theory to Marxism.

It is easy to show that Habermas' concern with historical materialism is central to his position. His interest in Marx and Marxism arises early in his writings and continues in various forms until the present, that is, over a period of some thirty years, in a wide variety of texts. It is possible to argue that his thought in part takes form as a result of his reading and critique of historical materialism. Since Habermas' position has already been discussed in a large and rapidly increasing literature, it is at least noteworthy that this facet of his position has so far attracted little attention.[1]

Obviously, the conclusion that Habermas offers a significant contribution to Marxism through his reading of historical materialism cannot be justified on an a priori basis; it can only be justified in the course of the discussion that follows. We can, however, note at present some of the difficulties which arise for the comprehension of his own position and for its relation to Marx and Marxism when the role of historical materialism in the evolution of his position is minimized or otherwise misunderstood. These include the uncritical acceptance as valid of his own reading of Marxism,[2] although his view of its nature has changed greatly over time and is merely one of the many available interpretations of Marx, Marxism, and critical theory;[3] the equally uncritical conflation of his view on the one hand and Marx and Marxism on the other,[4] despite the fact that at present he rejects in principle even the potential viability of historical materialism; and the inability to identify the nature and limits of his own contribution to historical materialism.

An appreciation of his comprehension of historical materialism is further important, indeed arguably indispensable, for an understanding of his own theory of communicative action. It is fair to say that the widespread failure to appreciate the significance of historical materialism for the constitution of his theory has impeded, and continues to impede, the comprehension of Habermas' position. The theory of communicative action, which has been nascent in his writings ever since his early book on the logic of social theory,[5] has recently assumed more definite, but—according to its author—still not definitive form in a massive treatise.[6] Now, almost since the beginning of his discussion of Marx and Marxism, Habermas was engaged in formulating a series of criticisms which culminated in the proposed rejection of historical materialism as a theory in the latter treatise. Significantly, he rejected the theory, but he did not reject its supposedly intrinsic intention which, he maintained, can be better reached through the medium of a paradigm change to his own position.[7]

Accordingly, the significance of Marx and Marxism for Habermas' thought is not only, as has been asserted, that the latter is one of the theories in the background of his own.[8] With respect to his own position, the importance of his reading of historical materialism is that he specifically intends his own theory to overcome difficulties he claims to diagnose in Marx and Marxism. It follows that, independently of whether or not one believes that Habermas throws light on historical materialism, his own theory in inseparable from his reading of that view, and can fairly be evaluated by its success in attaining the goals of Marx and Marxism by other means.

The present book has several features which we can usefully mention. First, in an obvious sense, any discussion is provisional since it can always be surpassed by further work which builds upon it. As concerns Habermas, his tendency to present his writings as unfinished attempts, adds to their apparently provisional nature and accordingly discourages any effort to draw general conclusions. This tendency is explicable by the fact that he is still actively writing and he is constantly engaged in rethinking earlier facets of his view. He frequently employs the controversy swirling around his thought as a way to determine the relative success of ideas which, following criticism, he often modifies. This tendency is also in part a conscious strategy to parry possible criticism.

The provisional nature of the present discussion should not, however, be exaggerated. In particular, it should not be allowed to undercut the possibility of a careful reconstruction and evaluation of Habermas' writings on Marx and Marxism. Habermas has not yet ceased to publish; but we can be confident that his reading of historical materialism has now reached its final point in which he rejects the theory in favor of his own view, although he continues to regard himself as a Marxist. The only possible further step, which he cannot take and still call himself a Marxist, is to reject not only the theory, but its supposedly intrinsic goals as well. Although it is possible that he will at some future moment break with what he holds are the goals intrinsic to Marxism, this will not basically alter his view of the nature of historical materialism as a theory and of its relation to communicative action.[9] Hence, it seems unlikely that in future writings there will be any basic changes in his attitude toward Marx and Marxism.

At this late date, for reasons intrinsic to his understanding of Marx and Marxism, Habermas has now turned his attention to other concerns. Since it would surely be incorrect to attempt to close a discussion that has not even seriously begun, the present essay remains provisional with respect to possible further debate on this and related themes. But we can be confident that insofar as any study is not merely provisional, conditions now exist which permit a serious study in depth of Habermas' approach to historical materialism.

Second, it is important to repeat that this is an essay on Habermas' reading of historical materialism. There will be discussion of Marxism and even more of Marx; and we are obviously concerned here with Habermas' own form of Marxism. But this is not meant as a study of Marx and Marxism as such. Nor is this a work specifically about Habermas' position in general, either early or late. Although such themes are not irrelevant to this inquiry, those who are specifically interested in such matters are advised to look elsewhere.

Third, we can note that the present discussion will be critical. Ordinarily it would be superfluous to identify this aspect as such, since philosophy itself is necessarily characterized by a critical attitude. Indeed, Habermas tacitly agrees with this point in his adoption of a quasi-Kantian perspective in his analysis of historical materialism. But even if he represents himself as a critical thinker, the reception of his writings has not always been rigorous, especially in Anglo-Saxon circles.[10]

Habermas must bear some of the blame for the occasionally hagiographic character of the debate he has engendered, which at present includes a semi-official bibliography of his writings as well as discussion about them, and an unfortunate tendency to transform the appearance of his recent work into quasi-media events, with the rapid publication either of materials concerning the book or a series of studies of it and the author's response.

The prevalence of an uncritical attitude toward a supposedly critical thinker is not useful; in fact, by creating the illusion that a substantive discussion has occurred, or even could take place in a relatively brief lapse of time, it retards the development of a more significant debate which can only occur at a temporal remove. Any thinker who introduces basically novel concepts cannot be understood quickly; and any thinker who is quickly 'understood' is not profoundly novel, or is in fact misunderstood. Fundamentally new ideas, which are not mere modifications of others but break with received views, can only be comprehended when they have been assimilated in the course of a lengthy critical discussion. The highest praise one can bestow on a supposedly rigorous position is to consider it in rigorous, that is, scrupulously fair but critical, fashion. Anything less is a tacit admission of the uncritical character of the view under study.

At the present stage of the debate on Marx and Marxism, a critical discussion may possibly also have a further effect, beyond the immediate relation to Habermas' writings. Marx was arguably a profound thinker, but he was not a careful writer. Marxism has not often been equal to his intellectual standards. In general it has been characterized by generations of special pleading on the grounds of social relevance, obscurely meant to take the place of rigorous debate; and frequently acrimonious, but unenlightening internecine conceptual strife, often culminating in rival claims of orthodoxy among its adepts.

The generally weak character of the Marxist literature has been largely paralleled by a recent tendency, when Marx and Marxism have not simply been ignored, to refute their views in a conceptually cavalier manner which, like much of Marxism, ignores, or even willfully flouts, the best standards of philosophical discussion. It is not necessary to hold that Marx is above reproach to believe that there is something to be gained, perhaps even in the possible stimulation of a more interesting and satisfying debate, in the limited defense of some of his ideas against indecisive critique.

Hence, another reason to be critical of Habermas' reading of historical materialism—beyond the fact that to fail to do so is to abandon the claim for critical thought for something intellectually less interesting—is that at this late date it may still be possible to show by example that there are philosophically substantive issues in Marx's position worthy of close and even sustained discussion. In that spirit, we can follow Habermas' own example. After many years of effort to provide a responsible reading of historical materialism, he has now turned his attention to other matters. But it is a premise of this study that he was once deeply concerned with close interpretation, critique, and reconstruction of Marx's thought.

Fourth, it is useful to mention the Habermas secondary literature. At present, we have arrived at a stage where the preliminary shape of the reception of his view has begun to appear before he has stopped, or even slowed, his production. There are, for instance, works available for many aspects of his position, including the bibliography of his writings and their reception,[11] his early[12] and later thought[13] in general, their relation to the German idealist background,[14] the question of critical social theory,[15] his view of modernity,[16] etc.

There will be almost no mention here of the bibliography concerning Habermas for several reasons. These include the fact that little of the discussion in the secondary literature bears directly on the present theme and that, as he himself recommends, it is always preferable to exhaust the primary texts before turning to the literature about them.[17] Someone who desires to learn about the discussion concerning Habermas would be well advised to read another book, since that is not the task at hand. If, rather, this essay leads to careful reflection on Marx and Marxism, on Habermas' discussion of them, and on his own position, it will have been useful.

The present study comprises a description and critical evaluation of Habermas' reading of historical materialism. The discussion begins with an account of the background of his approach to Marx and Marxism in the nineteenth century German tradition and in recent analytical philosophy of science (in chapter 1). It is followed (in chapters 2–6) by a general description of the development of his reading of the theory in various articles and books over several decades in a series of four interrelated phases. These include his initial interpretation of historical materialism, followed by its critique from a quasi-Kantian perspective, succeeded by an attempt at reconstruction, and ending in his rejection of the theory as such in favor of an alternative position arguably better suited than historical materialism to reach its intrinsic aim. Since his approach to Marx and Marxism is not well known, it seemed useful to postpone direct criticism of it, but not of his interpretation of other writers, until after it has been described. The final three chapters concern the evaluation of various facets of his views of Marx and Marxism, especially his contribution to the Marxist theme of the relation of theory and practice.

This study of Habermas' reading of historical materialism is centered on a single main theme: the relevance of reason. This theme runs throughout the history of philosophy in the widespread conviction about the social utility of rigorous thought. It is a staple of Marxism under the heading of theory and practice [Praxis], as a concern which supposedly separates critical social theory from the remainder of the intellectual tradition. It is further central in Habermas' approach to Marx and Marxism and in his own theory of communicative action.

In respect to the former it is basic to his claim for the characteristic difference between Marxism and so-called *Ursprungsphilosophie*, as well as to his classic discussion of the relation of knowledge and interest. As concerns the latter, it is ingredient in his claim to reach the aims of Marxism understood as critical social theory by the introduction of another, but still socially relevant, theoretical paradigm.

The description and analysis of Habermas' reading of historical materialism builds toward a critical discussion of his view of the relevance of reason. This theme, which is present throughout this study, is most sharply focused in the last chapter and in the Conclusion. In the context of an evaluation of his contribution to historical materialism, the concluding chapter addresses the link between his own view of theory and practice and its traditional Marxist analysis. The Conclusion studies Habermas' view of the relevance of reason and the problem as such.

It might be useful to anticipate a possible objection here. In part, the critical analysis of Habermas' reading of historical materialism rests on a comparison of his interpretation of Marx and Marxism to the texts in question. Now it might be thought, as Habermas implies in his occasional comments, that he is unconcerned with textual exegesis, that close textual interpretation is irrelevant.[18] These remarks amount to a tacit suggestion that there is a distinction to be drawn between historical-philological study and systematic thought, such as philosophy or social theory.

For some kinds of discussion this is arguably true, but it is false as concerns the complex effort to understand the nature and limits of historical materialism in order to surpass it in another theory. Like Hegel, who is Habermas' direct predecessor in this regard, the claim in fact to surpass an earlier position—in this case the views of Marx and Marxism which he examines under the general heading of historical materialism—must meet the test posed by textual interpretation. Otherwise, there is no basis, other than simple assertion, for the conviction that a later theory goes further down the path opened by its predecessor. For this reason, and despite Habermas' claim not to be concerned with exegesis as such, he cannot avoid and must meet this particular standard.

We can end this Introduction with a final note about the nature of the discussion to follow. Habermas is a difficult writer; his texts are filled with complex arguments and intricate accounts of the history of philosophy, especially German idealism, one of the most rewarding but demanding portions of the philosophical tradition, as well as asides on a variety of other disciplines. His reading of historical materialism, with which we are occupied here, primarily concerns Marx's at least equally difficult writings as well as selected portions of the Marxist tradition. Every statement says less than it intends, and conceals as well as reveals. Nevertheless, every effort has been made to provide as full an account as possible and to write clearly, in a manner which finally reveals more than it conceals. It will be a measure of the usefulness of this book if it is finally 'available,' not only to the happy few, those specialists who earn their living in writing about Marx and his followers, but also to the wider variety of intellectuals who, we may hope, are still concerned about the relevance of reason to the social world.

HABERMAS ON
HISTORICAL
MATERIALISM

I

THEORY RECONSTRUCTION
AND THEORY REPLACEMENT

Our task in the present chapter is to start the discussion. Even if the proper way to begin is to begin, not all beginnings are equally useful for the discussion to which they lead. In the present case, a suggestion of where we can usefully start arises from consideration of the nature of our theme: Habermas' critical reading of historical materialism. Since Habermas interprets this theory in terms of its possible reconstruction and ultimate replacement by another theory, reflection in general on his comprehension of issues concerning the relation between a theory and its successors will aid in understanding the particular angle of vision from which he comes to Marx and Marxism. This vantage point further presents the advantage of providing a way into Habermas' thought, as it specifically relates to historical materialism, that does not depend upon, and in fact casts light on, his reading of Marx and Marxism, which we shall study below.

As a result of his wide awareness of preceding and contemporary thought, Habermas' position includes influences from numerous sources. As concerns the reconstruction and replacement of historical materialism, two of the central themes in his discussion of Marx and Marxism, the main background for Habermas' approach lies in two disparate, but not unrelated areas: classical German idealist philosophy, especially Kant and Hegel, and recent analytic philosophy of science. It has perhaps been insufficiently noticed that in independence of each other, both the idealist philosophical tradition and recent analytic philosophy of science address the problem of theory development in ways which yield similar views of theory reconstruction and theory replacement. Since Habermas draws on these sources in his study of historical materialism, it will be useful, to initiate the discussion, to comment on them in order to characterize his approach to Marx and Marxism in general.

We can start with the theme of science in Habermas' writings. His concern with theory reconstruction and theory replacement is clearly related to his general interest in science. Beyond the obvious presence of a sociological dimension in many of his texts, his corpus reveals a persistent interest in science on several levels, including the social role of science, which he studied in an analysis of its relation to ideology;[1] the theory of the social sciences in general, which is the topic of a detailed inquiry into their intrinsic logic;[2] and recent analytic philosophy of science. The latter is a recurrent theme in specific discussions of particular points, where Habermas indicates a firm command of the necessary texts,[3] and as the unnamed framework for his investigation of issues not often investigated from this angle of vision, including Marx's thought. We can find various indications of the significance of Habermas' concern with analytic philosophy of science for his comprehension of Marx's view in the incorporation of specific themes from recent controversies concerning analytic philosophy of science in the discussion of Marx's position, particularly in his remarks on theory reconstruction and paradigm replacement; and in occasional comments which reveal that Habermas in part invokes philosophy of science as a standard, or arbiter, of the nature of acceptable theory.[4]

The concepts of theory reconstruction and theory replacement are obviously related as two ways to improve upon the original formulation of a position. The former provides the theoretical basis for the revision of the original view in order better to meet its intrinsic goal; the latter offers a theoretical basis in which the original view is discarded in order better to attain its supposedly intrinsic aim through an appeal to a different kind of view, or new theoretical paradigm. The similarity between these two approaches is that in both cases the purpose is to achieve, or to achieve better, the end toward which the original theory presumably aspired, but which it arguably failed to attain. As concerns the amelioration of the original theory, the difference between theory reconstruction and theory replacement is that from the former perspective this can be brought about through a better version of the original theoretical model, whereas for the latter the original must be discarded in favor of another, incompatible type of theory.

Interest in this theme does not originate with Habermas. In a general sense, the notions of theory reconstruction and theory replacement are constant companions throughout the philosophical tradition since its origins in ancient Greece. For the most part, attention has usually been focused on the replacement of an arguably defective view by another, supposedly superior alternative. Already in Plato's early Socratic dialogues we find the effort, unfortunately only rarely duplicated in later thought, to confront incompatible ideas in order to choose between them. From this perspective we can regard the entire later philosophical tradition, including the views of Plato and his successors, as a clash between different theories which represent the effort, constitutive of philosophy as an ongoing enterprise, to surpass previous views in the pursuit of truth.

This attitude prevails as late as Kant who, since he maintained that systematic and historical considerations could and must be sharply separated,[5] was unable to take a historical approach to the growth of theory.[6] It is well known that Kant presents his Copernican Revolution in the form of a rationally justified shift from one epistemological model to another, in effect as a form of theory replacement. According to Kant, the failure of the rationalist approach in previous attempts suggests the adoption of an inverse strategy,[7] which has the further advantages of explaining the possibility of a priori knowledge and of furnishing adequate, a priori proofs for the laws of nature.[8] It is fair to say that the quasi-Kantian ahistorical attitude, which regards systematic thought as in principle unrelated, or at most only distantly linked, to historical factors, is still widely represented in contemporary philosophy, in both phenomenology[9] and in analytic thought.[10]

On this specific point, Hegel sharply disagreed with the author of the critical philosophy. As a result, he substitutes a view of theory reconstruction for the more widely prevalent view of theory replacement. Hegel differs from Kant and from preceding thinkers in the philosophical tradition in his understanding of the growth of knowledge as an ongoing process of the reconstruction of earlier, imperfect theories in order better to attain their goals. His goal is not simply to replace one theory by another one, namely his own; it is rather to carry forward the aims of prior positions in his own thought. His view is not intended as a better, but incompatible alternative; rather it is meant to build upon and incorporate all that is valid in earlier theory in a new synthesis continuous with, and an improvement upon, its predecessors.

As part of his insistence on the relation of thought to time,[11] Hegel insisted on the inseparability of philosophy and the history of philosophy. His new perspective introduces at least two major changes in our understanding of the preceding tradition. First, it provides a way to grasp the history of philosophy as a unitary process, unfolding over time. According to Hegel, almost from its inception philosophy has always been concerned with the problem of knowledge. Since Parmenides, a long series of philosophers has approached this problem through the analysis of a supposed identity between thought and being. Although this identity has often been asserted, Hegel believes it has never been demonstrated.

Second, and as a direct consequence, he introduces teleology into the development of the philosophical tradition. According to Hegel, later positions build upon their predecessors, which they cannot ignore. He believes that the aim of philosophy is not to replace one type of theory by another; it is rather to bring together in a single analysis all that is of value in the preceding tradition, in order to prove, and not merely to assert, the identity of thought and being. In a word, Hegel differs from Kant and from preceding thinkers in the philosophical tradition in his understanding of the growth of knowledge through the reconstruction of earlier, imperfect theories in order better to attain their goals.

There is a clear difference in these two analyses of theoretical progress. We have seen that, by maintaining the separation of thought and history, Kant follows many others in arguing that such progress occurs when an earlier, explanatorily weaker view is replaced by a later, explanatorily stronger one, incompatible with the earlier analysis. This attitude is only the latest form of the pre-Socratic doctrine of the incompatibility of opposites. On the contrary,

Hegel's denial of the separation of philosophy and the history of philosophy results in a new understanding of progress as the result of the further development of a given form of theory.

The disagreement between Kant and Hegel concerning the growth of theory is not a mere historical curiosity, but is further of contemporary interest. The issues surrounding the growth of theory have long been a central concern in philosophy of science. It is not sufficiently known that the recent controversy in analytic philosophy of science between proponents of theory replacement and proponents of theory reconstruction in effect prolongs on a different terrain aspects of the dispute described between Kant and Hegel.

In part because of the pronounced antihistorical bias of contemporary philosophy of science, at present the discussion concerning the growth of theory is mainly between representatives of different versions of the concept of theory replacement. This controversy in analytic philosophy of science opposes a long list of participants, too numerous even to mention. For present purposes it will be sufficient merely to indicate several recent variants of the concept of theory replacement in briefest fashion by referring to the views of Popper, Kuhn, and Stegmüller.

In connection with his fallibilist approach, Popper insists on falsifiability as the criterion of a scientific theory. According to Popper, the growth of science occurs through a series of conjectures and refutations, which require the later introduction of another, incompatible view.[12] In an influential argument, in part directed against Popper, and which has led to a protracted dispute between them and their supporters, Kuhn maintains that different types of theory, for which he uses the ambiguous word "paradigm," are not refuted, but abandoned.[13] Despite their disagreement on other issues, Popper and Kuhn agree that scientific progress occurs through the replacement of one type of theory by another.

In reaction principally to Kuhn, a competing view, located midway between the concepts of theory replacement and theory reconstruction, has been sketched by Wolfgang Stegmüller, a West German philosopher of science.[14] According to Stegmüller, we can provide a rational reconstruction of a theory by discarding its irrational content and reconstructing its rational core in a manner that conforms to general criteria of rationality. The resultant concept of rational paradigm replacement he develops is clearly related, through its attention to the reconstruction of the rational core of the theory, to the idea of theory reconstruction.

The alternative views of progress through theory reconstruction or theory replacement provide a convenient framework to consider Habermas' discussion of historical materialism. His writings are characterized in general by a consistent effort to combine historical and systematic concerns. From his earliest texts until the present he has constantly sought to articulate his own position against the background of other views. In his writings on historical materialism, the concepts of theory reconstruction and theory replacement are presupposed in the various phases of his discussion: initially in the context of his attempt over many years to interpret, to criticize, and to revise the theory; and in the course of his later effort to reject Marx's position in order better to attain the goals intrinsic to historical materialism from the perspective of a new theoretical paradigm.

The alternative between theory reconstruction and theory replacement provides a framework for Habermas' discussion of historical materialism that was not explicitly present at its beginning. The dialogue with Marx and Marxism began in 1957 in a lengthy survey of the current philosophical discussion.[15] Habermas only turned directly to the problem of theory reconstruction in the introduction to a volume of occasional essays, entitled *On the Reconstruction of Historical Materialism (Zur Rekonstrucktion des historischen Materialismus)*, which appeared nineteen years later when his own discussion had already passed through several phases, including interpretation and criticism.[16] Here in brief compass he articulates a metatheoretical justification for the reconstruction of prior theory, including historical materialism.

Habermas begins his introduction by recalling that in recent years he has been attempting to develop a reconstruction of historical materialism at the same time as he has been engaged in developing a theory of communicative action. According to Habermas the simultaneous work on these projects is not a mere accident. He attributes what he calls the "prominence" of the latter theory in his writing of the same period to "the contribution that communication theory can, in my view, make to a renewed historical materialism."[17]

This statement, taken out of context, is ambiguous. It is clear that Habermas believes there is a relation, as part of a larger scheme, between his interest in historical materialism and communicative action, although the nature of that connection is not further defined. If communicative action is to make a contribution to historical materialism, there are some obvious ways to construe the link between the two views. For instance, it could be the case that Habermas intends communicative action to found historical materialism, in order to make it possible. It is well known that Sartre, for instance, has suggested the existence of this kind of relation between existentialism and Marxism. Or perhaps Habermas regards communicative action as a further and necessary consequence of historical materialism, as neo-Kantianism was intended to develop further the spirit of the critical philosophy. A third possibility, suggested by the idea of reconstruction, which figures in the title of his book, is that the intrinsic weaknesses of historical materialism require a restatement of the theory somehow related to the view of communicative action. In fact, as we shall see below, in different ways Habermas has in mind each of the relations between the theory and his own canvassed here.

The reconstruction of theory, including historical materialism, suggests the need to characterize this task. As early as the first paragraph, Habermas draws a series of distinctions which circumscribes a general outline of theory reconstruction. His view is based on a triple distinction between notions of the restoration, renaissance, and reconstruction of prior theory. Since this is the only explicit statement of his understanding of theory reconstruction in his pub-

lished work to date, it seems useful, despite its length, to quote the entire statement. Habermas writes:

> The word *restoration* signifies the return to an initial situation that had mean-
> while been corrupted; but my interest in Marx and Engels is not dogmatic, nor
> is it historical-philological. *Renaissance* signifies the renewal of a tradition that
> has been buried for some time; but Marxism is in no need of this. In the present
> connection, *reconstruction* signifies taking a theory apart and putting it back to-
> gether again in a new form in order to attain more fully the goal it set for itself.
> This is the normal way (in my opinion normal for Marxists too) of dealing with
> a theory that needs revision in many respects but whose potential for stimula-
> tion has still not been exhausted.[18]

    This passage is rich in information about Habermas' reading of the views of
Marx and Marxism, his understanding of his own relation to them, and his
idea of theory reconstruction. Since Habermas is concerned here with the relation of Marx and Marxism, even at this early stage of the discussion it will
be useful to describe Habermas' reading of historical materialism in the context of some main approaches to the theory as an aid in comprehending his
effort to reconstruct and to replace it.
    Obviously, it is not easy to characterize the relation of Marxism to Marx's
theory, particularly not easy to do so rapidly. The discussion on Marx and
Marxism has by now been underway for more than a hundred years in a massive and rapidly growing literature whose dimensions surpass the capacity of
even the most industrious student. It is difficult to describe this discussion adequately,[19] and impossible to do so even in outline here. For present purposes,
we do not require a characterization of Habermas' approach to historical materialism, since that will emerge in the discussion below. We can limit ourselves here to several brief remarks on the relation of Marxism to Marx.
    In an obvious sense Marxists in general are followers of Marx's thought.
The relation of the thought of a disciple to that of a master thinker is often
complex. It is well known that Kant claimed to understand Plato better than
he understood himself.[20] This claim in part determined the later reception of
the critical philosophy, in which a series of post-Kantian thinkers routinely
made the claim to be the only correct interpreter of the critical philosophy.
    It is a major mistake to conflate the doctrines of the disciple and the master.
In the same way that Kant is not a Kantian, nor Plato a Platonist, Marx is
not a Marxist, as he is reputed to have observed. Marxism is the intellectual
and political movement begun in Marx's lifetime by Friedrich Engels, his long-
time colleague, and that continues today. Marxists in general have always regarded the relation of Marxism to Marx and Engels as continuous and unbro-
ken. An example of this Marxist attitude is Lenin's influential description of
Marxism as the science of Marx's views, which are continuous with those of
Engels and their extension in the later Marxist tradition. This belief in an alleged continuity between Marx and Marxism has long been a source of the
political legitimacy claimed exclusively by various Marxists; it has further

provided the question of conceptual orthodoxy, which would otherwise be a simple problem of textual hermeneutics, with great practical importance.

In broad terms, we can say that Habermas shares the Marxist view of the relation of Marxism to Marx. This view consists in the rejection of an approach to Marx limited merely to Marx's writings as well as the rejection of what we might see as a further approach stressing the continuity between Marx and Engels. On the contrary, for Habermas there is no apparent distinction between the views of Marx and their extension in the writings of Engels and later Marxists.

In recent years much attention has been paid to the differences between the positions of Marx and the various Marxists,[21] but this is not an issue which apparently concerns Habermas. In the course of his lengthy study of Marx and Marxism, he raises a large number of questions, which are often of basic importance for an understanding of historical materialism; but significantly he never addresses the question of the degree of the continuity of Marx and Marxism, and hence the necessity, or even the utility, of a possible distinction between their views. In this sense, his reading of what he calls historical materialism is clearly Marxist.

Habermas' adoption of a generally Marxist approach to Marx and Marxism does not mean that he is otherwise uncritical about them. Like many other writers in this domain, he is relatively unconcerned with close textual interpretation, which he rejects, in the quoted passage, as "historical-philological." As a result, his discussion is on occasion framed in general terms whose precise link to the texts is difficult to establish. But he also points out that his interest is not "dogmatic" or vulgar. In the context of the study of historical materialism this assertion does not mean that his interpretation is supposedly genteel; it rather means that his reading is not determined by political criteria and is accordingly politically unorthodox or critical.

Except in politically orthodox circles, where any doctrinal deviation is suspect, Habermas' espousal of a nondoctrinaire attitude toward Marx and Marxism will not arouse concern. A more controversial move, closely related to his Marxist understanding of the relation of Marxism to Marx, is his constant reference to "historical materialism." From the vantage point of the Marxist debate, this allusion presupposes a basic distinction between Marxist 'sciences', where this term is used in a sense different from the more widespread domains of natural and social sciences.

It is usual within Marxism to distinguish historical materialism, or the science of history, from dialectical materialism, or the science of nature. As concerns Marx's position, this distinction is questionable on several grounds. It is known that Marx never employs either term to refer to his own systematic view,[22] which in turn raises questions about the description of his position in this manner. In fact, it has recently been shown that neither term occurs in Marx's writings, since both were coined only after his death.[23] It may be the case that various forms of the protean species called Marxism, especially Engels's later thought, fall under the heading of materialism as an ontological

designation; on the contrary, other than as an imprecise way to differentiate
Marx's view from some forms of idealism, the term "materialism" is inappro-
priate to refer to his position. In his writings, when Marx speaks of idealism
he almost invariably has in mind Hegel's position only.

This analysis depends in part on a separation between Marx and Marxism.
Although Habermas, as noted, is in general not concerned with this distinction, he does want to differentiate, as also noted, between critical and dogmatic, or vulgar, forms of Marxism. Now, following Stalin's reported inter-
vention in the discussion,[24] dialectical materialism was briefly promoted to
coequal status with historical materialism, although it later fell into disrepute
as dogmatic. Since Habermas is interested in evolutionary theory, not the philosophy of nature, and is further concerned to distance himself from so-called
dogmatic forms of Marxism, we would not expect him to favor dialectical
materialism. It is, hence, not surprising that he routinely, in fact apparently
indiscriminately, employs the term "historical materialism" to refer to Marx
and Marxism.

Habermas' critical stance toward Marx and Marxism is directly responsible
for his concern with the reconstruction of historical materialism. Obviously,
there is no point in reconstructing a theory which is already adequate and,
hence, is not in need of correction or amelioration of any kind. Now, since
the beginning of the Marxist movement Marxists have always been interested
in the reconstruction of Marx's position. In this sense, Marxism is like the
wider philosophical tradition, which can be regarded as a series of efforts,
born of the dissatisfaction of those thinkers who come on the scene after the
formulation of the original doctrines, to reformulate certain key ideas, which
continue to recur under different forms.

Obviously, as soon as Marxists declined merely to explain Marx's thought
and tried to alter it, either by adapting it to changed conditions or attempting
to extend it to areas not even considered by either Marx or Engels, they were
in effect reconstructing it. Habermas' interest in the reconstruction of historical materialism does not constitute a break with the Marxist tradition, in
which this kind of effort is a main concern, indeed central to its very existence.
He is merely the most recent in a long list of Marxist writers who, through
their discussion of various themes, have participated in this ongoing task.
What is new in his writings is the metatheoretical examination, from a quasi-
Kantian perspective, of the meaning and conditions of theory reconstruction
as this concept applies to historical materialism.

In the quoted passage, Habermas' triple distinction resonates with echoes
from the history of philosophy. The terms "restoration" and "renaissance"
designate approaches to a position other than its reconstruction. In recent
thought, the idea of restoration is closely associated with an attitude toward
the philosophical tradition exemplified by Heidegger, and following him,
Gadamer. It is well known that both believe that philosophy in effect 'lost its
way' early on, perhaps as early as the pre-Socratics. In stating that his interest
in Marx and Marxism is not dogmatic, Habermas rules out a merely political

relation to historical materialism and signals that his interest is critical, or at least potentially so. In refusing a historical-philological approach, he indicates that for him the tradition of Marx and Engels, whose views he does not differentiate, is still, or is at least in principle, viable, and hence need not be studied only retrospectively.

Habermas pointedly reaffirms this attitude toward historical materialism in his refusal of the idea that it requires restoration. In the context of the Marxist tradition, he here allies himself with those writers, mainly Marxists but including non-Marxists as well, who see a direct continuity of Marxism with Marx. From this perspective Marxism is not a deformation of the Marxian position, since the Marxists, or self-professed followers of Marx, have continued to tread the path which Marx had blazed. Now the role of discipleship is always perilous, since what Glucksmann has recently called the master thinker can always complain of misunderstanding by his followers. Kant, for instance, rejected Fichte's claim, which was accepted by Schelling and Hegel, to carry the critical philosophy to new heights. On the contrary, by implication Habermas accepts the Marxist view for the essential continuity of Marxism with Marx's thought.

In virtue of his conviction that historical materialism has not been corrupted, Habermas' refusal of its need for restoration is clearly linked to his belief that the theory is not in need of a renaissance. It may be helpful to note that the German vocabulary has two closely related words, both of which, in English, are often translated indiscriminately as "renaissance": "Aufklärung," from "aufklären," which literally means "to teach someone concerning a situation," or "to set aside a lack of knowledge or prejudices, especially concerning political, religious, or wordly matters." The noun "Aufklärung" is often used in German to refer to the rise of modern science and culture in the revolt against the strictures of religious superstition and lack of knowledge [Unwissenheit] in the eighteenth century. In French, the parallel term is "éclaircissement," from "éclaircir," meaning "to cast light upon," as in "éclairé," a term used to describe someone who is enlightened.

"Renaissance" is a word on loan from the French language, where it has a long history going back to the fourteenth century. In French, the term originally had a primarily religious connotation of rebirth (from "renaître," composed of "re," meaning "again" and "naître," meaning "to be born"). But since the seventeenth century it has acquired a secondary meaning of something that has a reappearance, or a new surge [nouvel essor]. In French usage, this word refers to the beginning of modern times in the movement which originated in fifteenth century Italy and spread throughout Europe, especially through the return to artistic canons, to Greco-Latin themes, and to perspective in painting which broke with medieval esthetics.

In German, the same word "Renaissance" has a closely related, but not identical meaning of the reawakening of an exhausted or spent form of culture, with special reference to the movement that began in fifteenth century Italy. The idea that a form of culture, like a flower, in effect blooms and then fades is well known in German intellectual circles. A characteristic example in the field of history is Spengler's famous analysis of Western culture, appropriately linked to the metaphor of the setting of the sun;[25] in philosophy, Hegel described different national cultures as reaching a high point, in which they incorporate the world spirit which, at their decay, then passes to another culture.[26]

Habermas here speaks of renaissance in the specifically German sense, in order to deny that historical materialism is in need of a reawakening of a meanwhile exhausted theoretical option. By implication, for him at this point historical materialism remains what it has always been as a lively, unexhausted approach, which still presents further possibilities for development. We can comprehend the significance of his conviction here if we realize that, after later changing his mind, he will go on to argue that historical materialism belongs to a part of the philosophical tradition that has exhausted its theoretical avenues for further progress and must now be relegated to the oblivion of history.

Habermas' stress, before he changes his mind, on the intrinsic vitality of a tradition which has been neither corrupted nor forgotten—apparent in his refusal in the quoted passage to accept either restoration or renaissance as the proper approach to historical materialism—does not preclude him from taking a critical stance toward Marx, Engels, and their followers. His critical, non-dogmatic attitude, upon which he himself insists, is evident in the concept of reconstruction, through which he addresses the various issues linked with the improvement upon any given theory.

In English, the word "reconstruction," which comes from the German "Rekonstruction," has a strong association with the process of the reorganization of the southern states in the period after the Civil War, obviously lacking in the German cognate. It further means "constructing again, rebuilding, or making over" and "to build up, from remaining parts and other evidence, an image of what something was like in its original form," for instance in memory. Both of these latter denotations are present in the German term, which also has the additional sense, not present in the English word, but upon which Habermas relies, of the recapturing of a prior, even primitive, situation.

In German, the terms "Rekonstruktion" and "Renaissance" share a reference to something originally present, but now dormant or worse, which can be recaptured. In view of his insistence on the continuity of Marxism with Marx, Habermas cannot approach the reconstruction of historical materialism in this manner. On the contrary, he employs the concept of reconstruction to mean the "dismemberment and reconstitution of a theory in order better to reach its intrinsic, but unattained goal."

If this is a fair interpretation, then there are obvious precedents for this kind of approach in the history of philosophy, especially in German idealism.[27] Hegel, as noted, maintains that the history of philosophy can and should be regarded as a series of increasingly adequate analyses of the problem of knowledge in terms of the claimed relation of subject and object, or thought and being. A possible weakness of Hegel's view is that it appears to impose an external conceptual framework on the position to be interpreted, instead of discovering its intention immanently. Kant speaks directly to this difficulty in his well-known distinction between the letter and spirit of a theory.[28]

In his effort to reconstruct a position in relation to its intrinsic intention, Habermas seems to be following Kant more than Hegel. In a well-known passage, Kant, who had in mind the reception of his own position, insists that a theory must not be judged by isolated passages torn from context; rather, a position is to be measured in terms of its intrinsic spirit, whose comprehension presupposes the idea of the whole.[29] Although this idea of how to evaluate a theory is attractive, it is difficult to state in acceptable form. Certainly, from the perspective of the critical philosophy a claim to know the intrinsic spirit of any position is controversial. If we identify the letter with the appearance of the theory, it is clear that any effort to comprehend the whole obliges us to surpass the phenomenal plane in order to grasp the thing-in-itself, or essence, which, Kant maintains, lies outside the bounds of possible experience and hence cannot be known.

The identification of a tension between Kant's distinction and the critical philosophy only means that the distinction is not wholly consistent with other aspects of Kant's position. But if we consider the difference between the letter and spirit of a theory in independence of the critical philosophy, we can discern further difficulties, connected with Habermas' related claims that a theory sets goals for itself and that such goals can be identified. These difficulties cast doubt on the version of theory reconstruction on which Habermas relies.

According to Habermas, reconstruction aims to attain more fully the goal a theory has set for itself. But obviously theories do not do anything on their own, much less set goals for themselves; their authors do that. This is less a conceptual difficulty than a verbal slip, although it points toward a more serious question concerning the kind of interpretation necessary to make sense of the claim to reconstruct a given theory. Now in order to maintain that a later view in fact offers what can legitimately be regarded as a better version of the original view, the intrinsic spirit of the latter must be identifiable. But it is doubtful that the goal of a theory can be unambiguously identified. If this were possible, then at least in principle it would be feasible to specify a univocal interpretation of a given theory. Indeed, a claim of this kind is routinely presupposed in all forms of orthodoxy: philosophical, political, religious, etc. Any thinker who makes the claim of orthodoxy presupposes the capacity to identify and to follow the intrinsic idea of a position, as for instance neo-Kantians, who differed widely in their respective readings of the critical philosophy, but invariably claimed to follow Kant.

Certainly, the idea of theory reconstruction presupposes that we can in fact know the intrinsic goal, and hence establish the correct interpretation, of a given theory as a necessary precondition of its reformulation. But can we even conceive of a univocal, correct reading of an important philosophical position, such as those of Plato and Aristotle, or Kant and Hegel? An empirical counterargument is furnished by the many, often incompatible interpretations of the views of these thinkers. While on textual grounds we may be able to rule out some proposed readings, it is inconceivable that we could establish a single comprehension of a position as correct and exclude all other possibilities as false. Now this inevitable failure counts against the very idea of theory reconstruction. While it is perfectly plausible to state that a later writer is inspired to elaborate a view by an earlier theory, there is no reason to accept a stronger claim.

This remark is not intended to refute Habermas' idea of theory reconstruction; it is rather meant to focus in passing on some of the difficult issues that arise within it. Attention to the historical background enables us to see that the concept of theory reconstruction has solid precedent in the history of philosophy; it further helps us to perceive that and how Habermas presumably relies on earlier views of theory reconstruction, especially Hegel's, in order to provide a framework for the reconstruction of historical materialism. The difficulties that arise within the idea of theory reconstruction may have led Hegel to dissociate his own efforts to improve upon earlier positions from any claim to grasp their intrinsic goal. We may further speculate that Habermas' realization of the nature and importance of the problems inherent in the proposed reconstruction of historical materialism as well as in the concept of reconstruction which this attempt presupposed were factors in his later turn from theory reconstruction to theory replacement.

The premise of theory reconstruction is that the position under study still possesses undeveloped conceptual resources which can be utilized to reach to its intrinsic goal. After a period in which he tried to reconstruct historical materialism in satisfactory fashion to attain its self-specified aim, Habermas changed his mind about the possible success of this effort. In the most recent and arguably final phase of his discussion of historical materialism, he has consistently argued that historical materialism has already exhausted its potential for further stimulation.

The later shift in Habermas' attitude toward historical materialism does not eliminate the difficulties associated with the concept of theory reconstruction, but rather generates a new series of problems. From Habermas' perspective it is clearly not meaningful to reconstruct a theory which is lacking further intellectual potential. But he has so far not indicated whether he now thinks that his own earlier efforts in that direction were misguided; nor has he indicated whether he now feels that the proper attitude toward Marx and Engels is to be found among the two remaining alternatives of his triple distinction, that is, in a choice between restoration or renaissance.

In recent writings, Habermas' approach toward historical materialism has changed in basic ways. He has criticized the theory in a manner he regards as fundamental.[30] In virtue of his belief that historical materialism has exhausted its capacity for further growth, its decisive critique is a sufficient reason to abandon the theory. Now, if the theory is to be abandoned in favor of another view, we require a metatheoretical analysis of the concept of theory replacement. Not surprisingly, since Habermas now holds that historical materialism cannot be further developed, he has recently silently abandoned his earlier concept of theory reconstruction, which governed his unsuccessful attempt to reconstruct the theory, in favor of an alternative, largely implicit, incompatible concept of theory replacement.[31]

In our discussion of his comprehension of theory reconstruction, we were aided by Habermas' brief but explicit metatheoretical reflection on this concept, in the passage quoted. Unfortunately, in Habermas' later writings there is as yet no single passage that provides a clear metatheoretical analysis of theory replacement as he understands it. This does not mean that such a passage will not be forthcoming; it only means that he has not yet provided one. In the absence of the needed clarification, we can at least infer the outlines of his comprehension of theory replacement from his effort to put forward his own theory of communicative action as a replacement for historical materialism, or even for post-Kantian philosophy in general. Obviously, his practice in replacing another theory or set of theories by his own refers to an implicit, as yet unarticulated metatheory governing the relation between theories incompatible in principle.

His main argument in favor of his own position is made in the course of a sweeping analysis of the post-Hegelian moment in modern philosophy. According to Habermas, this period is marked by the clash between two incompatible philosophical strategies: so-called rationalistic subject philosophy, which reaches its presumed high-water mark in Hegel; and an ongoing effort, set in motion by Nietzsche, and later extended by Heidegger and Derrida, Foucault and Bataille, and others, to escape from subject philosophy through the decisive critique of reason. Simplifying only a little, we can say that Habermas reads the post-Hegelian period as the theater of a gigantic struggle waged by later writers to emerge from the folds of Hegel's position by the decisive criticism and rejection of its underlying paradigm in favor of another alternative.[32]

In maintaining that post-Hegelian thought is mainly concerned to react against Hegel's view, Habermas offers an analysis of the structure of modern philosophy in which the roots lie ultimately in Hegel's position.[33] The latter's well-known tendency to read all prior thought as leading up to his own system gave rise in the literature to a well defined tendency to interpret later philosophy in relation to absolute idealism. This tendency is in part justified by the importance of Hegel's position. Even if he did not actually end philosophy by bringing it to a close, as some Young Hegelians and early students of Hegel believe,[34] it is difficult not to see Hegel as occupying a central position in modern thought. Examples of writers who have tried to comprehend later philosophical thought mainly through Hegel's position include Karl Löwith's reading of the period from Hegel to Nietzsche[35] and more recently Richard Bernstein's account of some contemporary developments against the background of absolute idealism.[36]

Although he also regards Hegel's influence on later thought as immense, Habermas sees the tradition from Nietzsche to the present, from an almost

Freudian perspective, as composed mainly of a series of negative reactions to absolute idealism. This controversial reading is simplistic. Certainly, there are aspects of recent philosophy which bear a mainly negative relation to Hegel's thought. A well-known instance, which Habermas does not mention, is the rise of British analytic philosophy in the course of the revolt against British idealism. Further, he provides an overly flattened or foreshortened image of certain figures he does mention. Although Heidegger's relation to Hegel is complex, Habermas presents the former simply as reacting against the latter. In a word, even if Habermas arguably highlights an insufficiently appreciated aspect of the post-Hegelian evolution of philosophy, his reading of this period is only in part reliable as a general interpretation since its contrasts are too sharply drawn to fit his thesis.

Habermas implicitly acknowledges this objection through his distinction between the explicit intent of the thinkers loosely grouped around Nietzsche and their collective result. As he reads the modern tradition, despite their individual achievements, those writers in revolt against Hegel failed to preserve the separation between the wider paradigm, or subject philosophy, which he also calls "the philosophy of consciousness," and a discernably different alternative.

He believes that none of these thinkers was successful in the attempt to escape from the subject philosophy which, in each case, reentered through the back door, so to speak. Although the 'official' reason to oppose Hegel was in principle to reject subject philosophy, Habermas holds that in practice the resultant critique of reason always led to a form of theory which remained within the rationalist paradigm of subject-centered thought. According to Habermas, at the limit, and despite the best efforts of talented thinkers in the post-Hegelian tradition, the attack on subject philosophy is only another form of it; for one paradigm collapses into another. He believes that the only way to escape from the subject philosophy is through the adoption of his own view of communicative action, which avoids the mistakes of his predecessors.

In any analysis of theory replacement, a key issue is how rationally to justify the decision to change from one model of theory to another. Kant, who proposed an earlier view of theory replacement, was obviously aware of this problem. He clearly presents his Copernican Revolution in the form of a rationally justified shift from one epistemological model to another. According to Kant, the failure of the rationalist approach in previous attempts suggested to him the adoption of an inverse strategy, which has the further specific advantages of explaining the possibility of a priori knowledge and of furnishing adequate a priori proofs for laws of nature.[37] He also describes his Copernican Revolution as an experiment, which he compares to the experiments of Galileo, Torricelli, and Stahl.[38] In an uncharacteristic use of hyperbole, he further maintains that even the smallest change in the theory that results from his Revolution would cause all of human reason to totter.[39]

Since Kant describes his own theory as transcendentally ideal and empirically real, we can expect him to argue on both the a priori and a posteriori levels. On reflection, we can see that Kant offers two main arguments in favor of a rational change from one type of theory to another: a pragmatic analysis, closely related to his own experimental view of theory, based on the supposed failure of another, rival alternative; and a quasi-transcendental analysis, which rests on the exclusion of what is supposedly the only other possible alternative. Now, in different ways, both of these strategies are problematic. The pragmatic approach is questionable, since it needs to be shown that the alternative theory is a better choice than the one it is supposed to replace. The difficulty in the quasi-transcendental argument is to show that the *reductio* has been carried out successfully and that all other possibilities have in fact been excluded.

In his discussion of theory replacement, Habermas restates both arguments we have identified in Kant's position, further proposes a new strategy Kant does not mention, and finally rejects a fourth argument he does not consider. The four arguments concern, respectively: the rational rejection of the paradigm of reason, which Habermas regards as the main thrust of the writers influenced by Nietzsche who argue for the rejection of the subject philosophy; Habermas' view that the old philosophy of consciousness is exhausted; his further claim that his own view of communicative action represents the only way out of the *aporia* of the subject philosophy; and finally his assertion that his own theory is inherently better than its alternatives.

Habermas rejects the antirationalist subversion of the rationalist tradition he correctly associates with Nietzsche's spiritual progeny on the grounds that it has led, and must lead, to a hopeless confrontation between Hegel and Nietzsche; he sees the Nietzschean line of argument as a merely negative critique which leaves no way out of the dilemma.[40] More generally, this critical approach is hopeless since a radical criticism of reason remains tied to the presuppositions of reason.[41] This point, which is well taken, can be strengthened: an antirationalist critique of reason is bound to fail, as it always presupposes what it rejects, that is, reason. Although it may be that there are other ways to develop Nietzsche's critique than those Habermas identifies, there is no way to provide a rational objection to reason.

In place of the strategy he rejects, Habermas proposes three further arguments in favor of a rationally justified theory replacement, in this case a change from the subject philosophy, which in his view includes historical materialism, to his own theory of communicative action. His assertion that the old philosophy of consciousness is exhausted[42] is a restatement of Kant's belief that rationalism has hitherto failed. He further shares Kant's predilection toward an experimental comprehension of philosophical theory. In a recent interview, he has expressed his conviction that there are no longer any metaphysical truths, so that philosophy, like the sciences, can be compared to an ongoing process or program of research in which all arguments are in principle permanently open to revision.[43]

The difference is that Habermas maintains—as Kant should have, but did not, as a condition of his argument in favor of the Copernican Revolution—that rationalism cannot be reconstructed in satisfactory form. Now, if

Habermas were able to demonstrate that the old paradigm had been exhausted—so that there were no possibilities for further development that could bring it nearer to its theoretical goal—then he would have a reason to invoke a new form of theory, although not necessarily his own. But a pragmatic survey of what has been attempted does not circumscribe what could be done. Since this kind of analysis has only retrospective value, no conclusion can be drawn as to future possibility. Accordingly, this line of argument does not provide a rational justification of theory replacement.

Habermas' second line of argument in favor of theory replacement is that his own theory constitutes a way out of the problems which arise between the Scylla of absolutism, that is, the subject philosophy, and the Charybdis of relativism, or the Nietzschean-inspired critique of the philosophy of consciousness.[44] This strategy, which resembles Kant's argument in favor of the Copernican Revolution as a possible solution, can be successful only if it can be shown that the difficulties in the original theory are intractable and that the proposed view constitutes a possible alternative. Although Habermas in fact demonstrates that the *aporia* of the Nietzschean line of criticism cannot be overcome, he does not prove this point, as he must, for the subject philosophy. But the mere fact that there is a possible alternative is not a sufficient reason either to abandon the original paradigm or to opt for a specific alternative to it.

The final type of strategy Habermas proposes in favor of theory replacement is a clearly pragmatic suggestion that a better form of theory is preferable. This kind of argument is not straightforwardly present in Kant's writings, which invoke the failure, not the relative weakness of the rationalist alternative. According to Habermas, his theory of communicative action is preferable to the paradigm associated with Hegel since, among other things, it provides for the reconstruction of Hegel's theory of the ethical life in independence of the premises of the philosophy of consciousness,[45] it takes over the role played by Marx and Western Marxism in the philosophy of practice [Praxisphilosophie],[46] and it contributes to the analysis of the free market economy characteristic of capitalism. In a word, the better theory, which hence ought to be adopted, is the one which does better, according to unspecified criteria, what the other theory or theories were arguably meant to accomplish.

This kind of strategy for theory replacement cannot be rejected simply on theoretical grounds. It can only be faulted in a specific instance on the practical grounds that the superiority of the alternative in question has not been demonstrated. Since this is a discussion of the framework of Habermas' study of Marx and Marxism, we do not require a detailed evaluation of the comparative merits of his theory of communicative action. Suffice it to say that, regardless of the merits of his view, he does not go far enough in his argument for its comparative advantage for us to choose it as an acceptable alternative to the subject philosophy.

We can end this account of the framework of Habermas' consideration of

Marx and Marxism with a final comment in order to anticipate a possible objection that Habermas is inconsistent and to situate his perspective. We have identified two general strategies in his approach to historical materialism: a concept of theory reconstruction according to which Habermas takes historical materialism as the raw material out of which to produce another, better form of the theory; and a view of theory replacement, to which Habermas implicity later turns in order to provide a rational justification for the acceptance of his own view as a better alternative to historical materialism and subject philosophy in general.

So far we have been treating the notions of theory reconstruction and theory replacement as alternative views of conceptual progress. But it would be an error to regard the distinction between these concepts as absolute. As we can see from the examination of the latter idea, in the final analysis an argument for theory replacement depends on the comparative examination of competing alternatives with respect to a given aim. In other words, in the transition from theory reconstruction to theory replacement Habermas does not alter his original intent, which is constantly to do better what historical materialism, as he understands it, was meant to accomplish. What does change is the means he chooses to carry out this task and perhaps even the specific source of the inspiration for the wider framework he employs. Although throughout his writings he is more critical of Hegel than Kant, in the effort to show that his own view is better adapted to reach the goal of prior theory, in effect he employs a Hegelian strategy.

II

PHILOSOPHICAL ANTHROPOLOGY OR THEORY OF HISTORY?

The aim of the preceding chapter was to clarify Habermas' framework for the reception of Marx and Marxism through remarks on its background in the German idealist tradition and in recent analytic philosophy of science. We have seen that like Hegel Habermas considers the philosophical tradition as an ongoing experiment, in which later writers strive to improve upon earlier theories in order better to reach the goals for which such views were formulated. This general perspective provides the framework for Habermas' initial approach to historical materialism as an important but flawed theory, susceptible of improvement.

Habermas' discussion of what he calls "historical materialism" is interesting in itself and for the comprehension of his position. It is surprising, since the discussion on Habermas is considerable and growing rapidly,[1] that comparatively little attention has so far been devoted to his reading of Marx and Marxism. Obviously this aspect of his position has not been entirely ignored. In particular, it plays a role in studies of his thought in relation to critical theory, a form of neo-Marxism elaborated by the members of the Frankfurt School, whose earlier representatives included Adorno, Horkheimer and Marcuse.[2] Wellmer, for instance, has emphasized the significance of Habermas' identification of the latent positivism in Marxism.[3] But although at present the burgeoning literature on Habermas contains several articles and a single book concerning his comprehension of historical materialism, to the best of my knowledge there is as yet no satisfactory, full-length study of his reading of Marx and Marxism.[4]

As his discussion of Marx and Marxism has emerged in piecemeal fashion over a period of many years, we will need to reconstruct its broad outlines and to differentiate its main stages. Since Habermas' reading of historical materialism is not widely known, it will be appropriate to let its main lines emerge before discussing it in detail. This does not mean that the present account of Habermas' comprehension of Marx and Marxism will be uncritical; it only means that, except for some critical remarks on his interpretation of other positions, for the most part a critical examination of various elements in his understanding of historical materialism will be temporarily postponed in order to allow a clear statement of it to emerge.

Since Habermas' reading of historical materialism spans some thirty years, we can begin with a comment on the degree to which it remains constant. It is not always the case that an interpretation of one thinker by another changes over time. Hegel, for example, who often spoke of the positions of his predecessors and contemporaries, rarely revised his views of them. His readings of Kant and Fichte, which he stated as early as the *Differenzschrift*, his first philosophical text, are later restated frequently and deepened, but not significantly altered in later writings. Habermas, on the contrary, has often modified his reading of Marx and Marxism.

In part, he is aware of this fact. In a recent interview he has indicated that he has always regarded Marx as a political theoretician; but it is only since 1958 that he began to take Marx seriously as an economic thinker, which in turn led him to abandon an anthropological approach to Marx's writings.[5] But since the alteration in the main lines of Habermas' comprehension of Marx and Marxism is possibly greater than even he realizes, or wishes to acknowledge, it will be helpful to stress the differences in the successive stages of his examination of historical materialism.

Habermas' interest in historical materialism appears in a variety of ways in his corpus. In some texts, it is nearly absent, or at least not overtly present, for example in writings focused on the elaboration of his systematic position. But even here, Marx and Marxism are present, although not named; for a constant feature of Habermas' work is his desire to overcome the problems he sees in historical materialism. Other writings fall under the heading of what we can call 'applied' Marxism, where Habermas utilizes ideas borrowed from Marx and Marxism to shed light on contemporary society. Examples include his repeated discussions of reification, scattered at intervals throughout his writings,[6] which derive from Lukács's well-known, productive misunderstanding of Marx's concept of alienation, and the analysis of contemporary science as a form of ideology.[7] In still other texts, the discussion is linked in whole or in part to the interpretation, criticism, reconstruction, and rejection of the views of Marx and Marxism.[8]

Depending on the perspective adopted, we can distinguish a variety of different stages in Habermas' examination of Marx and Marxism. But whatever the vantage point, it is clear that the initial phase takes shape in a lengthy paper, whose somewhat unwieldy title is only slightly more felicitous in German: "Report on the Literature Concerning the Philosophical Discussion about Marx and Marxism" ("Literaturbericht zur philosophischen Diskussion um Marx und den Marxismus").[9] This detailed discussion first appeared as an article in 1957 in the *Philosophische Rundschau*, a leading German philosophical journal, and was later republished as an Appendix [Anhang] to a collection of papers by Habermas entitled *Theorie und Praxis*. Surprisingly, despite the importance of this text as the beginning of Habermas' lengthy discussion of

Marx and Marxism, it was not taken up in the English version of this book and seems never to have been translated.

This paper, including 135 notes, is 76 pages long; it is divided into nine sections which, beginning with remarks on three typical approaches to Marx's *Paris Manuscripts* (1844), take up a number of related topics, before ending with comments on the immanent critique of Marxism. Speaking generally, we can characterize Habermas' discussion here as proceeding from Marx to Marxism, and from a reading of the *Paris Manuscripts* as a form of philosophy to the issues that such a reading raises, with special attention to three areas: the existentialist approach to Marx, the way in which historical materialism supposedly answers the question of the meaning of history, and a series of critical observations about historical materialism.

This text is unusual since, as the title obliquely indicates, at this point Habermas possessed a greater mastery of the secondary literature on Marx and Marxism than of the primary sources. Here we find a fair but selective command of Marx's writings, mainly of the early texts, and a wide awareness of their interpretation and of Marxism in general. At this point Habermas' knowledge of the secondary literature on Marx's position includes a good grasp of its German language discussion, a selective acquaintance with studies in French, with particular attention to Sartre and Merleau-Ponty, but little awareness of its discussion in English. In his examination of the different readings of the *Paris Manuscripts* and in the later development of his discussion, Habermas assumes the quasi-Hegelian pose of the neutral observer, whose concern is to envisage all the possibilities from a perspective which, by implication, is entirely neutral.

In part because of the overtly political nature of historical materialism, there are as yet no generally agreed upon guidelines for the interpretation of Marx and Marxism. Issues which either do not arise or have long been settled with respect to other positions are still very much alive, or even central to the study of Marx's thought. Concerning such figures as Kant or Hegel, or Husserl and Heidegger, the relevant question is not the nature of their positions, about which there is little dispute, but their respective claims to truth. But when we turn to Marx, the questions of the nature and truth of his view are inseparably connected.

The nature of Marx's theory has long been, remains, and probably will continue to be a central issue in the Marx discussion for both Marxists and non-Marxists. More than one hundred years after Marx's death, although progress has indeed been made in the comprehension of his thought, there is no reason to believe that we are closer to agreement as to the nature of his theory. A number of well-known, often incompatible analyses have been proposed as descriptions of Marx's position, such as philosophical anthropology, critique, political economy, idealist philosophy, historical and/or dialectical materialism, and philosophy of history.

Habermas' discussion here is centered on the interpretation of the *Paris Manuscripts*, which have often been associated with an anthropological approach[10] to Marx and the series of issues known collectively as Marxist humanism.[11] In the discussion of Marx's view, it is usual to consider approaches to it as philosophical anthropology or as historical materialism as mutually exclusive. The former is a form of philosophy, centering around a theory of subjectivity, whereas the latter is often regarded as nonphilosophic, and hence ranged elsewhere, for instance under the heading of scientific theory. It is difficult to be more specific since there is no general agreement in Marx studies, even on such an apparently simple, but in fact complex, issue as to the nature of Marx's position.

The incompatibility between the two approaches mentioned here follows from alternative interpretations of the significance of the initial period of Marx's position for the position as a whole. In general, the debate between readings of Marx's position as philosophical anthropology or historical materialism does not focus on the anthropological character of the early Marxian writings, which was only recognized rather recently due to the tardy publication of several important texts such as the *Paris Manuscripts* and the *Grundrisse*. Rather, the disagreement concerns the significance of the anthropological flavor of such early Marxian texts for the interpretation of his thought in general.

The most influential rejection of the anthropological perspective is due to the French Marxist, Louis Althusser. Although Althusser acknowledges the presence of an explicitly anthropological perspective in the Marxian writings from the early 1840's, he nevertheless minimizes their permanent importance within the position, and hence the weight of Marx's early interest in philosophical anthropology, by arguing for a break [coupure] in Marx's thought; according to Althusser, this break precisely separates Marx's initial, supposedly immature philosophic and later mature scientific points of view.[12]

Marxian philosophical anthropology is mainly formulated in the early writings, especially the *Paris Manuscripts*. The central body of doctrine known as the Marxist approach to history takes shape in the series of texts beginning with the *German Ideology*, where Marx and Engels stress a concrete form of social theory intended to avoid abstract philosophical assertions.[13] Those who favor an anthropological approach to Marx's position argue that the later writings are not independent of, but rather depend on, the concept of human being, which is a central theme in the early Marxian texts, and is arguably at least implicit in later writings.[14]

Most writers, as noted, regard the approach to Marx's thought as either philosophical anthropology or historical materialism as exclusive alternatives. But Habermas' initial examination of Marx and Marxism is an effort to combine both approaches within a single description of the Marxian position. The result is a possible tension either in Marx's view, as reflected in its depiction, or in Habermas' account of it. As concerns the latter, this apparent tension was rapidly dissipated through Habermas' decision, linked to his increasing interest in Marxian political economy, to abandon the anthropological reading of Marx's position. What remains unclear is which form of interpretation is most faithful to Marx's thought. For if, as Habermas here believes, Marx's view in fact encompasses both a concept of the subject and a theory of history centered on the economic dimension of society, a resolution of the resultant tension cannot be provided through giving up an aspect inherent to the position; it can only result from the kind of integrated reading of its various dimensions within the framework of a single, synthetic approach which Habermas offers here.[15]

In his discussion Habermas elaborates his understanding of Marxian philosophy mainly through a reading of an early, seminal text, "Contribution to the Critique of Hegel's Philosophy of Right. Introduction" ("Zur Kritik der Hegelschen Rechtsphilosophie. Einleitung"). This article is not to be confused with Marx's incomplete "Critique of Hegel's Philosophy of Right" ("Zur Kritik der Hegelschen Rechtsphilosophie. Kritik des Hegelschen Staatsrechts"). These two texts, both from 1843, are largely dissimilar, despite similar titles. In the former, Marx states a number of themes in telegraphic or aphoristic form which will later guide the evolution of his thought, such as man is the root of man, religion is opium of the people, you cannot abolish philosophy without realizing it, etc. In the latter, Marx provides a detailed, systematic commentary, in a scholarly manner, on paragraphs 261–313 of Hegel's *Philosophy of Right (Grundlinien der Philosophie des Rechts)*, paragraph by paragraph.

Habermas' approach to Marx's text is strongly influenced by the existentialist view of Marx, especially by Marcuse's variant of critical theory.[16] Now, in part this designation is misleading, or at least a source of possible misunderstanding. Marcuse, of course, was never an existentialist in any clear sense of the term. His relation to phenomenology was mediated through Heidegger, who directed his doctoral dissertation,[17] but who specifically dissociated his own thought from existentialism.[18] Although he later became sharply critical of Heidegger, Marcuse's peculiar form of Marxism never entirely lost its phenomenological tone, which does not mean that it ever took on an existentialist tone.[19]

Although phenomenological themes continue to occur in his more recent texts, in later writings on historical materialism Habermas has sharply rejected his own, earlier espousal of the phenomenological understanding of Marx's thought.[20] At this point Marcuse's influence on Habermas' initial understanding of Marx is evident on several different levels. These include an interest in the relation of phenomenology and historical materialism, evident in the discussion of the existentialist approach to Marx; his attention to the theme, posted in clearly Heideggerean terminology, of the question concerning the meaning of history; and the articulation of the discussion as a progression from a general philosophical reading of Marx to the existentialist approach, before turning to some problems of the materialist dialectic and the immanent critique of Marxism.

Habermas, as noted, begins his discussion by considering three alternative readings of the *Paris Manuscripts*. Although this text was written by Marx almost at the start of his career in 1844, it was not published during his lifetime; it emerged in print only in 1932. This belated appearance caused a sensation in Marxist circles, since the insistence on philosophical themes, especially alienation, ran counter to many well established interpretations of Marx's thought. The result was the emergence of the so-called humanist interpretation of Marx, which stressed the importance of his early writings in distinction to the received tendency to focus attention on his later texts, especially *Capital*.[21]

In his understanding of historical materialism as philosophy, Habermas follows Marcuse's pioneer review (in 1932) of the just recently published *Paris Manuscripts*. Marcuse here called attention to what he regarded as the philosophical dimension of historical materialism.[22] Habermas further develops this philosophical reading of historical materialism in terms of Marx's famous claim that philosophy must realize itself. Rejecting the Soviet view of Marx's thought as dialectical materialism, he concentrates on the notion of a self-realizing philosophy of history. According to Habermas, what he describes as Marx's philosophy of history and of revolution is a revolutionary humanism [revolutionärer Humanismus] rooted in the analysis of alienation [Entfremdung], whose intention is to change social relations in order to overcome alienation.

Merely to characterize Marx's theory as philosophy is to take sides in a debate that has its origins in the beginning of Marxism in Engels's thought. Marx's critical remarks on philosophy in general, the Young Hegelians, and Hegel have led to a series of different, incompatible interpretations of his position. The differences in interpretation can be summarized for present purposes in the form of an exclusive alternative: either Marx rejects philosophy as such as ideologically flawed in all its forms, as Engels, and following him, numerous later writers, including most Marxists, believe; or he rejects a particular kind of philosophy, but not philosophy as such. In the latter case, his intention is not to refuse philosophy as such; it is rather to object to certain forms of philosophy. For Habermas, who favors this approach, it is obviously important to specify the particular character of Marxian philosophy.

In this connection, Habermas makes several remarks. To begin with, he reaffirms Marx's familiar claim that philosophy can only be sublated through it own realization.[23] Now this idea of philosophy is susceptible of more than one interpretation. It can be taken to mean that the aim of philosophical theory is not, as has sometimes been believed, to furnish disinterested knowledge, or truth for its own sake. According to the latter view, philosophy has no other goal than itself; philosophy literally is its own purpose. The only reason to pursue philosophy in the pure sense of the term, that is, knowledge of first principles, is to satisfy one's curiosity; for this discipline is not socially useful.[24] In a word, from this perspective philosophy is unconcerned with practice.

This kind of comprehension of the philosophical task, which emerges as early as Aristotle's view of metaphysics, is related to a complaint that Marx makes against Hegel and his followers. Marx goes beyond the Aristotelian suggestion that philosophy as such is not socially useful to maintain that in fact it can further be harmful as a sort of mystification.[25] According to Marx,

in virtue of the principle that life is determined by consciousness and not consciousness by life, some kinds of philosophy, in particular absolute idealism,
have the social function of impeding any basic change.

On the contrary, Marx invokes a different image of philosophy as socially
relevant, because self-realizing. This alternative view of philosophic theory as
intrinsically concerned to relate theory to practice,[26] to which Marx appeals,
does not originate with him. It is already present in Plato's concept of pure
theory as socially relevant, which Aristotle is concerned to deny in his own
account of pure theory as irrelevant; and it is further present, in the modern
tradition, in views of the relevance of reason proposed by Kant and Husserl,
which influence Habermas' own reflections on this topic.[27] In his comment
here on the need for philosophy to be relevant by realizing itself, Habermas
for the first time touches on a theme that will determine his future development, including his later effort to elaborate a theory of communicative action
as a proposed replacement for historical materialism.

If Marx's theory is philosophy, it is obviously important not to conflate its
distinguishing characteristics with those of other views. In part following the
lead of Marcuse as well as other commentators too numerous to mention,
Habermas is critical of many of the ways Marx and Marxism are ordinarily
characterized. In his description of historical materialism as philosophy, at this
point in his development Habermas has in mind a theory of society and not
the theory of evolution he will later invoke. Here he carefully distinguishes
his understanding of the Marxian view from the Soviet-influenced view of dialectical materialism and other varieties of materialism, such as those represented by the eighteenth century Encyclopedists and the Monists at the end
of the nineteenth century.

He is equally unwilling to accept without comment what he regards as the
attempted 'philosophical' appropriation of Marxism in order to understand the
relation of Hegel to Marx. According to Habermas, it is only through a per-
ceptible distortion that Marx's theory can be simply reduced to pure philosophy. He believes that even if Marx misunderstood Hegel—who in fact had arguably already arrived at ideas which Marx found independently in the
course of his own effort to think against absolute idealism—we cannot overlook the specific difference between them, apparent in Marx's empirically-
secured, revolutionary philosophy of history.[28]

Habermas does not now elaborate this idea, which he will later develop.[29]
He mentions it here to warn against the negative consequences of a proposed
philosophical appropriation of Marx. He believes that an appropriation of this
kind fails to draw the distinctions necessary to preserve the differences between Marx's theory and what Habermas here calls "pure" [reine] philosophy,
and which Marxists have traditionally called "bourgeois thought." According
to Habermas, who is probably influenced by Korsch on this point,[30] Marx's
intention is not to criticize from the perspective of philosophical presuppositions, but rather from that of their sublation. From this angle of vision
Habermas pretends that as concerns traditional philosophy Marx's categories,

philosophical problems, and form of reflection change. It follows that for Habermas merely to contemplate Marxism from the angle of vision of philosophy as it is usually understood is to miss the specific nature of Marx's theory.

At this point Habermas believes that the so-called 'Young Hegelian interpretation' is characteristic of even the best philosophical readings of Marx. The perhaps unintended effect is to suggest that in his own insistence on the philosophical element of historical materialism as against the misunderstandings he rejects, Habermas alone offers a correct reading of the theory. Although even in his most enthusiastic moments Habermas was never a dogmatic Marxist, it is difficult to overlook his implicit claim to orthodoxy, which always presupposes the quasi-mystical belief of superior insight into an otherwise misunderstood position.

Habermas' treatment of other commentators is doubly important: for his critical comments, which are frequently insightful, and for the light they shed on his own reading of Marx and Marxism. His attitude towards most philosophical interpreters of historical materialism at this stage can properly be described as critical, even dismissive. Merely to characterize those who approach Marxism from the traditional philosophical perspective as unwittingly adopting a Young Hegelian attitude supposedly rejected by Marx is to propose a blanket refusal of other philosophical readings. Hence, it is significant to note an important exception to Habermas' negative comprehension of other readings of historical materialism in his treatment of what he calls "The Existentialist Attempt in Marxism."[31]

This section mainly concerns Sartre and his younger colleague, Merleau-Ponty. In his remarks on Sartre, Habermas refers only to writings up to and including *Search for a Method*. Accordingly, he omits any mention of the *Critique of Dialectical Reason*, of which it is the preface, or of any later texts, where Sartre further developed the effort to fuse Marxism with his own existentialism. Here Habermas considers Sartre as an interesting case of an erroneous tendency to conflate the philosophical reading of historical materialism with so-called pure philosophy.

He believes that Sartre's understanding of Marxism rests on a mistaken reading. According to Habermas, Sartre shares Marx's view that philosophy cannot merely add on or attach to [hinzufügen] a revolutionary dimension, which must be intrinsic to it. As he reads Sartre's position, the latter differs from Marx in regarding the appropriate beginning point as immanent to philosophy, resulting in the identification of philosophy and revolution, or more precisely the self-grounding [Selbstbegründung] of philosophy as an anthropology of revolution.

In Habermas' *Discourse on Philosophical Modernity*, he criticizes Marx for an exaggerated attention to the economic dimension of capitalism, which provides an unsatisfactory view of modernity. At present, he argues that Sartre's philosophy of revolution is wholly abstract; it is allegedly not concerned with the transformation of a particular society, but with the nature of society in general. Now this criticism is doubly ironic since Habermas will later describe

Marx's position as a theory of the evolution of society; and he will later characterize his own theory of communicative action, which he in part intends as another, more adequate means to achieve the goal intrinsic to the old philosophy of history, as a theory of the social context.

In part because of the brevity of his mention of Sartre, Habermas apparently here confuses the existentialist concept of "fondement" with the German idealist idea of "Grund." The two terms are indeed similar, and certainly share a similar range of connotations, but the philosophical denotations are not the same. German idealism was concerned with the problem of an epistemological foundation, or ground, in a quasi-rationalist sense; this epistemological concept is associated less with the quasi-religious notion of a divine ground in the views of Böhme and Schelling, than with the Cartesian cogito, in order to provide for knowledge in the full sense of the term.[32] Now Sartre does not regard Marxism as even a possible source of absolute knowledge, as is evident in his allusions to hermeneutics. Although he holds that Marxism is a philosophical anthropology, he also believes that it is missing a concrete idea of human being. The result is a lack, which he proposes to correct by offering the existentialist notion of human being to Marxism in order to prevent its collapse, but not to found it in any further, epistemological sense.[33]

In sum, we can say that in his discussion of Sartre Habermas is concerned with an argument which is arguably not present in Sartre's writings on Marx and Marxism or is in general even foreign to them. We can further note the irony attaching to a reproach based on a supposedly abstract perspective, since Sartre's own critique of dogmatic Marxism makes a similar point. Now Habermas' complaint is not directed to what Sartre does, which is to attempt to specify general, ontological conditions of social life; rather, he objects to what Sartre does not do, but presumably ought to have done, which, from Habermas' perspective, is to formulate a replacement for the Marxian theory. We can see that Habermas' later effort to replace Marx's theory by another, better view is already implicit here, at the onset of his discussion of Marx and Marxism, in his rapid critical remarks on Sartre's comprehension of Marxism.[34] Yet since Marx has already provided a specific link between revolution and a particular kind of society, it seems reasonable for Sartre, whose interest is not to replace Marx's position but to supplement it, to attempt to uncover what can be called "the ontological presuppositions of revolution in general."

There is evidence of an interest in Marxism as early as the end of Sartre's essay on "The Transcendence of the Ego," where he rejects so-called metaphysical materialism as a foundation for historical materialism, in order to drive an implicit wedge between Marx and Marxism.[35] This nascent interest develops later when he turns to Marxism after the Second World War in an important article, "Marxism and Revolution." His later return to Marxism is due to several factors, including the strongly critical discussion of his thought offered by Merleau-Ponty.[36]

The appreciation of Merleau-Ponty is more positive. Habermas argues that in virtue of Merleau-Ponty's critique of the alleged inconsistency in Sartre's position between the early, ahistorical dialectic of *Being and Nothingness* and the later, historical dialictic of his Marxist period, Merleau-Ponty differs from all other philosophical interpreters in taking seriously the specific problem raised by Marxism: "[Merleau-Ponty] regards this as the problem of an empirically secured philosophy of history and likewise of a theory of society in the form of a 'last' philosophy in general."[37]

Habermas believes that Merleau-Ponty correctly recovers the understanding of Marxism as a practically oriented philosophy of history. In Habermas' view, Merleau-Ponty shares Marx's thesis that philosophy must be immanent, and he further shares Marx's inability to understand the relation of philosophy to practice. But Merleau-Ponty's approach is said to fail because of an inner contradiction between his awareness of historical contingency and what Habermas sees as a quasi-Husserlian demand for a transcendental ground. In a word, Habermas believes there is a tension in Merleau-Ponty's thought in the latter's insistence on the openness of history and the denial of historical closure on the one hand and the supposed desire to provide a transcendental grounding of historical meaning on the other.[38]

This way of reading Merleau-Ponty's position requires a comment. Clearly, Habermas finds in Merleau-Ponty the general outlines of a philosophical view of historical materialism that he accepts at this point and which he regards as coming closest among the various philosophical interpretations to the practical intentions of Marxism. Unlike his remarks on Sartre, his immediate aim is not to discredit Merleau-Ponty's reading of Marxism; it is rather meant to point to the supposed incompatibility of Merleau-Ponty's radical view of philosophy with the traditional, phenomenological approach which he allegedly also adopts.

In his criticism of Merleau-Ponty, Habermas attempts to disjoin as exclusive alternatives the phenomenological approach to transcendental justification exemplified by Husserl and the Marxian concept of empirically secured philosophy of history. Now, in principle, his intention is justified; there are obvious dissimilarities in the positions of Husserl and Marx, such as their respective concepts of truth, which have long been seen as irreconcilably different.[39]

But the interpretation of Merleau-Ponty's own view as a form of transcendental phenomenology is controversial. For Merleau-Ponty's entire effort was directed against any attempt, such as that associated with Husserl, to provide a transcendental justification for claims to truth in the traditional, apodictic sense. More precisely, Merleau-Ponty's insistence on perception leads him to reject the ideas of apodictic evidence and atemporal thought.[40]

The immediate result of the discussion of the so-called existentialist attempt in Marxism is to identify a philosophically plausible reading of historical materialism. In later writings on Marx and Marxism Habermas does not come back to existentialism directly, although he repeatedly comments on phenomenology, from which existentialism springs, most recently in the course of an extended philosophical discourse on modernity. With respect to Marx and Marxism, such comments in his later writings serve a double function: to warn against possible misreadings from a phenomenological perspective, and to 'locate' concepts he can appropriate and reinterpret for his effort to develop further the spirit, if not the letter, of historical materialism.

In the present text, after his remarks on existentialism, Habermas turns immediately to a clarification of the approach to historical materialism as a philosophy of history in terms of the question of the meaning of history. His way of stating the problem further betrays the influence of phenomenology in his writings here, more precisely Heidegger's concern with the question of the meaning of Being.[41] Habermas' remarks also reveal a specifically Heideggerean influence in other ways at this point, including the concern with the future dimension of time, the refusal of other alternatives as insufficiently radical, and the insistence that the Marxian theory surpasses the philosophical tradition. In later writings he seems more interested in the Husserlian form of phenomenology, and above all in the extra-phenomenological critical philosophy. Here, when these later influences have yet to emerge, Habermas further takes Heidegger's position as the standard for Marx and Marxism. After a sketch of the Heideggerean view of historicity, he asks rhetorically if historical materialism can really provide a solution for what the "being-historical interpretation" [seinsgeschichtliche Deutung] promises.

In his response, Habermas draws a comparison between Kant and Marx centering on the concept of practical reason. According to Habermas, an application of the concept of practical reason to the problem of history yields the intended aim of the philosophy of history, that is, a view that the conditions of a possible revolution can be verified empirically since theoretical claims lead to practical results. This perspective enables Habermas to point to two ways in which historical materialism qua materialism differs from what he calls first philosophy [prima philosophia]: through its renunciation of the goal of self-grounding, and through its further abandonment of the intent to fulfill itself merely within philosophy. The result is neither a philosophy concerned with the question of the meaning of Being or with ontology in general. On the contrary, he believes that historical materialism is a fundamentally practical theory, or critique [Kritik].

In comparison with earlier discussion, the remarks on the relation of historical materialism to the views of Heidegger and Kant draw attention to a possible source of the familiar, but obscure, Marxian idea of practice [Praxis] in the concept of practical reason. Although in the text as a whole Habermas is officially concerned with the philosophical appropriation of Marx through the relation of Marx to Hegel, this comparison is important in showing that Marx can be usefully understood against a wider philosophical background.[42]

This passage is further significant in making clear that as early as the initial stage of his examination of Marx and Marxism Habermas follows Korsch's lead in interpreting historical materialism as a practical philosophy, or critique. Habermas insists often on the influence Lukács had in opening his way to Marx and frequently recalls specific Lukácsian vocabulary and themes; but although there are many other influences, in his general approach to historical materialism as an empirically secured philosophy of history, which accordingly differs from other forms of philosophy, he primarily relies on Korsch's view of Marxism as critique.

Through the adoption of a basically Korschian reading, tinged with numerous other influences, Habermas to his satisfaction distinguishes his own understanding of Marx and Marxism from various other efforts to provide a philosophical interpretation of historical materialism. Now, since Korsch's approach, which he never names in this essay, is a well-known form of Marxism, in effect Habermas rejects non-Marxist, philosophical interpretations of Marx and Marxism in favor of a particular Marxist reading of the theory. In sections devoted to the problem of a materialistic dialectic and the immanent critique of Marxism, he devotes the remainder of his "Literaturbericht" to differentiating his comprehension of historical materialism from those found in other, competing forms of Marxism.

Under the heading of the materialistic dialectic, Habermas considers four themes: the materialistic critique of philosophical foundationalism, ideology and revolution, the dialectic of work, and the relation of materialistic dialectic to the social sciences. The remarks on Adorno make plain Habermas' indebtedness to the former's refusal of any association between historical materialism and *Ursprungsphilosophie*, which is roughly synonymous with philosophical foundationalism in its various forms. Habermas interprets the renunciation of the requirement of philosophy to ground and to fulfill itself as philosophy to mean that through the unity of theory and practice theory can achieve both goals. Although he differs from many Marxists in his belief that historical materialism is a form of philosophy, he here denies that other, weaker standards of theory need to be invoked.

According to Habermas, who here silently adopts Lukács's well-known analysis, the development of the view that historical materialism can only attain the aims of founding and fulfilling itself by unifying theory with practice lies in the doctrine of ideology.[43] He describes the notions of ideology and of revolution as forming a conceptual circle, in which each is the presupposition of the other. In his comments on the dialectic of work, after contrasting the views of Engels and Lukács, he suggests that through his refusal of abstraction Marx distanced himself from Hegel. According to Habermas, "materialistic dialectic" means that "the dialectical logic must emerge from the relations of work without understanding work in a metaphysical sense."

His intention at this point would seem to be to differentiate Marx from Hegel, who also proposed a dialectical understanding of work, by preserving the supposed distinction between materialism and idealism. Habermas here rethinks this distinction under the heading of founded or foundationalist and nonfounded or nonfoundationalist forms of philosophy. But it is not unclear how Habermas can deny, as he must to make out the distinction he seems to have in mind, that work is an ontological category, in fact a central category of social ontology.[44]

Although Habermas in part adopts ideas borrowed from Lukács, he is critical of the latter's celebrated form of Marxism. In the discussion of dialectic, he strongly criticizes Lukács's views of class consciousness and of the proletariat as the subject/object of history. He continues this criticism in his remarks on the relation of materialist dialectic to the social sciences. His intention here is to clarify the relation of philosophy and the sciences as Marx describes it. According to Habermas, these nondialectical sciences are unsuited to the comprehension of their object since they cannot grasp its developmental tendencies. This point is an application to the social sciences of Lukács's neo-Kantian claim that so-called bourgeois philosophy cannot know its object.[45] As distinguished from the social sciences, Habermas sees the task of philosophy as being to sublate the objectification of the nonobjectifiable in a whole in the Hegelian senses of the term "sublation." But he rejects Lukács's theory of proletarian class consciousness because of an alleged association with Soviet orthodoxy, in favor of a renewed insistence on the need for empirical falsifiability.

Habermas continues his attack on Lukács's form of Marxism in remarks on the problem of class consciousness, in a section devoted to the immanent critique of Marxism which closes his essay. After some comments on the differences between Eastern and Western forms of Marxism, he addresses the question of the contemporary relevance of proletarian class consciousness for revolution. According to Habermas neither Sartre nor Marx successfully handles this problem. He ends his study with a quotation from Marcuse in order to illustrate what has emerged as the central theme of the discussion, that is, that what Habermas calls "the philosophical approach [der philosophische Ansatz] of historical materialism demonstrates its fruitfulness in connection with empirical research only if the elements of Marxism receive a needed critique without any reserve [vorbehaltlos]."

In the present context this statement has a double implication. On the one hand, Habermas is clearly reiterating his unorthodox approach, which means that he rejects the temptation to mute his criticism on grounds of political orthodoxy. By implication, then, he at this point reaffirms his concern with the discovery of the truth by pursuing his argument wherever it may lead. Since this attitude is certainly a general prerequisite of any scholarly endeavor, it would normally not attract further attention. But since ordinary scholarly standards are not often observed in the discussion of historical materialism, it is at least useful to note Habermas' implied intent. In this way he signals his intention to disregard any special pleading for historical materialism on any grounds whatsoever. The theory, insofar as it makes claims to know, must meet generally accepted standards for all theory. His conviction that historical materialism needs to meet the same criteria for theory as other views will later be a silent presupposition of the criticism he will bring against it from a quasi-Kantian angle of vision.

On the other hand, he suggests that he is willing to understand historical materialism on its own terms, that is, through its well-known concern to relate theory to practice, which he here interprets as mandating an empirical evaluation. In principle this means that since it is a practically oriented theory, if its evaluation is to respect its intrinsic aim, historical materialism cannot be evaluated in a theoretical manner. In the sense, historical materialism differs in kind from traditional philosophy, or what Habermas, following Adorno, also calls *Ursprungsphilosophie*, for instance the critical philosophy, whose claims are wholly a priori. On the contrary, the theory can and must be studied in an empirical manner. In practice, there is a clear implication, which closely follows Korsch's effort to judge the theory of historical materialism through its practical results, that the criteria of historical materialism must also be applied to itself. It is accordingly not by accident that in the immediately succeeding texts on historical materialism Habermas amplifies his effort to understand Marx and Marxism from an empirical perspective, that is, as an empirically falsifiable form of philosophy.

This detailed description of Habermas; "Literaturbericht" is justified by its inherent importance, its present unavailability in English, and its role in the further evolution of his study of Marx and Marxism. An aim of the present discussion is to demonstrate that we find in this text the first phase of what is arguably one of the major readings of historical materialism in our time, as a serious effort to come to grips with the nature of this theory and problems it poses.

In his later writings on Marx and Marxism, as will be seen below, Habermas alters numerous aspects of his interpretation. But there are many features which do not change, and hence which are represented in the present and in later phases of the discussion. These include his general reading of historical materialism as an empirically secured philosophy of history, which he later refines; the many-faceted but continued revolt against the early Lukács's general approach to Marx and Marxism; the constant attention to Kant's critical philosophy as a criterion for the assessment of philosophical theory in general; and the continued consideration of phenomenology and a phenomenological reading of historical materialism. More generally, it is fair to say that most of the other themes that he later raises in the course of his extended study of Marx and Marxism are at least anticipated in this early essay. In this sense, we can say that Habermas' later discussion of historical materialism takes shape in the conceptual space created by its initial phase.

III

THE TRANSITIONAL PERIOD

The later phases of Habermas' discussion of historical materialism reflect the further development of the discussion begun in the "Literaturbericht." After this text, there is a period of transition in which Habermas revises his first approach to the theory at the same time as his own theory of communicative action begins to emerge. This chapter will be concerned with a description of the transitional period falling between his initial reading of historical materialism and its later critique. Here we will study the evolution of his approach to Marx and Marxism through the reconsideration of familiar themes, such as his attitudes toward Lukács and Korsch, and the introduction of new ideas, including the emergence of his epistemological objection to Marx's theory, his distinction between work and interaction upon which it is based, and his analysis of the relation of knowledge and interest.

The transitional period in Habermas' discussion of historical materialism will be studied here in three main texts: the important account of Marxism as critique,[1] where he identifies the basic elements of his reinterpretation of the theory from an economic perspective and further identifies the basic criticisms he will advance against it; the celebrated inaugural lecture Habermas delivered upon assuming a lectureship in Frankfurt,[2] where he offers a systematic analysis of the relation of knowledge and interest fundamental to his critique of historical materialism as well as to his own theory of communicative action; and a short text on Hegel[3] where he 'discovers' his own distinction between work and interaction in Hegel's early thought.

In general, in the transitional period Habermas further develops his interest in the relation of theory and practice. Already in the "Literaturbericht," as noted, Habermas utilized the Marxist concern with this relation in two ways: as a standard to explain the difference between historical materialism and other forms of philosophy and as a description for the theory itself. In the transitional phase, Habermas further develops this theme in a paper entitled "Between Philosophy and Science. Marxism as Critique," published in 1963.

At this point we can identify three specific changes in Habermas' approach, concerning the influence of Korsch and contemporary philosophy of science, and the attempted resolution of an earlier, unresolved tension. In the first place, Habermas now strengthens his reliance on Korsch's approach to Marx and Marxism in the elaboration of his own on historical materialism as critique. His understanding of historical materialism at this point is in effect a modification of Korsch's view, which Habermas now supplements through the adoption of the concept of fallibilism borrowed from contemporary philosophy of science.

Since Korsch plays a significant role in this phase of Habermas' discussion and is also an important interpreter of Marxism, it might be useful here to locate the Korschian approach to Marxism within the context of the rise of Hegelian Marxism. The development of Hegelian Marxism is mainly due to two influential works, which both appeared in 1923: Lukács's *History and Class Consciousness* and Korsch's *Marxism and Philosophy*. In general, Korsch's reading of Marx is closely related to Lukács's early Marxist phase.

Korsch here exercises a particular effect on Habermas' understanding of historical materialism. In *Marxism and Philosophy,* like *History and Class Consciousness* an early work, Korsch argued that Marxism is neither philosophy nor science, but critique. Habermas now follows Korsch's insistence on the status of historical materialism as critique excluding philosophy and science, although he resists the later's effort to drive a wedge between Marxism and philosophy as such in order to preserve his earlier distinction between it and so-called first philosophy.

The second innovation in Habermas' transitional phase follows from his interest in philosophy of science. In order to understand the opposition between Marxist and non-Marxist forms of philosophy Habermas turns at this point to the stress in contemporary analytic philosophy of science on empirical refutation, especially to the Popperian view of fallibilism. In his influential discussion of the so-called demarcation problem, Popper argues that science in general, by which he primarily means natural science, especially physics, differs from philosophy in that it can be empirically refuted.[4] In Habermas' discussion the result is a novel comprehension of historical materialism as an empirically based philosophy of history, susceptible of empirical refutation. In this way Habermas attempts to preserve his earlier insistence that as philosophy Marxism rejects the traditional concern with first principles while characterizing it—following Marx's emphasis on practice and his own version of the presumed difference in kind between traditional philosophy and Marx's thought—as empirically rooted.

The third new feature is the effort to dissipate a possible tension that arose in the "Literaturbericht" in the grasp of historical materialism as both philosophical anthropology and a theory of history. If these twin perspectives are incompatible, then obviously they cannot coexist within a single theory or interpretation of it. Habermas attempts now to overcome this possible problem by shifting his focus from the anthropological issues characteristic of, or at least more apparent in, Marx's youthful writings to the economic concerns which become an increasingly dominant theme as early as the *German Ideology*. At the same time, he shifts his attention from the early writings to later texts from the *German Ideology* onward, with increasing emphasis on *Capital*.

The result is an understanding of historical materialism which combines classical Marxist and novel features in a single reading. The classical Marxist emphasis is mainly visible in the stress on the economic comprehension of the Marxian position reminiscent of the approach associated with Engels and numerous later representatives of politically orthodox Marxism.[5] The novel features include a concern to link the understanding of historical materialism to developments in recent analytic philosophy of science and, above all, an increasingly clear intention, which is a permanent feature of Habermas' later discussion of Marx and Marxism, to criticize historical materialism from the vantage point of the critical philosophy.

In the "Literaturbericht" Habermas was concerned to clarify the relation of historical materialism to philosophy by arguing that in virtue of their practical orientation and corresponding empirical basis, the views of Marx and Marxism differ from first philosophy, or ontology. This theme, as noted, motivates his turn to Korsch and Popper in order further to clarify the status of Marxism with respect to philosophy, or at least traditional philosophical thought, and the sciences. But although Habermas is indeed in part successful here in clarifying the status of historical materialism, he at the same time creates additional problems for his consistent insistence on the theory's philosophical status, which so to speak runs against the tide of Marxism in general, including Korsch's view.

In part, he has already abandoned this point in his adoption here of Korsch's view that Marxism is located between philosophy and science. Nevertheless, he continues to maintain that the theory is philosophy when he describes it as a philosophy of history with political intent. The result is a tension, which Habermas is unable to resolve, between the approach to historical materialism as an empirically based form of philosophy, and the insistence on its 'location' between philosophy and science. Certainly, Habermas' later tendency to refer to historical materialism as a social theory does not resolve this issue, since it leaves open the problem of the status of social theory.

As noted, the present discussion places new emphasis on the link between critique and political economy which becomes increasingly prominent in Marx's later writings. The interest in critique derives from Korsch and also Kant, and Habermas' concern with political economy is also related to Korsch.[6] The result is a discussion that now dwells on several topics mentioned scarcely, if at all, in the earlier text, including the concept of critique, the labor theory of value, the analysis of economic crises, the critique of ideology, and the presuppositions of a materialist philosophy of history.

As in his previous discussion of historical materialism, Habermas is now concerned to reject other approaches even as he develops his own reading of Marx and Marxism. He begins here by retracing some of the ground already covered in the earlier essay. After noting four historical facts which preclude acceptance of the Stalinist theory of dialectical materialism, he then rapidly surveys typical forms of the reaction to Marxism, such as Sovietology, as well as theology and philosophy. He rejects the latter as an adequate approach to Marxism for its alleged failure to renounce the philosophical presuppositions supposedly suspended by materialist critique. In an obvious allusion to Heidegger, he further rejects the approach associated with the critics of *Ursprungsphilosophie*, since they concern themselves with questions of Being, while Marx's interest allegedly lies in the specific historical and social context.

According to Habermas, in part because academic thought has become positivist and lost the Marxian capacity to envision society as a historical whole, the economic and sociological debate with Marx has been at a standstill for decades. In a clear reference to Korsch, who is not otherwise named, Habermas states that a formal designation of Marxism as 'between' philosophy and science does not provide a clarification from the perspective of philosophy of science. In a tacit reference to Kant's claim to understand Plato better than he understood himself, Habermas now defines his task as the comprehension of Marxist theory as a philosophy of history formulated with an explicit political intent, and scientifically falsifiable.[7]

Habermas continues his discussion by observing that Marx called his own theory "critique." He distinguishes three meanings of the term, including an original Greek sense; an allegedly Hegelian view of dialectic as the logic of crisis to be resolved theologically; and what he describes as a specifically Marxian, materialist theory in which crises are thought to be resolved through the dialectic of social labor. By implication, the specifically materialist nature of historical materialism lies in its rejection of the idealist effort to provide no more than an illusory solution to social problems. From this perspective, Marx's position is a critique of political economy. According to Habermas, the Marxian critique differs from other forms of political economy in its recognition of the historical character of political economy and in its concern with the practical solution of real social crises. In a word, as he states, the theory of political economy is a genuine theory of crisis.[8]

Habermas' shift from a philosophical to an economic interpretation of historical materialism raises significant questions concerning the unity of the position and of his reading of it. The problem of continuity arises naturally within Habermas' discussion in view of his own turn from the philosophical to the economic aspects of historical materialism. As concerns the theory, this problem is clearly present in his difficult insistence on the philosophical status of the position even as he stresses its economic side.

This problem can be formulated in various ways, each of which has received extensive discussion in the literature on Marx, such as the relation of the earlier and later Marxian writings, or the link of philosophy, especially philosophical anthropology, with economics, or political economy. Habermas does not consider this issue directly in any of its forms at present or in later writings; but he often comments on it obliquely, for instance in his earlier remarks meant to clarify the relation of Marxism to philosophy. Here he turns immediately to a detailed, but brief, analysis of Marxian political economy, with special attention to the labor theory of value.

Habermas does not say so, but it is at least reasonable to assume that his attention here to the labor theory of value, as well as his critique of it elsewhere,[9] is meant to correct the failure of earlier sociology to take the labor theory of value as the systematic point of departure.[10] He notes that the Marxian value theory arises out of the simple consideration that the transformation of money into capital presupposes that the capitalist can buy and sell commodities at their true value, and still accumulate value. He then proposes two related theses. On the one hand, the value theory is linked to the analysis of crises, which arise from the process of utilization, or investment, of capital accumulated as surplus value. On the other hand, this doctrine presupposes that we can consider and resolve these crises from the economic point of view. According to Habermas, Marx elaborates these theses in different parts of his position. The first thesis is developed in political economy as the theory of crisis and the second thesis occurs in historical materialism as the doctrine of ideology.

Since we will return to this topic, we do not need to provide a detailed account of his remarks on the labor theory of value at present. It is sufficient merely to note that an important result of his silent decision to take the labor theory of value as the systematic point of departure for the study of historical materialism is that in his discussion here and in the future the validity of the entire Marxian position stands or falls in terms of the controversial Marxian value theory. He does not now make this argument, which will be the presuppostion of his later effort to reject historical materialism through a critique of Marxian value theory.[11] The discussion in the remainder of this essay consists in a critical examination of two theses he sees as linked to the Marxian value theory as well as the presuppositions of the so-called materialist philosophy of history.

To begin with he examines the Marxian view of the economic crises supposedly intrinsic to capitalism. Marx's understanding of the crises of capitalism has been criticized in recent years from various perspectives. At present Habermas follows the frequent objection that Marx's theoretical model is overly simplistic since capitalism is more resilient than he believed. In a complicated discussion drawing in part on supposed differences between the *Grundrisse* and *Capital*, Habermas here advances various objections related to different kinds of economic crises. He suggests in passing that the classical formulation of the labor theory of value is insufficient to explain the actual growth of value.[12] And he envisages a post-economic situation in which, since it would be possible to satisfy both 'necessary' and 'superfluous' needs, capital accumulation would cease.[13]

His critical examination of the Marxian understanding of the crises of capitalism represents an indirect attack on the latter's value theory, which in retrospect clearly foreshadows a later, more direct effort to refute it. Habermas' equally skeptical reading of the concept of ideology depends on a controversial parallel he discerns between Schelling and Marx. Now, Schelling's influence on Engels is clear, although not often noted. Examples include a series of early articles by Engels on Schelling[14] as well as a shared interest in the philosophy of nature. But there is no evidence that Marx was ever influenced by Schelling in particular or by the mystical tradition in general. Nevertheless Habermas feels no hesitation in claiming that the celebrated, but unclearly defined, priority of the base over the superstructure in historical materialism derives from a prejudgment similar to Schelling's thought and the mystical tradition.[15]

Marx's concept of ideology rests on the claim that a socially distorted form of society tends to produce a distorted apprehension of itself on the level of consciousness. This idea has been widely influential in the Marxist discussion, for instance in Lukács's theory of class consciousness and, in different form, in Mannheim's sociology of knowledge.[16] Habermas' earlier remarks on ideology, in the "Literaturbericht," were neutral in tone. His criticism here represents the continuation of his earlier objections to Lukács's theory of class consciousness, which obviously depends on the concept of ideology.

According to Habermas, the relation of ideology to politics and economics cannot merely be assumed; it must be demonstrated.[17] He regards Marx's supposed failure to prove this relation as a special case of a more general epistemological deficiency. In voluntarily Kantian language, which inaugurates the quasi-Kantian attitude that will henceforth be a constant feature of his writing, he describes a supposedly inherent epistemological deficit of the Marxian theory: "Marx never explicitly posed for himself the epistemological question concerning the condition of the possibility of a philosophy of history with political intent."[18]

This criticism constitutes a clear turning point in Habermas' examination of historical materialism. Beginning at this point the subdued epistemological concern present in the earlier "Literaturbericht," especially in the polemic against Lukács, becomes fully manifest as a leading theme of Habermas' discussion of Marx and Marxism here and in later writings. In the present context, there is a shift from the reading of Marx's theory as critique, influenced by Korsch, to the concept of critique as the standard of nondogmatic, epistemologically adequate theory, derived from Kant. For Habermas, the latter, quasi-Kantian concept of critique will continue to function in all his later writings as the epistemological criterion from which to consider Marx's theory as well as to elaborate an alternative theory of communicative action presumably resistant to the criticism he here raises against historical materialism.

Habermas' turn to an epistemological concept of critique has an important consequence for his comprehension of Marx's view. His original effort to interpret Marx's position as a novel form of philosophy is maintained in the present essay in the claim that it is neither traditional, or first, philosophy, nor science. His proposed rejection of traditional philosophy in the name of historical materialism is put in doubt by his acceptance of the Kantian transcendental turn as the standard of all philosophy, including Marx and Marxism.

There is an obvious tension in his desire to reject a supposedly traditional form of theory while at the same time continuing to employ it as a standard of rigorous thought. And in his turn to the Kantian view of critique Habermas blurs the traditional distinction which, in imitation of various forms of Marxism, he has constantly sought to maintain in different ways between Marx and traditional philosophy. These include his description of Marxism as an empirically secured philosophy of history, its capacity for empirical refutation, its location between philosophy and science, its intrinsic political intent, etc.

Habermas' turn to Kantian standards of theory is clearly linked to his critical reading of the texts of Marx and Marxism. An implication of the view that Marx's position is relevantly different, which has always been drawn by Marxists, is that historical materialism must be judged by different standards.[19] But a consequence of the introduction of a quasi-Kantian, transcendental model as the criterion for theory in general, including Marx's position, is to reject the claim that the latter view can or even ought to be judged by standards not employed for philosophy in the wider sense. In the resultant denial of all forms of special pleading for Marx's theory on the grounds that it is relevantly different, Habermas clearly indicates that the position must stand or fall by the same criteria as other forms of philosophy.

Habermas only pursues the metatheoretical criterion of critique in later writings. At the close of this essay he returns briefly to the theme, already mentioned in the "Literaturbericht," of the relation between Marx and Kant. The discussion in this passage is controversial and derivative. Despite Habermas' claim, there is no reason to believe that Hegel was familiar with Vico's position, which he never mentions. We can also note that Marx adopts the perspective of the proletariat; but the epistemological justification for this move only emerges in Lukács. Nevertheless, Habermas confidently asserts that Marx reconciles Vico, as preserved in Hegel, with Kant,[20] in a theory supplemented by the epistemological justification of the proletarian perspective.[21] It would seem that Habermas does not understand this assertion from an epistemological angle of vision, but rather from a more Sartrian approach to Marxism as the philosophy of our time. According to Habermas, it is only with the rise of capitalism that historical materialism has achieved its historical preconditions, that is, that the world has become a unity and that history can be made.[22]

In sum this essay continues the approach to historical materialism as an empirically secured philosophy of history, and adds a series of new dimensions. These include an emphasis on empirical disconfirmation already implicit in the attention to the theory's empirical character, a description of the theory as critique which is neither philosophy nor science, and a turn to the Kantian concept of critique as the epistemological standard.

A consequence of the emergence of an epistemological reading of historical materialism is to suggest two related tasks: a deepening of the critique of the theory from a Kantian angle of vision, and a wider analysis of the relation between critical and noncritical forms of philosophy within the context of the German tradition. In a word, the epistemological criticism Habermas raises here points to a historical progression, which receives a systematic evaluation in the objection raised.

This double task is the focus of the next stage of Habermas' examination of Marx and Marxism in two texts bearing nearly the same name: "Knowledge and Human Interests. A General Perspective," his inaugural lecture as a professor at the University of Frankfurt, delivered in 1965; and *Knowledge and Human Interests,* a historically oriented expansion of his systematic analysis, which appeared in 1968. As the titles indicate, the discussions in part overlap; but there are significant differences between them which point to the need for separate treatment of each text.

Despite the continuity with his earlier treatment of Marx and Marxism, Habermas here breaks significant new ground in various ways. Even as he continues to deepen and to develop his understanding of historical materialism, he is starting to develop a new theory ultimately intended to replace it, or more precisely meant to reach the goals supposedly intrinsic to historical materialism, but which it is arguably unable to attain. With the exception of some later essays specifically directed to the reconstruction of historical materialism,[23] in these and in later writings Marx and Marxism are never studied in isolation and always considered in terms of more general questions.

The discussion here of the connection of knowledge and human interests concerns a theme studied under different headings in Marxism as the relation of theory and practice, and by Kant as the *conceptus cosmicus,* or concept of philosophy as the science of the relation of all knowledge to the ends of human reason.[24] It follows that for Habermas Marx's thought is not only linked to the wider tradition through absolute idealism from which it is often held to emerge; it is also connected to the surrounding history of philosophy through a theme it supposedly shares with the critical philosophy. It further follows— since Kant and Marx allegedly pursue a similar goal—that it is permissible to criticize the latter from the former's perspective and to attempt to surpass Marx's thought, toward the presumed common end in view, by relying on a different, quasi-Kantian theoretical model. It remains, however, to be shown that Kant and Marx are in fact concerned with precisely the same goal.

We have noted that Habermas' criticism of Marx from a broadly Kantian vantage point commits him to a quasi-transcendental concept of theory. In the inaugural lecture he takes up this topic in typically oblique fashion through remarks on Husserl's transcendental phenomenology, with special attention to the idea of objectivism. Husserl was initially critical of Kant, and his followers were always concerned to distinguish his theory from the critical philosophy.[25] But as he became more aware of the latter view, he came to see the positive relation between it and his own form of phenomenology.[26]

Habermas is less interested in the relation of Husserlian phenomenology to the critical philosophy than in the critique of the positivism inherent to modern science, which Husserl sketches in his final period under the heading of objectivism. But he is dissatisfied with the relation of Husserl's own position to the concept in question. As concerns Husserl, Habermas' aim at this point is to turn the Husserlian concept of objectivism against transcendental phenomenology in order to sketch out a valid version of critical theory, in this case a theory which possesses causal efficacy due to the intrinsic link between knowledge and human interests.

The systematic treatment of the relation of knowledge to human interests provides, as the title suggests, a general perspective on a concern as old as philosophy itself. The essay is divided into a series of seven short sections. Habermas begins with a statement of the central thesis to be examined in this discussion: "The only knowledge that can truly orient action is knowledge that frees itself from mere human interests and is based on Ideas—in other words, knowledge that has taken a theoretical attitude."[27] He then contrasts two recent views of knowledge: Horkheimer's attempt, representative of the Frankfurt School approach to critical theory, to make out a distinction in kind between traditional and critical forms of theory, and Husserl's defense of a form of the traditional idea of pure theory as relevant.

This contrast concerns what we can call two views of the relevance of reason. Horkheimer and many other Marxists regard traditional theory as socially irrelevant, and believe that critical and other forms of Marxism are socially relevant. Husserl, on the contrary, argues that only theory which is critical in a closely Kantian sense of the term is worthy of the name, and he further maintains that pure theory is in fact inherently relevant. With respect to the thesis under discussion here, Horkheimer represents the Marxist rejection of the relevance of the traditional form of reason, which Husserl, on the contrary, still strives to uphold.

Habermas adjudicates the dispute between the two views of reason by scrutinizing Husserl's brief remarks on objectivism in his last, unfinished work, *The Crisis of European Sciences and Transcendental Phenomenology*. Husserl here studied the crisis of the sciences as science due to the fact that they have become largely irrelevant to life, which he attributed to the turn away from the Platonic ideal of theory. Habermas, who follows Dilthey's differentiation of the natural and social sciences in his own distinction between empirical-analytic and historical-hermeneutic sciences, correlates the social irrelevence of the sciences to their relation to the Greek concept of theory. He believes that they maintain the traditional idea of science, although they have abandoned the Greek mimetic understanding of the relation of *theoria* and *kosmos* presupposed in the relevance of theory for *bios theoretikos*.

Habermas here offers a controversial reconstruction of Husserl's critique in three steps. According to Habermas, Husserl criticizes the objectivism of the sciences, or their failure to free themselves from prescientific interests rooted in the life-world; and he further identifies transcendental self-reflection, or phenomenological description, with traditional theory. The disagreement concerns the relevance of forms of reason. Husserl believes that phenomenology can lay claim to the title of pure theory unjustly claimed by the sciences. But Habermas refuses phenomenology's claim to practical efficacy. According to Habermas, traditional theory derives only 'pseudo-normative' power from the concealment of its real interest. It follows that in his critique of the objectivism of the sciences Husserl falls prey to another objectivism.

Habermas' objection to Husserl rests on a controversial interpretation of the latter's notion of objectivism. We need to distinguish between Habermas' criticism and the interpretation on which it rests. In his brief discussion, Husserl contrasts objectivism with transcendentalism. He believes that objectivism consists in taking the world as an unexamined given, whereas transcendentalism demands a radical clarification of the subjectivity of the life-world which underlies and makes possible the realm of scientific discourse. According to Husserl, since the rise of epistemology the history of philosophy has been the scene of a constant struggle between objectivistic and transcendental philosophy.[28] In accusing Husserl of objectivism, Habermas uses this term in a different, non-Husserlian sense linked to the supposed failure to clarify the supposed connection of pure theory with life. Although he is perhaps correct that the proposed relation requires clarification, this point is independent of his effort to utilize the concept of objectivism in a nonstandard manner against its author.

In order to clarify the relation of pure theory to life Habermas returns indirectly to a concept of critical theory. He now proposes a rival concept of theory whose normative power derives from an acknowledgment of its intrinsic interest. He argues for this view by 'discovering' it in the roots of the philosophical tradition and in contemporary science. He believes that even in Greek thought the supposed divorce of knowledge from interest was at best a fiction. Clearly his intent is to change the usual understanding of conceptual geography by abandoning the distinction between disinterested and interested forms of theory since, as he holds, all forms of theory are ultimately interested.

He now applies this conviction to correlate types of theory with corresponding kinds of interest by rethinking the distinction between types of science, to which he adds a third division, modeled on Horkheimer's view of critical theory.[29] According to Habermas, the empirical-analytic sciences possess a technical cognitive interest, whereas the historical-hermeneutic sciences have a practical one, and the critically oriented sciences incorporate an emancipatory cognitive interest.

We can usefully understand the force of Habermas' claim by comparing his revised notion of critical theory with the original version. From the perspective of the link between knowledge and human interests, his point is that traditional theory cannot demonstrate this connection, which is, however, inherent to critical theory. But in his understanding of self-reflection, he extends the latter beyond its original bounds. Horkheimer, who drew the original distinction, maintained that the future of humanity now turned on the existence of a critical attitude. But he also believed that the concern for social justice did not guarantee that claims for truth were not corrupted by ideology, including the claims of critical theory.[30] In terms of Habermas' own predilection for a Popperian form of fallibilism, we can say that Horkheimer acknowledges the continued possibility of an empirical disconfirmation of any statements of empirical truth. As he does not differentiate between the concern for social injustice and the result of this concern, Habermas makes a stronger claim than classical critical theory in the assertion that self-reflection in fact is causally efficacious.

That the latter concept can be understood in two ways reflects a change in Habermas' focus at this point. In the earlier essays on Marx and Marxism he was anxious to establish the difference between historical materialism and other kinds of theory, particularly different types of philosophy, and then to link the theory to the external world and to philosophy of science. In writings after his criticism of the supposed Marxian failure to pose the epistemological question, Habermas seems to draw closer to Kant and to traditional philosophical concerns in general. Although he does not abandon his interest in the relation of theory to practice, which he here maintains under the heading of knowledge and human interests, he begins to insist on the centrality of the traditional epistemological question of truth in the full sense.

Habermas believes that his version of critical theory as both relevant and true provides the first successful analysis of the social interest of theoretical truth. In effect, he thinks that through cognitive self-reflection a theory that possesses an emancipatory cognitive interest can sustain the traditional philosophical claim for truth. Since the concern with a theory that combines relevance and truth is as old as Plato, there is a clear implication that in his revised concept of critical theory Habermas intends in a sense to bring the Platonic tradition to a successful close.

Habermas does not draw out this implication, but turns immediately to further consideration of his notion of emancipatory cognitive, or as he now refers to it in an even less felicitous term, knowledge-constitutive human, interests. His remarks on this topic are severely compressed, almost telescopic, although retrospectively helpful in understanding the further evolution of his thought. He now proposes five related theses, of which the first three concern the link of the transcendental subject to what Husserl would call the life-world and to history, the instrumental uses of knowledge, and the forms in which this interest takes shape.

The former is an effort to rethink the Husserlian concept of the subject in terms acceptable to historical materialism. The reference to instrumental uses of knowledge is meant to deflect any criticism for possible reductionism. On the contrary, Habermas here suggests, parallel to his triple distinction between types of science, an irreducible distinction between knowledge related to human preservation and knowledge related to other goals. Finally, the latter thesis provides the basis for Habermas' later investigations of ego development and the process of socialization.[31]

The fourth, perhaps most interesting thesis asserts the coincidence of knowledge and interest in self-reflection. In a severely reduced compass, he here describes the epistemological basis of his claim that self-reflection [Selbstreflexion] leads to socially relevant knowledge. According to Habermas, who not by accident here employs the Kantian term "Mündigkeit,"[32] the human interest in maturity (or adulthood) is not a mere fancy, since it can be verified a priori.

Habermas develops this thesis as the basis of a linguistic theory of relevant reason. He holds that in the use of language, which is the medium for knowledge-constitutive interests, we necessarily presuppose maturity. He maintains that even the first sentence intrinsically contains the intention of a general and unforced consensus [einer allgemeinen und ungezwungenen Konsensus]. He believes that maturity is the only idea which we really possess in the sense of the philosophical tradition. And he remarks that the term "reason" [Vernunft] as used in German idealism contains both the notions of will [Willen] and consciousness [Bewußtsein], since reason means as well the will to reason. Through this chain of reasoning he arrives at the view that in self-reflection knowledge comes together with the interest in maturity.

This argument can in part be elucidated through some remarks about its background in the history of philosophy, which Habermas constantly presupposes. In his view of maturity Habermas reconstructs a Kantian notion with roots in Aristotle. In his teleological view of ethics Aristotle argues that as the highest good, happiness [eudaimonia] is self-sufficient [autarkes, from autarkeia], hence lacking in nothing.[33] From the opposing perspective of his deontological ethical theory Kant reinterprets "self-sufficiency," in terms of the problem of the Enlightenment, as the capacity for independent moral action without the guidance of others.[34] According to Kant, this capacity is the necessary prerequisite of moral maturity and further describes the sense in which human being differs from a mere machine.

Although Habermas employs the same term as Kant, he transforms what in the latter's theory is a thesis about a prerequisite for the exercise of practical reason into a claim of the truth and utility of self-reflection. Whereas Kant cautiously argued that we can only hope that moral action will render us happy, and hence be socially useful, Habermas believes that in self-reflection knowledge and human interest coincide. In a word, he holds that self-reflection is intrinsically socially relevant.

Habermas bases this conviction on his understanding of the concept of consensus, which is only mentioned here,[35] in the fifth and last thesis, that is, his assertion that the proof of the unity of knowledge and interest is provided in the dialectical reconstruction of the historical traces of suppressed dialogue. He intends his claim as a revised form of the Socratic assumption, which functions normatively in the entire philosophical tradition, of dialogue as a source of truth. In effect he restates this Socratic view in his claim that in principle all discussion, as rooted in language, intrinsically aims at universal agreement as the result of unconstrained, nonauthoritarian dialogue. Habermas' innovation is to insist that the failure to realize that the necessary conditions for such dialogue do not always exist is to transform theory into ideology. Accordingly, he maintains that the truth of statements is based on the anticipation of the good life, and he further argues that a retrospective reconstruction of the obstacles to unconstrained communication reveals the unity of knowledge and interest.

In fact the suggestion that the conditions of dialogue do not always exist agrees with Socrates's view, as depicted by Plato.[36] It is accordingly controversial to assert that from the beginning philosophy has always assumed that the conditions for mature discussion are actual, and not virtual. But Habermas clearly surpasses Socrates's hypothesis of the utility of dialogue in his even more controversial claim that under the proper conditions discussion does produce truth.

In part, Habermas' argument is ambiguous here. He follows Kant's lead in insisting on moral autonomy as a condition of fruitful discussion. But the claim that the truth of statements is grounded in the anticipation of the good life[37] has two distinct meanings. On the other hand, it suggests that the precondition of effective dialogue is the establishment of moral autonomy, or perhaps even what Hegel would call mutual recognition. Depending on how this suggestion is interpreted, the kind of discussion Habermas has in mind is dependent on the prior achievement of the good life, to which it is intended to lead. In that particular sense, the suggestion is counterfactual, since it presupposes conditions which do not presently obtain. On the other hand, this claim tends to create a confusion between the view that the truth is useful, which Habermas asserts, and the contrary view that the useful is true, which, if asserted, would render trivial the argument that dialogue arrives at truth.

There is a further ambiguity in the expressed conviction that the retrospective reconstruction of the obstacles to unconstrained communication reveals the unity of knowledge and interest.[38] An awareness of the obstacles to non-repressive communication provides knowledge of a sort, which is different from that supposed to emerge from appropriate dialogue. Despite the compressed nature of his discussion, Habermas needs to preserve the distinction between uncovering the hindrances to discussion useful to the individual, for instance through the dialogue of psychoanalytic treatment, and the more general kind of dialogue in principle useful to us all which then becomes possible.

Habermas ends his discussion with some remarks on science in part relevant to his changing evaluation of historical materialism. Noting that in its self-understanding science retains the philosophical illusion of pure theory, he evokes this illusion with respect to types of science. Unlike Husserl, he believes that objectivism is not problematic as such, since it enables science to function without reflection. He holds that scientific objectivism only becomes problematic in the nomological sciences when technique is substituted for enlightened action; and it is questionable in the hermeneutic sciences when the possibility of rational agreement on goals is surrendered in favor of what he regards as the mere decision among objectified values and uncomprehended beliefs.

Like Husserl, Habermas is concerned with the practical consequence of the lack of a self-reflective dimension in science, although the two diagnoses differ.

Husserl complained that the objectivistic nature of the natural sciences prevents them from securing their own status as science, whereas Habermas argues the different point that the sciences do not consider their relation to human interest. Clearly there is an important difference between the scientific status of the various sciences and their relevance for human beings.

Habermas applies his interest in the social relevance of science to historical materialism and to theory in general. In connection with the former he warns against the appeal to a dogmatic philosophy of history, which he describes as the obverse of mere decisionism. More generally, he asserts that the proper way to go beyond the limited self-awareness of the sciences is to destroy the illusion of objectivism, not as Husserl thought through the renewal of pure theory, but by revealing the connection of knowledge and interest. According to Habermas, to be true to the philosophical tradition means to renounce it by abandoning ontology.

In different form, these points were both anticipated in Habermas' earlier discussions of Marx and Marxism. The reproach that historical materialism needs to refuse authoritarian decisionism, like the earlier complaint that it lacks an epistemological dimension, is a form of Habermas' general appeal to Kant's critical approach as a standard of theory in general. Here he extends this view to include self-criticism, or self-reflection. The point which closes the essay is a warning against the assumption of the utility of knowledge which remains hidden in the dogmatic adherence to the ideal of pure theory. This is a widening of the point already made that a socially relevant theory cannot hold ontological pretensions.

In comparison to his earlier discussion of Marx and Marxism, Habermas' adoption of the critical perspective enables him here to rethink his interest in relevant social theory in terms of the history of philosophy, which is no longer dismissed. His examination of the concern of historical materialism with the link between theory and practice, which he now studies under the heading of knowledge and human interest, reveals the roots of this problem in the Greek notion of pure theory. As in his previous writings, he continues to defend a modified version of historical materialism, in this case in the opposition of critical theory to Husserl's yearning for pure theory as relevant. Against Husserl, Habermas maintains that theory cannot be and never was wholly disinterested; and he further maintains that there is no guarantee of the social relevance of knowledge as such.

The force of this argument is to bolster Habermas' contention in prior writings that in virtue of its social relevance historical materialism is incompatible with so-called pure theory, or ontology. He believes that since all forms of knowledge are interest-laden, socially relevant truth must result from unconstrained dialogue that is not pure, but which inclines toward human emancipation. Through the development of his argument against the background of the history of philosophy, he here deepens the link he discerns between relevant social theory and the critical attitude even as he develops a framework for further inquiry into historical materialism and social theory in general.

In later writings on diverse topics, Habermas pursues his discussion with Marx and Marxism even as he considers topics whose link to historical materialism is sometimes distant or even difficult to perceive. In "Labor and Interaction: Remarks on Hegel's Jena Philosophy of Mind," which appeared in 1967, Habermas indirectly continues his interpretation of historical materialism in an inquiry devoted mainly to the study of an early Hegelian manuscript. This is the text of lectures that Hegel presented at Jena in 1805-1806, when he was still engaged in studies of political economy. As Habermas points out, Lasson regards this manuscript as a prior phase of the *Phenomenology,* and accordingly emphasizes parallels between the two texts. In contrast, Habermas argues that we have here the effort to develop a theory of the formative process of spirit which Hegel later abandoned.

Habermas' discussion concerns the evolution of the concept of the subject in German idealism and the related emergence of an analysis of the relation of work and interaction. In simplest terms, he believes that in the Jena period, in connection with his notion of spirit, Hegel proposed an analysis of work and interaction as irreducibly separate categories. He further believes that this analysis is not taken up in Hegel's later writings, but was rediscovered independently by Marx as a reductive relation which failed to preserve the Hegelian difference in kind. Habermas maintains that neither Hegel nor Marx offered an adequate clarification of this topic, which is fraught with practical consequences for contemporary life.

As concerns the comprehension of Hegel's thought, this argument is interesting as a way to link the emergence of the notion of spirit to his dissatisfaction with earlier, more abstract views of subjectivity in Kant and in Fichte. According to Habermas, Hegel desired to correct the concept of subjectivity in earlier German idealism through a notion of spirit based on mutual recognition. In this view, subjects that know themselves as nonidentical are united on the basis of reciprocity. Habermas sees the struggle for mutual recognition as a reconstruction of the suppression and reconstitution of the dialogue situation as a moral relationship. And he adds that the logical relation of communication distorted by force itself exerts practical force.[39]

If we accept Habermas' claim that the view of spirit of the Jena period does not remain in the later writings, his proposed reading is interesting in calling attention to an experimental side of Hegel's thought which is not apparent in the mature, polished texts. As a historical interpretation, the specific analysis of the emergence of Hegel's concept of spirit is less successful. In order to establish the distinction between Hegel and his predecessors, Habermas clearly exaggerates the extent to which Fichte remains bound to Kant's view of subjectivity as the transcendental unity of apperception.

In his remarks on Fichte Habermas ignores the dialectic of ego and non-ego that pervades the *Wissenschaftslehre* of 1794, as well as the important account of the relation of self and another self,[40] which is a clear predecessor of Hegel's analysis of mutual recognition. His reading is arguably more instructive as an indication of his intent in other writings. In particular, it casts light on his concern in "Knowledge and Human Interests" with unconstrained dialogue. In his description of the struggle for recognition as a suppressed and distorted dialogue susceptible of reconstruction, he does more than provide a novel interpretation of an important notion; he further discovers a close anticipation of his own comprehension of dialogue within Hegel's thought.

Habermas pursues his reading of Hegel's doctrine of mutual recognition as dialogue in a way which initially stresses the similarities to his own view. He introduces a distinction between strategic action and communicative action, or roughly the difference between individual and nonindividual processes of decision; then he identifies the latter as the medium for the formation of self-conscious spirit, which Hegel formulates in the categories of family, language, and labor. According to Habermas, Hegel sees an interrelation of labor and interaction in which neither can be reduced to the other;[41] and he further maintains that for Hegel labor and interaction are linked under the heading of the emancipation from the forces of internal and external nature.[42] There is a clear resemblance between Hegel's view of the emancipatory function of mutual recognition, or communication, as depicted here and Habermas' account of unconstrained dialogue as the locus for the coincidence of knowledge and interest.

Habermas connects his reading of mutual recognition with his criticism of Marx through the interrelation of work and interaction. He points out that since the Hegelian analysis of this interrelation was confined to the Jena period in manuscripts unknown to Marx, the latter was not directly influenced by their contents. He believes that under the heading of social praxis Marx independently rediscovered but failed adequately to explicate a relation in which he unfortunately reduces communicative action to instrumental action, or labor.[43] On this basis he concludes that neither Marx nor Hegel provides a satisfactory analysis of the interrelation of work and interaction which they correctly link to social emancipation.[44]

Habermas' conclusion is meant to apply equally to Marx and Hegel, although his respective treatment of them is distinctly different. Adopting a generally Marxist, or materialist, perspective, he accuses Hegel of idealism.[45] He here follows Marx's point that in the *Phenomenology* Hegel's achievement is to grasp the self-creation of man as a process.[46] He further follows Marx's criticism that Hegel provides only an abstract analysis of the historical process in virtue of the supposed reduction of all objects, including human life, and man, to objects of consciousness only.[47] According to Habermas, in virtue of the identity thesis Hegel interpreted the dialectic of representation and of labor idealistically, for instance in the alleged sublation of the distinction between objects as objects and as adversaries.[48] He further maintains that in the mature writings the 'transition' between internal will and the objectivity of law is guaranteed only through the dialectic of morality since labor has been deprived of its central role in the system.[49]

Habermas' treatment of Marx represents an extension and application of his prior, general criticism to a specific situation, that is, the interrelation of work

and interaction. In previous writings he has objected that Marx fails to pose
the general epistemological question from a Kantian angle of vision, and he
has insisted on the need for unhindered dialogue. He now combines both
points in his criticism that Marx reduces interaction to work, or communication to instrumental action. He believes that in the final analysis for Marx
everything is merely the relations of production, or work, which in turn led
in the Marxist tradition to a mechanistic misinterpretation of the dialectical
Marxian analysis of the relationship of the forces and relations of production.[50]
In other words, as Marx does not share Hegel's epistemological sensitivity,
he allegedly fails to separate communicative action from strategic action, and
as a result threatens the possibility of dialogue productive of truth.

This criticism is triply significant: for the analysis of the interrelation of
work and interaction, for Habermas' view of Marx, and for Habermas' own
position. If neither Marx nor Hegel provides a satisfactory analysis of this interrelation, we can expect Habermas to make the attempt; this effort is one
way to characterize the intent of the view he later evolves under the heading
of a theory of communicative action. But we must avoid the implication that
he now seeks to maintain an equal distance from Hegel and Marx. Although
he is critical here of both thinkers, he never explicitly denies a distinction in
kind between idealism and materialism; and he constantly seeks to maintain
an ever more tenuous identification with historical materialism.

Habermas does not now develop further either his rejection of a mechanistic
Marxian interpretation[51] or his objection to Marx's supposed reduction of interaction to work.[52] As concerns Marx there is a clear implication, which only
gradually emerges in Habermas' later writings, that the model of work, or
productive activity, at the heart of the Marxian position, is too narrow to provide a contemporary social theory. It follows, as Habermas later sees, that
someone interested in this task needs to provide an alternative more adequate
than the Marxian approach to its intrinsic goal. Hence another, fuller description of the purpose of the theory of communicative action he will develop
is to offer a social theory which both allows for the possibility of communication and otherwise fulfills the goals of the Marxian position.

IV

KNOWLEDGE AND
INTEREST AGAIN

In the transitional phase of his discussion of historical materialism, Habermas modifies his original interpretation and announces the basic epistemological critique which he will further develop in later writings. He elaborates his criticism of the theory's purported epistemological deficit in *Knowledge and Human Interests*. This complex study, published in 1968, constitutes the historical redevelopment of the systematic perspective outlined in Habermas' inaugural address.[1]

The status of this book within Habermas' corpus is at present difficult to determine. There is no question that it was widely discussed when it appeared and was regarded as his most significant work to date. In the wake of the publication of the more recent study, *The Theory of Communicative Action*, it is unclear which book is more important, especially since Habermas himself tends to see his major contribution as the eventual development of the theory of communicative action. That project received strong impetus in his huge study of this topic, but it remains dependent upon the earlier analysis of knowledge and interest. For this reason, and despite the fact that Habermas naturally stresses the interest of his more recent research, we can speculate that in time this text may again and finally come to be recognized as Habermas' most significant work.

In the present context it is unnecessary to provide a detailed account of its overall argument, even in outline. At present it will suffice merely to indicate in briefest fashion enough of the argument to make it possible to comprehend his remarks on Marx's position in this book. The book expands the assertion stated in the fifth thesis of the inaugural lecture, that is, that the unity of knowledge and interest mentioned in the title is proven in a dialectic which reconstructs the historical traces of suppressed dialogue. This assertion contains an important ambiguity. It is unclear whether Habermas means to bring out, or make apparent, what has been suppressed, and is presumably not known, or whether he also desires to reformulate, and hence improve upon, what has been suppressed. In other words, at stake is a difference between a reconstruction that is only retrospective, and one that is retrospective as well as prospective.

In other writings, Habermas endeavors to reconstruct the interpretation of historical materialism in the latter, richer sense through the identification and reformulation of a supposedly different approach.[2] Here he concerns himself solely with a retrospective reconstruction of the prehistory of what he describes as modern positivism in order to analyze the connection of knowledge and (human) interests.[3] As in his inaugural lecture, at this point he continues to regard positivism as the disavowal of reflection which he earlier criticized in Marx's position in the discussion of Marxism as critique.[4] A new feature here is the thematic development of his understanding of the lack of reflection, which he earlier raised as an objection against Marx's thought, throughout the post-Kantian philosophical tradition. In that sense, it is fair to say that Habermas now extends a theme which he initially identified in the discussion of the Marxiam position to the analysis of German philosophy in general.

Although he does not provide a new theory of knowledge in this context, his book is meant to play a prolegomenal role to a new, future epistemology. More precisely, the analysis of the link of pre-positivist views of knowledge with social interest is intended to show that a radical critique of knowledge is only possible as social theory.[5] The book is divided into three parts, entitled "The Crisis of the Critique of Knowledge [Erkenntniskritik]," "Positivism, Pragmatism, Historicism," and "Critique as the Unity of Knowledge and Interest."

For present purposes, we can restrict our attention to the first and last phases of the discussion. As concerns the initial section, we need to consider the reading of Marx's view of knowledge in the context of the German philosophical tradition, where Habermas extends his objection to the supposed epistemological deficit of historical materialism. As concerns the final section we must review his accounts of the relation of reason and interest in Kant and Fichte and of Nietzsche's view of knowledge. In the former, Habermas again takes up the topic of his systematic lecture; in the latter he provides the first version of a reading of Nietzsche which he will later elaborate as part of his rejection of German idealism in favor of his own, rival view.[6]

Habermas begins his discussion of "The Crisis in the Critique of Knowledge" with a remark[7] meant to tie together epistemology, the emancipation of modern physics from philosophy, and the relation of knowledge and interest. His analysis amplifies his previous concern with the reading and criticism of historical materialism against the double background of Hegel's position and contemporary philosophy of science. After asserting that the problem of reliable knowledge is the main theme of modern philosophy, he calls attention to the epistemological significance of the well-known change in the relation of science to philosophy resulting from the rise of modern physics as an independent discipline.

According to Habermas, the change in this relation enabled science to substitute itself for philosophy. He maintains that as late as Kant it was not possible to identify knowledge with science, which continued to derive its justification from philosophy. He further maintains that Hegel occupies a dual role in the future evolution of the problem of knowledge. According to Habermas, Hegel's metacritique of the critical philosophy did not alter the traditional claim of science's dependency on philosophy; it rather abandoned science entirely.

More generally, Habermas holds that since Kant, philosophy has no longer understood science. Now, developing his earlier remarks on objectivism and positivism, he accuses modern science of 'scientism,' or the nonreflective identification of knowledge with itself. He sees a consequence of its supposedly scientistic attitude in the fact that today an inquiry into the conditions of the possibility of knowledge must start with the view of analytic philosophy of science. But he does not accept the latter approach without further reflection, since he also holds that this positivistic approach is inherently uncritical and falls below the level of the critical philosophy.

As concerns epistemology, this line of discussion yields what in the first instance seems to be a traditional philosophical view of the relation of philosophy and science in which, since neither has a monopoly on knowledge, each has a role to play. In practice, this means that knowledge can be identified neither with science, nor with philosophy; and the possibility of knowledge cannot be reduced to an examination of methodological principles.

Like Husserl, Habermas here insists that science in fact lacks a reflective dimension. Accordingly, we can clarify his understanding of the link of philosophy and science to the traditional analysis in relation to a quasi-Husserlain dichotomy: either he must accept Husserl's version of the claim traditional in philosophy since Plato that in the final analysis scientific claims for knowledge are to be validated in philosophy, or he must demonstrate against Husserl that science can develop within itself the reflective dimension necessary to carry out this task.

Second, Habermas holds that Hegel's radical critique of epistemology opened up a possibility for future epistemology as well as for an understanding of the link of scientific knowledge to interest [Interessenbasis]. He accepts what he describes as Hegel's phenomenological self-reflection as a necessary radicalization of the critique of knowledge. But he believes that this possibility was later obstructed for two reasons. On the one hand, Hegel was allegedly prevented from its further elaboration by his preoccupation with the postulates of the identity philosophy. On the other hand, although Marx's theory supposedly required Hegel's self-reflection, according to Habermas Marx misunderstood his own conception [hat sein eigenes Konzept mißverstanden] and hence completed the decline of the theory of knowledge.

Habermas here clearly revises his view of Hegel at the expense of Marx. Whereas in earlier writings he rejected Hegelian idealism as such in favor of historical materialism, he now turns backward toward Hegel even as he turns away from Marx. As in the prior essay on knowledge and interest, Habermas here continues to insist on the supposed need to develop the unsatisfactory

analysis in Hegel and Marx in a way that takes up a hidden theme in their
views and goes beyond them. Beyond the implication that he understands
their views better than they did themselves, Habermas further implies that the
spirit, if not the letter, of their positions can be further elaborated.[8]

In the first section of his book, Habermas develops an analysis of the crisis
he discerns in the critique of knowledge in three chapters concerning Hegel's
critique of Kant, Marx's metacritique of Hegel, and the idea of the theory of
knowledge as social theory. The initial chapter reveals an important ambivalence toward epistemology in its full title, which reads: "Hegel's Critique of
Kant: Radicalisation or Sublation [Aufhebung] of the Theory of Knowledge."[9]

Habermas' ambivalence is significant, since as his position evolves it becomes clear that, despite his concern with Marx and Hegel, his primary allegiance lies with Kant. Hegel believed that he was fulfilling the intention of
the critical philosophy, and Habermas still understands Marx largely in terms
of absolute idealism. But if Hegel only incorrectly captures Kant's goal, and
like Habermas one is concerned to maintain the epistemological standards of
critical philosophy, the way forward must lead backward toward Kant. Accordingly a key step in that progression is to comprehend the effect of Hegel's
critique of Kant on the project of epistemology in general.

Habermas' analysis depends upon a tacit distinction between first philosophy and epistemology. He regards Hegel's critique of Kant as conclusive with
respect to the intention of first philosophy [Ursprungsphilosophie]. But he
holds that, despite Hegel's attack on epistemology, it is unclear that we need,
therefore, to abandon the critique of knowledge as such.[10] He develops this
point in a critical review of Hegel's critique of Kant, and through comments
on the Hegelian project. According to Habermas, Hegel's critique of Kant is
deprived of necessary force since he does not, and cannot, provide a full justification of absolute knowledge in phenomenological self-reflection.

In his discussion, Habermas objects to specific elements of the Hegelian critique of the critical philosophy. After noting that Hegel regards the critical
philosophy as invoking the model of an instrument or a medium, he accuses
Hegel of invoking a distinction which exists only with the latter's conceptual
framework. Hegel is more successful, in Habermas' view, in elucidating a series of implicit presuppositions of a critique of knowledge which is ostensibly
presuppositionless, including a normative concept of science, a normative
concept of the ego, and the distinction between theoretical and practical reason. According to Habermas the latter presupposition shows that Kant's abstract approach is untenable since on the levels of pure and of practical reason
he operates with different, incompatible ego concepts.

Habermas accepts Hegel's critique of Kant, but he rejects the claim, which
he controversially ascribes to Hegel, that the epistemological approach as such
is superfluous.[11] This claim is controversial since it is possible to regard Hegel's
approach to knowledge as another form of epistemology, intended to fulfill
the spirit of the critical philosophy.[12] According to Habermas the root diffi-

culty in Hegel's position is his preoccupation with the philosophy of identity,[13] which he assumes, but does not demonstrate.

Now shifting gears, he applies this point to the relation of philosophy to science. According to Habermas, in virtue of his assumption of the concept of identity Hegel causes a fatal misunderstanding in which philosophy usurps the legitimacy of the independent sciences by maintaining its claim to constitute universal scientific knowledge. This point is difficult since, as inspection of the texts demonstrates, Hegel rather makes the traditional Platonic point that as the science of sciences philosophy can assume nothing and must ground itself and all other sciences.[14] Nonetheless, Habermas maintains that the belief he ascribes to Hegel is at the origin of a positivism which only Marx could have contested; for Marx allegedly prolonged Hegel's critique of Kant without, however, espousing the philosophy of identity.

In sum, Habermas in part accepts Hegel's critique of Kant; but he restricts its value to first philosophy in order to insist on the continuing interest of the critique of knowledge, which he sees Hegel as rejecting. As a result, Habermas modifies his previous approach in two respects. First, he now attempts to specify the notoriously vague distinction between materialism and idealism, integral to his own reading of historical materialism, by 'locating' it in the acceptance or rejection of the philosophy of identity. Here he is close to some parts of recent Marxist discussion.[15] Second, he further attenuates the difference between historical materialism and philosophy in his depiction of Marx as a central participant in the discussion of knowledge arising out of the publication of the *Critique of Pure Reason*.

From the perspective of Marx's critique of Hegel in the last of the *Paris Manuscripts*, Habermas sees Marx as detaching consciousness from its framework in the philosophy of identity. For Hegel nature has mind as its presupposition, whereas for Marx, who supposedly inverts this relation, nature is the ground of mind. The alleged result of the inversion attributed to Marx is a sophisticated, transcendental form of materialism which understands the objectivity of objects of possible experience as arising out of objective activity, rooted in the real labor process. Hence work [Arbeit] is the fundamental category of human existence and an epistemological category.

With respect to his earlier discussion, Habermas continues to insist on the difference between idealism and materialism, although he now also acknowledges that the view of social labor as synthesis is inseparable from an idealist meaning of synthesis. The result is to attenuate even further the distinction in question. In previous writings, especially in the "Literaturbericht," he has called attention to the relation of phenomenology to historical materialism. At this point he warns against the danger of disregarding the idealist meaning of social work in favor of the Husserlian concept of the life-world, which he associates with a phenomenological form of Marxism in the writings of Marcuse, Sartre, and others.[16]

Now, his warning is puzzling since it is unclear that any of the proponents of phenomenological Marxism ever denies that for Marx social labor mediates objective and subjective forms of nature and does not constitute invariant meaning. Perhaps we can best construe it, then, as a sign that at present Habermas wishes to distance himself from his earlier approach. This interpretation of his intent is further reinforced by his remark that evolution unmasks both philosophical anthropology and transcendental philosophy as an illusion.[17]

Habermas here takes pains to specify the sense in which Marxian synthesis is materialist by articulating a concept which, he admits, Marx never makes explicit. He maintains, in terms of a Hegelian notion, that for Marx the self-reflection of consciousness discloses the structure of social work. From this angle of vision Marx's view of social labor is supposedly specifically materialist since it does not generate a logical structure; it is rather the empirical and transcendental accomplishment of a species subject which produces itself historically. In a word, Marx's materialism is said to consist in the fact that for the activity of thought he substitutes material production, in which political economy replaces formal logic.

Habermas sums up his discussion by stating that synthesis through social labor results neither in a logical structure, nor in an absolute unity of man and nature. Surpassing the frequent concern to understand the philosophical component of Marx's thought solely in relation to Hegel, he now develops an interesting comparison between Marx's position and Kant's. According to Habermas, Marx substitutes a unity achieved by actual manipulation for the unity attained through the categories of the understanding. But Marx supposedly remains Kantian through his insistence on an invariant relation of the species to the natural environment. Habermas further calls attention to the possibility of an instrumentalist theory of knowledge arising out of the Kantian component in the Marxian concept of synthesis, as elaborated by Peirce and Dewey.[18]

As compared to Kant's view of synthesis within an invariant relation, the first difference in Marx's concept of synthesis through social labor is said to lie in the substitution of work for mental activity. This is a variation of the well-known Marxist claim that in the turn to political economy Marx provides a way of addressing real social problems as distinguished from the putatively imaginary approach adopted by German idealism.[19] The point to note is that despite his increasing reservations about historical materialism, here Habermas still remains confident about the value of Marxian political economy, which he will later criticize and abandon.[20]

The other difference Habermas discusses emerges from a complex observation on the relation between Kant, Fichte, and Marx. Again bypassing Hegel, he assesses the significance for historical materialism of Fichte's revision of the Kantian notion of the subject. Here adopting Hegel's interpretation of his idealist colleague, Habermas maintains that Fichte does not arrive at, but rather begins from, a concept of the unity of self-consciousness in order to prove the identity of ego and non-ego. Now, Habermas' interpretation is controversial since it depends on the uncritical adoption of Hegel's own problematic reading of Fichte's thought. But he is correct to call attention to the largely unexplored relation of Fichte and Marx.

Habermas believes that Fichte's revision of the Kantian view of the subject illuminates the materialist understanding of the socially working subjects [gesellschaftlich arbeitender Subjekte]. He holds that the identity of consciousness, which Kant called a transcendental unity of apperception, is in fact achieved through work as an act of self-consciousness in Fichte's sense. With respect to historical materialism, the difference lies in Marx's restriction of Fichte's absolute ego to the contingent human species.

The entire analysis of this chapter is based on the way in which the materialist concept of synthesis, which Habermas identifies in Marx's theory, can be regarded as a successor to the idealist concept in the critical philosophy. The intended result is to 'locate' Marx within the epistemological discussion begun by Kant, while preserving the distinction between idealism and materialism. Now, other Marxists, in particular Lukács, have made this argument. The distinguishing features of Habermas' account include his concern to understand Marx's thought in terms of an invariant framework of synthesis shared in general by the entire German philosophical tradition and his specific emphasis on Fichte's role.

Habermas ends the chapter with an interesting juxtaposition of Marx and Hegel which leads up to a basic criticism of historical materialism. He here repeats his earlier claim that Marx adopts the intention of Hegel's critique of Kant without the presuppositions of the philosophy of identity. Now, this point has not been demonstrated, and is in fact rendered precarious by his own quasi-Hegelian reading of Fichte. He then remarks that the philosophical foundation of this materialism [dieses Materialismus] is insufficient to establish a so-called presuppositionless phenomenological self-reflection of knowledge. This statement clearly suggests that the Marxian form of materialism is insufficient, although another version of it could in principle be successful in this task. But other than the bare claim, Habermas does not in fact attempt to show that the effort at presuppositionless phenomenological self-reflection, which he correctly holds is Hegel's goal, is also intrinsic to Marx's theory.

Habermas' criticism of Marxian theory of knowledge at this point is a further refinement of his earlier objections to the lack of an epistemological dimension in Marx's thought. Here we can note attention to the intention supposedly intrinsic to Marx's view, the consequence of its epistemological deficiency, a restatement of the source of the problem, and its retroactive effect on Marx's understanding of his own position.

As noted, Habermas here attributes to Marx the intention to provide a presuppositionless phenomenological self-reflection. The result of Marx's failure is a supposedly positivist reduction of the act of the self-production of the human species to work. More precisely, Marx is allegedly forced to analyze such elements as symbolic interaction and the role of the cultural tradition, which are ineliminably required to comprehend domination [Herrschaft] and ideology, in terms of the instrumental approach from which it differs in kind. In a word, Habermas objects to the intrinsic reductionism of the Marxian theory which assimilates reflection to work on the grounds that Marx's materialist concept of synthesis is too narrow for its intended purpose and even prevented the author of the theory from understanding his own procedure [seine Verfahrensweise]. It is as if Marx's own theory were in fact an instance of ideology that brought about its own misunderstanding.

By contrast with the prior discussion, this version of Habermas' critique of historical materialism differs mainly in the ascription of a Hegelian intention to Marx and in the assertion that the latter failed to comprehend his own theory. It is doubly important for Habermas to view Marx as attempting to carry out a Hegelian task by other means: in order to preserve the crucial distinction between idealism and materialism, and to open the way for an epistemological reading of Marx's theory.

In asserting that Marx failed to comprehend his own theoretical approach, Habermas makes it plausible to reconstruct historical materialism in a manner that purportedly conforms, if not to its letter, to its intrinsic spirit. As Habermas reads Marx, the latter's concern is to carry forward the Kantian discussion, prolonged by Hegel; in arguing that Marx failed in his attempt, Habermas implies that a successful form of materialism must take shape as the legitimate successor to the critical philosophy, that is, in the guise of a critical epistemology. In a word, at this point he further develops his shift away from Hegel in favor of the interpretation of the nature and limits of Marx's theory in terms of Kant's position.

This shift, which was earlier apparent in the acceptance of the Kantian standard of critique, is further emphasized now by the Kantian structure of the argument. The assertion that Marx's theory is too narrow to comprehend the social context can be construed as maintaining that this type of thought is inadequate to know its object, which is hence unknowable. This kind of argument is familiar in Marxism, in Lukács's claim, influenced by Lask's form of neo-Kantianism, that bourgeois philosophy cannot know bourgeois society, which is, however, knowable from the perspective of historical materialism.[21] Habermas' innovation consists in making a similar claim about Marx's view which precisely denies the more usual Marxist assertion of its intrinsic superiority over so-called reactionary thought.

He states his view of Marxian epistemology in the third chapter, appropriately entitled "The Idea of the Theory of Knowledge as Social Theory." Here he elaborates his reading of Marx's position as an instrumentalist translation of the philosophy of absolute reflection which both surpasses Hegel and falls short of its own goal. In further remarks on the relation of Marx to Fichte, he takes up the epistemological dimension of historical materialism under the aspect of the relation of different types of science. After a comment on the relation of morality to class struggle, he closes the discussion with a reiteration of the epistemological theses sketched at the end of the preceding chapter.

In the preceding chapter, Habermas has already set out the main lines of his conception of Marx's relation to the ongoing inquiry into the problem of knowledge in the German philosophical tradition. Perhaps for this reason, since the main argument has already been made, the elaboration of his conception here, which combines the restatement of familiar themes with the introduction of new material, is less systematic. He begins with another look at the doctrine of reflection. Marx, he suggests, surpasses Hegel by disclosing the mechanism of progress in reflection, although he erroneously reduces it to labor.

It will be recalled that Lukács directed attention to the role of consciousness in Marx's view of history and revolution.[22] Habermas, who does not mention the idea of class here, further differs in his understanding of the role that consciousness plays in the Marxian theory. In terms of his belief that Marx reduces reflection to instrumental action, he identifies what he regards as a basic tension in Marx's position. On the one hand, tacitly following Lukács, he again claims that Marx retains the framework of the philosophy of reflection. Now returning to his earlier emphasis on Fichte, he argues that Marx's supposedly materialist reinterpretation of Hegel is mediated by the Fichtean philosophy of the ego, in a conception of reified products. On the other hand, Habermas maintains that because of Marx's relation to Fichte he renders reflection impossible by conceiving it on the model of production.

Identification of the alleged tension allows Habermas to expand his earlier critique from a Kantian perspective in two ways. First, there is the implicit claim that the critical standard he invoked is in fact required by, but impossible to comprehend within, the Marxian position. It follows that a reconstruction of the Marxian theory which provides an adequate notion of reflection can claim to carry out the intention of the theory. Second, he now expands the role attributed to Fichte, which becomes doubly significant for the constitution of Marx's thought: in the supposed rejection of the Hegelian philosophy of identity, and in the allegedly intrinsic limitations of Marx's erroneous appeal to production as the model of reflection.

In his earlier discussion of historical materialism Habermas has taken notice of the relation of Marx's position to science. In an abrupt shift, he now returns to this theme, which he greatly expands. The investigation here can be read as an elucidation of this facet of Marx's thought and as a further clarification of the notion of a critical social theory through its relation to science. From both angles of vision, the consideration of the connection of Marx's theory to science presupposes the distinction drawn in "Knowledge and Human Interests" between instrumental (analytic and historical-hermeneutic) and emancipatory, or socially critical, sciences.

From the familiar perspective of the suggested Marxian epistemological deficit, Habermas suggests that Marx did not entirely annul the distinction between the natural sciences and the sciences of man. Although Marx regarded his own view as critique, he tended to compare it to natural science, for instance, in the well-known demand, which Habermas cites and describes as positivist, for a natural science of man. According to Habermas this demand is astounding since it fails to acknowledge the self-reflective dimension which separates social science from the natural sciences.

He then turns rapidly to the issue of the social utility of science and general knowledge. In this regard, he makes an argument about Marx's thought analogous to his earlier identification of a part of the Hegelian view absent in the final version of the theory. Now pointing to a passage in the *Grundrisse* which, he believes, has no parallel in *Capital*, he summarizes Marx's analysis of the connection of scientific knowledge and human emancipation. According to the model sketched in the former text, as a result of technical progress, in time the entire labor process will be transferred from the human individual to mechanical surrogates, thereby emancipating the social subject from even necessary labor. Once again appealing to the allegedly equivocal influence of Fichte on Marx, he describes the Marxian model as the consequence of a materialist reinterpetation of Fichte's theory of knowledge, translated into a Saint-Simonian perspective.

Beyond the unsupported references to Fichte and Saint-Simon, this analysis is interesting in the light of the critique Habermas will later offer of Marxian value theory. In his allusion to a future period in which labor-time or labor-quantity will no longer function as a measure of value, he invokes a temporal limitation for the application of the labor theory of value and prepares for its possible rejection. Habermas, who does not pursue these points, concentrates on the importance of the argument described here for Marx's position in order to argue for its deep, but intrinsic, ambivalence.

As part of his argument, he contrasts two incompatible approaches within the wider position: the view that the development of the technological aspects of the labor process will emancipate the human species from necessary labor, and the contrary, better-known view that the technological transformation of the labor process will not by itself lead to the emancipation from labor since such emancipation further depends upon the relations of power which govern interpersonal relations. According to Habermas, this second analysis, which is also present in the *Grundrisse*, alone survives in *Capital*. He believes that the simultaneous presence of both theoretical models in a single text betrays an ambivalence at the heart of Marx's position.[23]

Habermas now relies on this supposed indecision to return to the interrelation of the concepts of work and interaction in Marx's thought. The link is provided in the difference between the two models present in the *Grundrisse*, which are respectively assimilable to an analysis in terms of material production on the level of work and a further analysis presupposing interaction. The force of this point is to insist again that Marx tacitly appeals to the concept of interaction, which he can only explain in an unsatisfactory manner through the model of production.

Now, distinguishing between development on the levels of work and interaction, Habermas maintains that the social self-formative process is unrelated to new technology. He describes it rather as an attempt, through critique, to secure free communicative action as such [kommunikatives Handeln als kommunikatives] by dispelling ideology and domination. According to Habermas, the two perspectives of self-production through productive activity and education [Bildung] through critical-revolutionary activity are interdependent within the theory; but because of his dependence on Kant and Fichte, Marx is finally unable to combine them.

Habermas develops the contrast he discerns between two allegedly insufficiently synthesized angles of vision within Marx's position by linking each component to different forms of knowledge. He sees work as correlated to productive knowledge arising from a theoretical-technical perspective, and further regards interaction in relation to the theoretical-practical attitude of reflective knowledge. According to Habermas, the best available model for the latter form of knowledge is to be found in Hegel's discussion of the dialectic of the moral life in his early Jena and Frankfurt writings. But since, as Habermas also acknowledges, this model was not taken up in the mature version of the system, it is difficult to understand why Marx "should have employed" it[24] in his economic analysis.

After his comment on Hegel, almost by association of ideas, Habermas now turns his attention to the theme of the moral totality in Marx's position. His remarks here are as important for the theory of communicative action he will later develop as for his insight into Marx's thought. According to Habermas, Marx understands the moral totality as a society in which people produce in order to reproduce the conditions of life in an exchange with other people and with nature. Habermas follows numerous Marxist and non-Marxist commentators in drawing attention to the relation between the Marxian theory of class struggle and Hegel's analysis of the master-slave dialectic. But he innovates in his descriptions of the dialectic of class antagonism as a moment of reflection[25] and of the commodity form of labor as ideology, as a dialogic relation.[26]

Communicative action is a type of social theory (not to be conflated with its genus), which Habermas will later develop in a major treatise. Since he does not yet possess his theory of communicative action, Habermas employs this facet of the discussion to address the question of the understanding of social theory implicit in Marx's scattered remarks on the science of man. He quickly characterizes the so-called felt disruption of the moral totality as the inequality between the degrees of repression enforced and in fact required for the development of the means of production. According to Habermas, the science of man is continuous with the self-reflection of class-consciousness and, like Hegel's *Phenomenology*, knows itself to be part of the process which it recollects. Now following Hegel, Habermas maintains that the science of man has as its task the extension of reflective knowledge transmitted to it from the prescientific context of the moral life, to which it belongs.

Habermas' normative description of the science of man against a Hegelian background allows him to describe and to criticize Marx's view of this science. He maintains that Marx shares with Hegel the phenomenological exposition of the appearing consciousness, which Marx does not understand from an epistemological viewpoint. Now relating Marx both to Hegel and to the earlier discussion of historical materialism as critique, he states that the science of man, which is critique, is only possible in a phenomenologically broken framework [in phänomenologisch gebrochener Einstellung möglich].

Since Habermas insists that Marx's materialist critique of ideology is embedded in a phenomenological framework,[27] we need to note the shift at this point in his understanding of the meaning of "critique." In the present context this term no longer refers primarily to a putative location between philosophy and science; it rather refers here to the critique of ideology from the vantage point of materialistic presuppositions. In a word, in his present interest in the comprehension of the aspect of the position advanced in the *German Ideology*, Habermas has now abandoned his initial view of Marx's theory as philosophical anthropology linked to the early writings, but not yet arrived at his subsequent concern with the political economy of the later writings.

The criticism advanced from the perspective of what Marx might have accomplished clearly indicates what Habermas believes needs to be done to improve the theory. The discussion here, because of its brevity, assumes almost telegraphic form as Habermas rapidly recalls a number of his main theses. From this highly compressed passage we can isolate several points, which require separate mention, on topics as diverse as the source of Marx's supposed error, the relation of history to the philosophical tradition, the contemporary role of philosophy, and the idea of a science of man.

Habermas' diagnosis of Marx's theory again points forward to his own later position. He believes that had Marx reflected on the methodological presuppositions of his own notion of social theory, Marx would not have conflated work and interaction under the heading of social practice. He further holds that Marx could have avoided the allegedly misleading identification of a science of man with natural science by relating the materialist concept of synthesis to instrumental action and to communicative action.

The suggestion is clear that an adequate social theory needs to differentiate between work and interaction and to relate them within a wider framework. It follows that Habermas regards his own later effort to elaborate a concept of communication wholly unconstrained by external influences as consistent with the form of social theory Marx would have developed had he reflected on the epistemological presuppositions of his approach.

Habermas addresses the question of the relation of knowledge to science through remarks on the Marxian science of man. Although he employs the term "science," it would appear from the context that he has in mind the more restricted problem, which recurs throughout his discussion of historical materialism, of the link between Marx's thought, philosophy, and science. Defusing the simple opposition of philosophy and science, he claims that science cannot simply negate philosophy. It rather preserves philosophy within itself as critique, that is, the critique of ideology which, he states, is its only right [Recht].

According to Habermas, despite his rejection of absolute idealism Marx failed to develop the science of man because of his equation of critique with natural science. In a closing reference to Marx's theory, Habermas now criticizes so-called scientistic materialism for its repetition of the sublation[28] of epistemology operated by absolute idealism, allegedly prolonged by Comte and other positivists.

The discussion of "The Idea of the theory of Knowledge as Social Theory," which terminates with this point, is as interesting for what Habermas does not say as for what he says. After the early "Literaturbericht," in previous writings on historical materialism, he steadfastly refused to distinguish between Marx and Marxism even as he maintained the Marxist thesis of the difference between idealism and materialism. Although he here redefines this thesis from an epistemological perspective, he significantly considers only Marx under the heading of materialism.

Now, from the vantage point of theory of knowledge, which Habermas employs here, there are significant differences between Marx and Marxism. To take a single example, Lukács, whose influence on Habermas' approach to historical materialism is constantly in evidence, long ago showed the naive nature of Engels's understanding of philosophy.[29] Habermas, who insists on the dimension of critique in social theory, could be expected to draw attention to the differences which separate the concepts of knowledge in the views of Marx and the Marxists. It is hence perhaps an indication of his ambivalence that although he here tacitly separates Marx from Marxism, he does not bring this separation into the open through comments on the differences in their respective approaches to the theory of knowledge.

So far in this chapter we have been considering Habermas' treatment of historical materialism from the perspective of knowledge and human interests first stated in the inaugural lecture and later continued in the book. We need now to expand the discussion beyond the immediate topic in order to take up two related themes: the relation of knowledge and interests, and the description of Nietzsche's position. Habermas returns to the former in chapter 11, entitled "Reasons and Interest: Retrospect on Kant and Fichte," and he discusses the latter in chapter 12 under the title "Psychoanalysis and Social Theory: Nietzsche's Reduction of Cognitive Interests."

The account of reason and interests is triply important as a return to the theme of the inaugural lecture from a more historical perspective; a retrospective clarification of the main angle of vision underlying the book, which further elaborates the themes of the lecture; and a positive, metaphilosophical standard for the relation of theory to the social context, which will continue to guide Habermas' later reflection leading to the theory of communicative action. In different ways, all of these themes, as well as others, are present in his retrospective glance at Kant and Fichte.

Habermas' return to the themes of reason and interest occurs in the wake of a lengthy discussion entitled "Positivism, Pragmatism, Historicism," which forms the entire second part of the book. He opens the chapter on reason and interest with comments of Peirce and Dilthey in reference to his own distinction between forms of science, and a restatement of his earlier assertion that Marx was unaware of the nature of his thought.

In a tacit reference to his triple distinction, Habermas maintains that Peirce and Dilthey carried the self-reflection of the natural and social sciences [Geisteswissenschaften] to the point where the basis of science in knowledge-constitutive interests [erkenntnis-leitenden Interessen] could be grasped. He further maintains that although they uncovered the roots of scientific knowledge in interest, neither reflected on it as such nor even understood what he was doing.[30]

Habermas now states his understanding of the notion of interest and then develops it through discussion of this concept as it presents itself in the views of Kant and Fichte. He comprehends the idea of interest, not as implying a naturalistic reduction of transcendental-logical properties to empirical ones, but rather as preventing it. He makes, as he notes, the undemonstrated claim that knowledge-constitutive interests mediate the natural history of the human species with the logic of the formative process. He reserves the term "interest" for the basic orientations contained in the so-called fundamental conditions of the possible reproduction and self-constitution of the human species, that is, work and interaction. According to Habermas, knowledge-constitutive interests can be defined as a function of the objective problems already resolved within the cultural form of existence.

This initial formulation is so broad as to include other related concepts, such as the doctrine of *conatus*, or the striving central to all living things to preserve oneself in being, which Spinoza made the basis of his rational psychology.[31] Unlike Spinoza, who refers to appetite or desire in general, Habermas restricts his attention to the link of interest with knowledge. But even this general description suffices to grasp the connection between the notion of interest Habermas describes here and Marx. In the context of his earlier critique of Marx's supposed failure to differentiate and to relate the twin themes of work and interaction, we can see that Habermas now proposes to accomplish the latter part of this task through his notion of interest.

To articulate his notion of interest, Habermas now considers this theme in the German philosophical tradition, first in a brief remark on Hegel, and then in more extended remarks on Kant and Fichte. He uses Hegel to discover the link of reason with interest, which he desires to analyze. His analysis makes rapid use of such Kantian concepts as the will to reason, reason, and maturity [Mündigkeit] and such Hegelian notions as reflection and self-reflection. According to Habermas, the process of reflection depicted in the *Phenomenology* describes the coincidence of the will to reason with reason. He believes that in self-reflection knowledge for its own sake coincides with the interest in maturity since the fulfillment of reflection presents itself as a movement of emancipation. He concludes with two claims: an assertion that reason stands under the interest in reason, which parenthetically supports his earlier denial that rea-

son and interest can be separated; and the further assertion, which also reinforces a point made earlier, that reason pursues an emancipatory interest directed at the completion of reflection.

This comment is more interesting in respect to Habermas' argument than
as an example of Hegel exegesis. When we paraphrase his reading as the Enlightenment claim that reason as such contains an emancipatory interest, we
see that Hegel never makes this claim and in fact strongly denies a related view
of the utility of abstract reason.[32] Habermas does not pause to argue for his
controversial interpretation of Hegel, although this forms the *terminus ad quem*
of his historical analysis.

After a comment that the interests of knowledge are to be understood in
terms of the intrinsic interests of reason, he immediately embarks on his discussion of Kant and Fichte. His aim is to demonstrate that the notion of the
interest of reason is already present in the critical philosophy, but that Fichte,
after his subordination of theoretical to practical reason, is the first thinker
to unfold [entfalten] the concept of an emancipatory interest, intrinsic to acting reason.

Habermas' demonstration rests on controversial interpretations of both
Kant and Fichte. His thesis is that reason as such has an intrinsic interest in
emancipation; but in his remarks on the critical philosophy he focuses on practical reason, Kant's term for the moral faculty. He begins by looking at Kant's
definition of interest and then retraces the latter's familiar analysis of freedom
in the *Fundamental Principles of the Metaphysics of Morals* with the help of unchar-
acteristically copious quotations.[33] Habermas' point seems to be that Kant has
no coherent view of the notion of interest in his moral thought, even if he
desires to attribute a form of pure interest, by generalization from the moral
capacity, to the other faculties of the mind as well. Although Kant desires to
subordinate theoretical to practical reason, Habermas regards this effort as unsuccessful since the concept of speculative reason remains ambiguous. He
maintains that it is only if the speculative interest of reason were taken seriously as a pure practical interest that theoretical reason would lose its role as
independent of the interest of reason.[34]

This line of argument, developed through the analysis of Kant's moral trea-
tises, is surprising. We have already noted that as early as the first edition of
the *Critique of Pure Reason*, that is, prior to his moral writings, Kant presents
a concept of pure philosophy, or the incarnation of pure reason in systematic
scientific form, as intrinsically practical.[35] Hence it is difficult to grasp why
Habermas believes that Kant only extends the concept of interest to the other
faculties from his theory of morality, and equally difficult to understand why
Fichte is supposedly the first to argue that pure reason is inherently practical.
In fact, the latter argument, which is present in the philosophical tradition as
early as Plato, is questionable as a reading of Fichte's view.

Habermas' complex discussion of Fichte is based on the *First and Second Introductions* (1797) to the *Fundamental Principles of the Science of Knowledge
(Grundlage der gesamten Wissenschaftslehre,* 1794). As he did with Kant, in his

discussion of Fichte Habermas concentrates on the relations of theoretical and practical forms of reason and the concept of interest. Perhaps because he is committed to understanding Kant from the perspective of the latter's moral writings, he does not consider Kant's efforts to subordinate theoretical to practical reason.[36] Now, it is arguable, as Habermas asserts, that Fichte succeeds where Kant fails in grasping the unity of reason. But it is too simplistic to see Fichte as merely subordinating theory to practice, since he argues that there is an interrelation in which each depends on the other.[37]

Habermas' main thesis concerns the role of interest in Fichte's thought. On the basis of Fichte's famous opposition between idealism and dogmatism, he suggests that idealism depends on the practical interest of the subject, or the will to emancipation by which it raises itself to intellectual intuition. According to Habermas, Fichte shows that self-reflection is both intuition and emancipation, and hence establishes the unity of theoretical and practical reason. From this perspective, the development of the notion of the interest of reason from Kant to Fichte leads from a concept of the interest in the action of the free will to the concept of an interest in the independence of the ego, operative in reason itself. In Fichte's view of reason as interested self-reflection, interest is allegedly both embedded in reason and constitutive of knowing and acting.

Habermas is correct that Fichte identifies the form of theory with the particular approach to knowledge. Like Marx, he was deeply committed to an activist understanding of the role of the philosopher.[38] In that respect, as Habermas points out, his view of knowledge conflicts with the more traditional, contemplative view. But it is questionable whether we can simply identify the concepts of interest and reason Habermas discusses in Fichte's thought with his own effort to relate knowledge and human emancipation. For Fichte holds that the difference between idealists and dogmatists concerns the difference in their interests, that is, their conception of self-interest, which should not be conflated with a desire to emancipate human being as such. And the process of self-reflection in Fichte's discussion is not the historical self-emancipation of the human species, present in Hegel's *Phenomenology*; it is rather the act of awareness through which the individual realizes that the subject is independent and self-sufficient.[39]

Habermas closes the discussion with a remark on Hegel and a brief summary which establishes the significance of this historical analysis for his own effort to clarify the relation of reason and interest. He asserts that Hegel substitutes phenomenological experience for the central self-intuition of an absolute ego as the source of the world and itself, that is, the view Habermas here attributes to Fichte. He further criticizes Hegel for a failure to perceive that the conditions of human life surpass those posited in the absolute movement of self-reflection.

The chapter ends with a restatement of Habermas' familiar attempt to correlate forms of knowledge with particular types of interest. In respect to other versions of this argument, the difference lies in the assertion, based on his analysis of Fichte's view, that it is in self-reflection that reason grasps itself as interested. In the present context, this point is doubly important, for a reason Habermas mentions and for another reason he does not invoke.

Both reasons concern the general connection of knowledge and interest which he has been examining since his inaugural lecture. Habermas tacitly justifies his historical analysis by drawing a connection to the problem of objectivism. He believes that in self-reflection, through the identification of the link between reason and interest, we dissolve the scientistic objectivism which suppresses the connection of knowledge with interest. Hence, the analysis of Fichte's thought is significant in indicating a way to escape from the phenomenon of objectivism, which Habermas, like Husserl, finds endemic in contemporary scientific thought.

The other reason, which Habermas does not mention, appears when we reflect on the relation between objectivism and the central theme of the discussion. Now, objectivism is an expression of the underlying problem, which is the connection of knowledge with interest denied in the traditional philosophical and scientific concepts of pure theory. This connection has so far been asserted, and even analyzed systematically, although its existence has not been demonstrated. The deeper function, then, of this complex historical analysis, in particular of Fichte, is that Habermas finds in so-called subjective idealism what he regards as a convincing argument for the connection under study. In Habermas' interpretation of Fichte, the latter provides a crucial element in the revision of Marx's thought: the necessary third concept, interest, which conjoins work and interaction in a manner that secures the connection of reason with human emancipation. In a word, for Habermas the way forward from Marx leads backward to Fichte's concept of interest.

The analysis of reason and interest is closely related to the discussion of historical materialism. The clarification of reason and interest is the theme of the first chapter in the third part of the book, which bears the overall title "Critique as the Unity of Knowledge and Interest." Habermas follows the clarification with two chapters on Freud's views of psychoanalysis and metapsychology. He ends the book with a chapter on Nietzsche entitled "Psychoanalysis and Social Theory: Nietzsche's Reduction of Cognitive Interests."

The connection between the interpretation of Nietzsche's thought and historical materialism is not evident in this work; it only becomes clear in the later study of modernity where Habermas situates historical materialism in the Hegelian tradition, and then opposes Nietzsche to Hegel, and, by implication, to Marx and Marxism. Since the later interpretation of Nietzsche builds on the approach begun here, it will be useful, in order to follow the further evolution of the discussion of historical materialism, to attend briefly to Habermas' remarks on Nietzsche in this context.

Much of this chapter continues the previous discussion of Freud, whose theory Habermas here contrasts with Marx's view. Habermas combines two distinct elements in his discussion: the traditional Frankfurt School concern with the synthesis of historical materialism and psychoanalysis,[40] which he shares, and his own concern with the concept of interest. He notes that Freud conceived of sociology as applied psychology and that he related ego conflicts to the economic foundations of society. Habermas sees this as suggesting a comparison of the world-historical process of social organization with the process of socialization of the individual.

He now introduces a comparison between Freud and Marx. He believes the views are comparable since Freud supposedly grasps culture [Kultur][41] as Marx does society, that is, as the means to rise above animal conditions. Tacitly appealing to his own notion of interest, Habermas locates the difference between the two positions in their respective conceptions of the relation of individuals to the institutional framework of society. For Marx this relation is based on social labor, whereas for Freud it concerns the repression of instinctual impulses.

Since his description of historical materialism as critique, Habermas has constantly been concerned with various aspects of its relation to science. He now extends his comparison of Marx and Freud, in terms of his own distinction between work and interaction, to include the question of science. He repeats in part his earlier critique of Marx for the inability to provide an account of reflective knowledge in general, with specific reference to the status of science as critique, from the angle of instrumental action. He then remarks that Freud's metapsychology provides a framework for distorted communicative action which Marx did not comprehend.

This comment presupposes that the problems of ideology and hegemony [Herrschaft] can be understood as instances of distorted communication [verzerrte Kommunikation].[42] According to Habermas, Marx could not see this point because of his unwarranted assumption that human beings differ from animals through the production of their means of subsistence. According to Habermas, the concepts of ideology and hegemony acquire a more substantial role [Stellenwert] when they are grasped as forms of distorted communication from a Freudian angle of vision. For Habermas, the advantage of the Freudian approach follows from the objection he has repeatedly raised against Marx for the latter's failure to distinguish properly between work and interaction. Unlike Marx's view, Freud's theory has the supposed capacity to comprehend the developmental process from the double perspective of work and distorted communication.

Beyond its intrinsic value, Habermas intends his discussion of Freud as an illustration of the point, following from his distinction between work and interaction, that the connection of knowledge and interest only manifests itself in the self-reflection of critical sciences. He views the analytic situation as an analogue of the unity of insight and emancipation which Fichte developed under the heading of self-reflection. But he further discerns an important difference in the specific understanding of the relation of reason and interest. Interest arguably inheres in reason only within idealism, which is concerned to ground reason. According to Habermas, if we understand the cognitive and critical capacities as derivative of the self-constitution of the human species, we perceive, as Freud supposedly showed, that reason inheres in interest, that is, interest in self-preservation.

Although Habermas here makes reason dependent on interest from the biological perspective assumed by psychoanalysis, he rejects the inference that his analysis is dependent on its proximate origin. He believes that the interest in self-preservation is indirect, nonempirical, and not a so-called system-property of the organism. He further protects his analysis against reductionism in two ways.

On the one hand, he associates his view with Freudian psychoanalysis, which no longer operates as a simple illustration for, but rather becomes a part of, the argument itself. Habermas maintains that Freud recognized the connection of knowledge with interest, which he also defended against the psychologistic misunderstanding that entails a subjectivistic devaluation of knowledge. In effect Habermas here cloaks his own theory in the prestige of Freud's.

On the other hand, he analyzes a well-known attempt to argue the opposite point of view in Nietzsche's thought. According to Habermas, Nietzsche provides a psychological reading of the relation of knowledge and interest which constitutes a metacritical dissolution of knowledge as such. Although in his discussion of modernity he will later oppose Nietzsche to Hegel, Habermas here maintains that Nietzsche carried to the end, as the self-denial of reflection [Selbstverleugnung der Reflexion], the self-sublation of epistemology [Selbstaufhebung der Erkenntnistheorie] begun by Hegel and continued by Marx.

From his quasi-Kantian, critical perspective, Habermas' reading of Nietzsche's attack on epistemology as a form of positivism consistently, but perhaps excessively, denies the value of the latter's view. For Habermas, Nietzsche's view of knowledge begins from positivist assumptions concerning the possible fulfillment of the critique of knowledge and the conception of science. Habermas regards the attempt to circumvent the possibility of critique and science through reflection as paradoxical; but this is only the case if the self-reflection must be total. Habermas hence fails to appreciate the weight of this objection which Hegel, following Herder and Hamann, brought against the critical philosophy for its impossible demand that reason sit in judgment on itself.[43]

The analysis of Nietzsche's comprehension of science is more detailed, but not more positive, and not wholly clear. Not surprisingly, since Habermas shares the same view, he does not seem to object to Nietzsche's conception that scientific progress overcomes metaphysics; he is disturbed rather by Nietzsche's insistence on the separation of science and morality, which results in technically exploitable knowledge with no firm relation to practice. In a word, science, which has the monopoly on knowledge, is itself useless. Since Habermas defends the social utility of scientific progress throughout his writings, he is consistent in his objection to the characterization of science, in a passage he quotes, as "sovereign ignorance."

Habermas develops this point through remarks on Nietzsche's polemic against historical science, which Nietzsche considers as meaningless as the natural sciences. He rejects as a minsunderstanding Nietzsche's objection that when historians search for the uses of history they think unhistorically. According to Habermas, the error consists in attributing historical scientism to the historical discipline as such. More generally, he maintains that Nietzsche's inability to appreciate the cultural and natural sciences derives from an inability to free himself from a positivist conception of science.

This latter point provides Habermas with the occasion to restate the outlines of Nietzsche's theory of knowledge. He believes that the central insight in Nietzsche's view is that science aims not at knowledge, but at the control of nature. In fact, as Nietzsche's epistemological perspectivism supposedly shows, the approach to science as a means of self-preservation negates the very possibility of knowledge; for nature in itself has no meaning and there are only different perspectives.

Habermas' objection has a transcendental flavor familiar from his interest in the critical philosophy. He maintains, again through the claim that Nietzsche applies Hegel's criticism of Kant to epistemology in general, that because of his positivistic perspective Nietzsche cannot understand that he employs reflection in an argument against reflection. In the immediate context, his critique of Nietzsche is not only meant to defend the utility of science. It is further intended to reject the supposed biological reductionism of Nietzsche's insistence on the interest of reason in human preservation.

The significance of this critique is apparent against the wider background of Habermas' reading of historical materialism and analysis of the relation of knowledge and interest. In his complex position, Habermas seeks to defend the notion of self-reflection that he claims to find in Fichte against Nietzsche's effort, which Habermas associates with Hegel, to turn the tool of reason against itself; and he further makes use of self-reflection, against the idealist identification of interest as intrinsic in reason, in order to argue that reason is inherent in the interest in self-preservation which informs all thought and action.

Habermas' description of Nietzsche's position as clearing the way for the rise of positivism, which in fact precedes it, may or may not be accurate. However, it illuminates his own critique of Marx from a Kantian angle. In general, and despite his complex reading of the history of modern philosophy, Habermas operates with a simple dichotomous model of epistemological thought. Like Kant, who distinguished between pre-critical, or dogmatic, and critical perspectives, he differentiates critical and positivistic approaches in relation to reflection. With respect to this model, there is no place for a putative third way represented by the views of Hegel and his most profound student, Marx.

Although Habermas follows Hegelian usage in the description of Hegel's grasp of epistemology as a sublation of the critical philosophy, he regards absolute idealism not as a higher stage, but as a regression to a lower level in virtue of its alleged rejection of absolute reflection. With respect to the theory of knowledge, Habermas' review of what he calls the pre-history of positivism reveals that Marx is located between Hegel and Nietzsche in the course of the emergence of the positivistic loss of reflection supposedly characteristic of post-critical thought. If Marx's position can be resurrected at all, Habermas believes it can only be on the Kantian basis of a fully critical theory of philosophy.

V

THE RECONSTRUCTION OF
HISTORICAL MATERIALISM

In *Knowledge and Human Interests,* Habermas elaborates his systematic critique of Marx against the wider historical background. The effect is to extend the objection originally raised against Marx—that his theory lacks a reflective dimension—to the entire post-Kantian philosophical tradition, beginning with Hegel's attempted sublation of the critical philosophy. The thematic analysis of positivism, which Habermas defines as a lack of a reflective moment and finds virtually throughout post-Kantian thought, is a generalized form of the complaint he has earlier made in his discussion of Marxism as critique. This line of argument follows from Habermas' belief, similar to his conviction that after Kant philosophy no longer understands science, that epistemology in the true sense of the term disappears after the critical philosophy.

This way of interpreting the post-Kantian development of the epistemological discussion is doubly useful for Habermas: it provides him with a standard, namely, a Kantian view of theory, by which to reject later forms of the theory of knowledge; and it suggests that further progress, including progress in historical materialism, requires a reconstruction of the latter theory from a Kantian perspective. Although Marx's critique of Hegel may be more relevant to Kant's position, which accordingly suggests a basic distinction between Kantian and Marxian forms of philosophical theory, Habermas implies that the distinction between the two approaches is at most relative, not absolute. For in his reliance on a Kantian criterion for the evaluation of the Marxian position, Habermas clearly presupposes that there is a common theoretical terrain which renders it legitimate to judge the status of historical materialism as a theory in terms of the standards of the critical philosophy.

From this angle of vision the anti-epistemological line of development supposedly set in motion by Hegel, and to which Marx allegedly belongs, ends with Nietzsche's epistemologically minded attack on the theory of knowledge. In relation to the problem of knowledge, Nietzsche can be seen as opening the way for the subsequent rise of positivism, including the reduction of epistemology to methodological discussion in analytic philosophy of science. In this way, Habermas prepares his later effort to transcend not only historical materialism, but post-Kantian thought in general, in the defense of a theory of communicative action which, in the insistence on absolute reflection, is intended as a legitimate successor of the critical philosophy. In effect, then, Habermas' later rejection of historical materialism and *Bewußtseinsphilosophie* is also an attempt to return to the Kantian inspiration on a new, higher plane.

At present, we need to consider Habermas' effort, after his critique of historical materialism, to reconstruct it in satisfactory form. His encounter with Marx and Marxism traverses a developmental path which never bears more than a rough correlation with its chronological expression in a series of texts. We have so far reviewed writings concerned more or less closely with his interpretation and critique of historical materialism. Obviously, these phases are inseparably related in the various books and articles. Even the earliest account of Marx and Marxism in the "Literaturbericht" strikes a critical note, and there is a clearly interpretative dimension to the critical consideration of Marx in *Knowledge and Human Interests*. In texts later than this book, although the hermeneutical and critical dimensions do not disappear, they begin to recede into the background in favor of the emergence of another theme at which Habermas has been hinting for some time: the effort to reconstruct historical materialism.

It is difficult to specify the origin of the reconstructive phase, since it overlaps with other parts of the discussion. There are scattered hints concerning the reformulation of historical materialism throughout Habermas' critical discussion of Marx's theory. As criticism obviously presupposes a point of view, merely to observe that Marx's thought lacks a critical dimension is to propose that a way be found to incorporate such a dimension into the position. In that sense, the basic revision of the theory is already present in the objections articulated in Habermas' initial account of Marx and Marxism. Nevertheless, it is only in a single, brief moment of his lengthy study of historical materialism, in the volume called *On the Reconstruction of Historical Materialism* (*Zur Rekonstruktion des historischen Materialismus,* 1976), that Habermas goes beyond statements expressing the need to reconstruct the theory by actually undertaking this task.

This volume is not a single, sustained argument; it is rather a collection of often disparate essays, covering a wide variety of topics, written for various occasions, which are here brought together within the covers of one book.[1] The studies in this volume share the perspective of Habermas' emerging theory of communicative action, which informs them all in different ways. It is reasonable to infer that this theory is ingredient in the attempted reconstruction of historical materialism, although the link between communicative action and the reconstruction in question requires clarification.

Now, in part this link was already apparent in earlier texts, such as *Knowledge and Human Interests,* where there are occasional direct references to the theory of communicative action. This link is only accentuated in later writings, where Habermas continues the elaboration of his own position even as he prolongs his discussion of Marx and Marxism. One way to clarify this link is to consider other examples in the history of philosophy.

Obviously Habermas is not the first thinker to approach another from the vantage point of his own view. As concerns historical materialism, the most prominent recent example is Sartre's later thought. We have already reviewed Habermas' remarks on the so-called existential attempt in Marxism. In his later phase Sartre, as noted, defended the controversial claim that existentialism founds Marxism as a philosophical anthropology that lacks a concept of man, which is arguably available in existential thought. Now Habermas cannot make this specific claim since in writings later than the "Literaturbericht" he rejects as misguided the anthropological approach to historical materialism. But it is still possible for him to understand his theory in a Sartrean sense as completing an intrinsically deficient theory.

In practice it is not easy to specify Habermas' grasp of the relation between his own theory and historical materialism, in part because his view of it alters over time as a function of the evolution of his reading of Marx. But it is correct to say that whereas initially Habermas thought of communicative action in a quasi-Sartrean sense as extending, and hence as completing, historical materialism, he later came to think of his position as supplanting the tradition emanating from Marx by offering a new and incompatible way to attain the goal intrinsic to, but not reached by it.

This interpretation is supported by two developments in the course of his dialogue with Marx and Marxism. On the one hand, there is the extension, as noted, of his critique of Marx's position to post-Kantian philosophy in general. Since Habermas refuses to relinquish the intrinsic relation of Marx's theory to philosophy, the immediate result is to make it impossible to reconstruct historical materialism on the basis of an already extant philosophical position. On the other hand, the slow elaboration of Habermas' view of communicative action as an independent theoretical entity, coupled with the decisive criticism of historical materialism, means that it is both possible and necessary to avoid further reliance on Marx's position.

The final phase of the relation between communicative action and historical materialism only arose after Habermas' later turn away from his initial effort to reconstruct the theory. He later will give up the effort as misguided in virtue of what he regards as the lack of further possibilities for development within historical materialism. The inference is clear that his failure to carry out the reconstruction in a satisfactory manner was due, not to his strategy, but to the intrinsic limitations of the particular theory. At present, he has not yet arrived at this negative reading of the inherent possibilities of historical materialism for further growth, which he is concerned to bring about from his quasi-Kantian, critical perspective.

The official topic of this book, as reflected in the title, is the reconstruction of historical materialism. In practice the essays concern a wide variety of topics whose connection, even indirect, with Marx and Marxism is not always evident. For the most part, with the exception of the actual effort to carry out the reconstruction in question, the discussion concerns Marx more than Marxism. In this volume, three texts directly relate to Marx's thought: the introduction, the occasional article on the role of philosophy in Marxism, and the essay for which the volume is named, on the reconstruction of historical materialism.

The range of issues under discussion in this book is especially evident in the introduction, whose purpose is to link together essays composed on a variety of themes and for different occasions. In order not to go beyond the present concern with historical materialism, it will be useful to concentrate selectively on those aspects of the introduction most closely related to this theme.

The introduction is entitled "Historical Materialism and the Development of Normative Structures." It opens, as noted, with a short, metatheoretical passage, linked to recent philosophy of science as well as the idealist tradition, tending to justify the reconstruction of philosophical theory. Habermas remarks that it is not by accident that the essays collected here belong to the period in which he has been engaged in working out his own theory of communicative action. He then immediately draws attention to the connection of his theory to historical materialism in a general statement. According to Habermas, his theory is intended to solve problems of a philosophical nature concerning the foundations of the social sciences, although he sees a close link to questions relating to a theory of social evolution.[2] The remainder of the introduction is devoted to the justification of his controversial assertion of a link between his own concern with communicative action and Marx's position.

We can pause here to anticipate an obvious objection to our review of Habermas' discussion. It might be objected that this statement is outside the scope of the present work. Habermas here speaks of social evolution and does not mention historical materialism. Nevertheless, we can infer that his intent at this point is to raise the question of the relation of his own position to historical materialism for several reasons. These include the fact that this passage immediately follows a discussion of the reconstruction of historical materialism in a book bearing this title; Habermas' explicit attempt to justify the reconstruction in question through a metatheoretical comment on the reconstruction of theory in general; and the comment that Marx understood historical materialism as a theory of social evolution of which the analysis of capitalism was a part only.[3]

The latter point marks a further elaboration of Habermas' understanding of Marx's thought, which is triply significant for the evolution of Habermas' interpretation of historical materialism, his effort here to reconstruct it, and his later attempt to refute the theory. As concerns the reading of the theory, we can note that in the period following his description of historical materialism as an empirically falsifiable philosophy of history, Habermas has steadily been concerned with two main issues: the lack of a critical dimension in the theory, which he increasingly extends to post-Kantian philosophy in general, and the relation of Marx and Marxism to analytic philosophy of science.

Now, throughout this period, Habermas' reading of the precise link of historical materialism with philosophy has remained unclear. He is neither willing to accept nor to deny the standard Marxist claim that philosophy is ideology whereas Marxism is science. He is hence unwilling either to accept or to reject a definitive description of the connection of historical materialism with philosophy. In *Knowledge and Human Interests,* he partially clarified this connection through the observation that philosophy survives in Marx's thought as the materialist critique of ideology. This move shifts the center of his reading of Marx from the early manuscripts to the *German Ideology*. He now reinforces his reading of Marx's thought from the vantage point of the *German Ideology* in the comment that Marx's position is primarily a theory of evolution which extends beyond the analysis of capitalism. It is well known that in this work Marx provides a sketch of a theory of social evolution in terms of different forms of ownership.[4]

The description of Marx's position as a theory of social evolution opens the way for Habermas to reconstruct it as a nonpositivistic form of social theory. Already in *Knowledge and Human Interests,* he suggested that the capacity of social theory for self-reflection enables it to avoid the scientistic objectivism of natural science. Now, it is a simpler task to provide the critical dimension allegedly necessary to turn Marx's position into a nonobjectivistic social theory than it is to reformulate a theory of capitalism in general. The latter, wider task requires a detailed account of the nature of modern society which Habermas did not yet possess when he composed this book. He only turns to this problem in subsequent writings, for instance in the wake of his attempted refutation of Marx's position, where he quickly sketches an alternative, arguably richer theoretical approach.[5] Since Marx's thought allegedly lacks a critical, or self-reflective dimension, its redescription as a form of social theory, in independence of the problems of the theory of capitalism, makes plausible the attempt to reconstruct historical materialism.

The description of Marx's position as a theory of social evolution raises a serious question about Habermas' later efforts, which effectively terminate the dialogue with historical materialism, to refute the theory. This attempt, as noted, is based on its identification as an economic position, centered on the labor theory of value. If, as Habermas here maintains, the theory of capitalism is merely a fraction of a larger position, then the theory as such cannot be refuted merely through the critique of its economic dimension. At best, a critique of this kind could merely refute the economic aspect of the position.

Habermas' elucidation of the claimed relation between the theory of communicative action and historical materialism is complex. He begins by pointing to three situations [Umstände]: the danger of bad philosophy in Marxism, the lack of clarity concerning the normative basis of Marxian social theory, and the felt need for the theory of communicative action within historical materialism. He then turns immediately to a theme frequently touched upon in earlier writings: the relationship of historical materialism and science.

His discussion here in part recalls, but further develops, specific points he has previously made. He notes that it is especially dangerous to employ a scientistic understanding of science, and states that Marxism can no longer appeal to the model of physics in order to block the road opened by the rise of social scientific theories of development. His warning against positivism echoes his earlier criticism of the problem of objectivism in writings since the inaugural lecture and his critique of the danger of Marx's appeal to physics as a standard in *Knowledge and Human Interests*. But he now goes beyond his earlier remarks in his suggestion that in abandoning the model of natural science Marxism would do well to turn to recent trends in the social scientific theory of development. This suggestion is only reinforced by his description in this context of Marx's position as a theory of social evolution which, by inference, can profit from later developments of this type of social theory.

Habermas' intent is to indicate that Marxism ought not to employ a mistaken analogy of physical theory to prevent historical materialism from such later developments as his own stressing of an intrinsically self-critical form of social science. The implication that later progress has in part outdated historical materialism is reinforced by a remark about the presumed lack of clarity in the foundations of Marxian social theory. Habermas maintains that Marx thought he had settled this problem through a materialistic appropriation of Hegelian dialectic. And he further maintains that today, if we are not to take up a metaethical position, we must develop general presuppositions of communication for the justification of norms and values.[6]

Clearly, at this point Habermas is close to Sartre's belief that as an intrinsically incomplete theory Marxism needs to be founded in another, prior view. He here recalls the point made in *Knowledge and Human Interests* that Marx misunderstood his own thought, which now takes the form of the failure to secure its theoretical foundations. But he goes beyond his earlier discussion in the implicit claim that the Marxian theory, which arguably reduces interaction to work on the model of production, can only be clarified from the level of interaction, or communication. In a word, there is a clear suggestion that the further elaboration of historical materialism requires as its necessary condition Habermas' own view of communicative action.

Habermas now draws this conclusion in an explicit comment on the relation between his own position and Marx's. He states that the discussion of the epistemological foundations of historical materialism demands a so-called 'communicative-theoretical reflection', or discussion from the plane of interaction, as distinguished from Marx's model of production. After this general comment, he identifies a particular issue on which communicative action can contribute to historical materialism. According to Habermas, Marx concentrates on the forces of production to the neglect of the phenomenon of the superstructure [Überbauphänomen], which is more important than Marx thinks. An instance is the problem of the learning processes which contribute to the development of productive forces, but which arguably cannot be understood on this level. More generally, Habermas believes that culture remains a superstructural phenomenon which is prominent in the evolutionary process of society. He adds that it is precisely this prominence that explains the contribution his communicative theory can make to the renewal of historical materialism.[7]

Habermas' announced intention to contribute to the understanding of culture within historical materialism is an extension of his earlier criticism of Marx's tendency to grasp interaction in terms of production. If culture, which cannot be grasped on the model of work, influences social change, in order to understand social evolution we require a richer view of this phenomenon than that available in Marx's theory. In this way, through further development of his previous critique of the limits of Marx's position, Habermas sees the need to focus on the concept of culture, and, hence, on the distinction between superstructure and base.

The proposed revision of the Marxian concept of the superstructure presupposes a reading of this aspect of Marx's thought in terms of the theory of communicative action. But here and elsewhere, Habermas consistently discourages the inference that his own theory has assumed its mature form. In a passage omitted from the translation, in the course of a rapid enumeration of his previous contributions to the concept of communicative action, he indicates that he is referring here to "fragments" [Bruchstücke].[8] This remark implies a theoretical whole to which the pieces belong, but which, as Habermas realized, was not yet explicit in this book. This claim, which is acceptable here, when his theory is obviously in an incipient state, becomes progressively less plausible as it is repeated in later writings, especially in the massive treatise directly devoted to the theory of communicative action.

Habermas now makes a suggestion about the proper approach to social theory, which he only attempts to work out in detail in the later discussion of communicative action. Obviously, there are many different approaches to social theory. It is equally obvious that analytic philosophy of science, which has consistently figured in his discussion of historical materialism, is closely related to analytic philosophy of language. Perhaps for this reason, he proposes to extend his approach to social theory in terms of communicative action by basing the latter on a version of the notion of a speech act theory, with obvious analogies to the classic work by John Searle.[9]

At this point Habermas apparently believes that society can be comprehended from the communicative perspective since it is literally produced by language. According to Habermas, the structures of linguistically produced intersubjectivity [sprachlich hergestellten Intersubjektivität] are necessary conditions for social and personality systems. It follows that social systems can be regarded as a series of communicative actions, and so-called personality systems, or human individuals, can be studied in terms of ability to speak and to act.[10]

The proposal to ground all social theory in a concept of language recalls Habermas' earlier reading of Hegel, as well as his description here of the relation of communication to interaction. As noted, language was one of the social universals which Habermas identified in the early version of Hegel's view, but which arguably disappeared in the mature version of his thought. In the present context, the emphasis on language provides a strategy for Habermas to make out his claim that although Marx reduces interaction to work, the clarification of work can occur only from the perspective of interaction, to which language belongs.

It is less problematic to determine why Habermas might want to argue that intersubjectivity is in some sense literally produced by speech than it is to justify this controversial claim. It is not, for instance, difficult to examine the homologies between the structures of the ego and of group identity, to which he next turns. There might be more resistance to his claim, in passing, that what he calls holistic concepts, such as productive activity and *Praxis*, need to be resolved into the basic concepts of communicative action and purposive rational action to avoid the conflation of the two processes of rationalization that determine social evolution.[11] But this statement is merely an application of the basic assertion that forms of work require analysis in terms of interaction. The deeper question, which we cannot even attempt to answer here, is whether some form of speech act provides an adequate basis for social theory.

As noted, Habermas is aware of the controversial nature of his approach to Marx's view. At the end of the introduction, he takes up two possible objections, as concerns the relation of his theory to the Marxist theoretical tradition and to historical materialism. Now it is curious that these topics receive separate attention here if he holds that Marx and Marxism form an inseparable entity. In writings earlier than the present book, although he has on occasion rejected forms of dogmatic or vulgar Marxism, he has never drawn a clear distinction between Marx and the Marxist epigones. In the present context, in which he concentrates increasingly on Marx's thought under the heading of historical materialism, we can construe this procedure as a hint that historical materialism cannot simply be equated with the Marxist theoretical tradition.

Habermas' treatment of these objections reveals a basic ambiguity in his comprehension of the connection of his own position to Marx's. He remarks that the analysis of capitalism is useful in developing a theory of social evolution. He then points to supposedly still useful elements in the theory of capitalism, including the account of the relation of wage labor and capital, the concept of class structure, the model of crisis in connection with the process of capital accumulation, and the mechanism of the legitimation of domination through bourgeois ideology. An identification of parts of the analysis of capitalism which are supposedly not yet outmoded suggests that Habermas' effort is not limited to the development of the notion of the superstructure beyond the point at which Marx left it; it is also, even centrally, an attempt to salvage what is still worthwhile in an allegedly outdated theory in order to produce a view of social evolution intended to replace Marx's position.

Now these two ways of reading the relation between Habermas' view and Marx's are not only different; they are irreconcilable. At this point Habermas does not even attempt to resolve this tension, which is finally only dissipated in his later study of communicative action. There he defends the conclusion—which by implication follows from the failure of his effort here to rework historical materialism in satisfactory fashion—that Marx's position and the general type of philosophy to which it belongs cannot be reconstructed or otherwise salvaged; it must rather be abandoned in favor of his own, alternative theory.

In sum, we see that the introduction is a complex document which functions to connect two distinct phases of Habermas' discussion of historical materialism: the earlier interpretation and criticism which are still committed to the identification of a viable form of the theory, and its later rejection as not possibly viable in favor of his own alternative position. Although there is an analogy with Sartre's approach to Marxism from the vantage point of existentialism, there is a difference in Habermas' eventual conclusion that his own position need not remain subservient to historical materialism. If the latter view cannot be reconstructed in satisfactory manner, then the theory of communicative action must become an autonomous entity, which preserves the viable pieces of Marx's theory, but leaves the theory itself behind. In a word, Habermas finally rejects not only historical materialism; he further rejects a Sartrean comprehension of the relation between his own theory and Marx's in favor of a more Hegelian approach.

The introduction to this book was written after the fact in order to link together the writings collected here. In this volume the two essays which concern Marx's thought are both occasional pieces. The essay entitled "The Role of Philosophy in Marxism" has not so far been translated. It was delivered at the Korcula Summer School in August, 1973 after a paper on the same topic by Gajo Petrovic,[12] a leading Yugoslav philosopher and a member of the so-called Praxis School, a group of Marxist intellectuals concerned with problems of humanism. Although Habermas' paper is short (11 pages), it is important as an indication of a connection he perceives between his own effort to reconstruct historical materialism and philosophy in general.

Habermas here again takes up a problem which has preoccupied him since the "Literaturbericht" and to which he has offered a series of differing responses: the relation of historical materialism to philosophy. This question is central to the Marxist tradition. Since Engels, it has always defined itself through the rejection of so-called bourgeois, or orthodox philosophy in favor of a revolutionary philosophy, or more often through the rejection of philosophy in all its forms in favor of science.

It is not surprising, in view of the wide variety of approaches which fall under the loose heading of Marxism, that there is no single, generally accepted understanding within Marxism of the relation between historical materialism and philosophy. With respect to this question, the single shared conviction within Marxism seems to be that historical materialism differs in kind from traditional philosophy. This difference is often described in terms of the distinction between idealism and materialism, although there is no agreement as to how to characterize it. The unclarity, which typifies the Marxist view of this issue, is present in all of Habermas' writings that touch on the topic, as they also presuppose a protean distinction between idealism and materialism whose contours vary over time.

In Habermas' prior writings we can discern a series of varying descriptions of historical materialism, including its description as philosophical anthropology, empirically falsifiable philosophy of history with a practical intent, neither a metaphysics nor an ontology nor a first philosophy, a theory of knowledge as social theory which preserves the concept of critique, and a theory of social evolution. These alternative descriptions derive from attention to different portions of the Marxian corpus and reflect Habermas' concern at different stages of the discussion with different issues.

There is no effort in his writings to show the interrelation of his various ways of understanding the link of historical materialism to philosophy. It does not, however, follow that he simply changes his mind or that there is not a single, underlying vision. But we can point out that the characterization here of historical materialism as a theory of social evolution fails to clarify the underlying question of how historical materialism relates to philosophy. For a theory of social evolution can be understood in various ways, for instance, as a form of social philosophy, or as a social analogue to the Darwinian theory of natural selection. While the former is a type of philosophy, the latter is a form of social science, more closely related to sociology, political science, or even social psychology.[13]

In his essay, Habermas is less concerned with the relation of historical materialism to philosophy than with the clarification of philosophy's possible role in the achievement of the objectives of Marxism. In a continuation of the approach he has frequently employed since his discussion of Marxism as critique, once again he employs science as a backdrop for his understanding of historical materialism. He begins by observing that Marxist theoreticians have always had a clearer view of the utility of science for the productive potential of the bourgeois world, which is supposed to become a new, socialist society, than they have had of the role of philosophy. After a brief summary of some of the various Marxist views of philosophy, he states the question that interests him here: is philosophy more a productive force or a false consciousness?[14]

The significance of this way of posing the question is to identify two alternatives rooted in Marxism: the frequent claim that philosophy is false consciousness, based on the influential discussion of ideology in the *German Ideology,* and the rival view of philosophy as a productive force. The latter refers to the idea that social progress is a function of the development of productive forces. This is a notion which Marx elaborates in the *German Ideology* and in later writings. The question suggests that there are conflicting interpretations of a theory which is finally incoherent. Habermas immediately acts to prevent this reaction by rejecting one of the alternatives as unacceptable, more precisely by drawing a distinction between the cultural tradition in general and ideological consciousness. The latter by definition occults the subjacent class structure and contributes to the legitimation of the present legal and power relationships. According to Habermas, Marx and Engels never understood the content of the cultural tradition simply [einfach] as ideological;[15] and the young Marx, who deeply respected Hegel, only regarded as ideological the premises of foundationalist philosophy.

The intent of this clarification is to cast doubt on the proposed alternative as an adequate framework to understand the role of philosophy within Marxism. Habermas next calls into question the utility of a determination of the precise nature of the classical view of this issue. He maintains that if his rough sketch is correct as a description of the role and the relation of philosophy and the sciences, then today a Marxist kind of analysis [eine marxistisch angeleitete Analyse][16] must lead to another conception. In order to justify this conclusion, he briefly comments in the remainder of the paper on three problem areas: the changed situation of culture in recent capitalism, the ruling scientism and the reactions to which it has led, and some important tasks of contemporary philosophical thought.

He quickly describes the supposedly new constellations of bourgeois culture through comments on religion, morality, and art, as well as technology [Technik] and science. He suggests that religion is in the process of coming to an end and that increasingly less attention is directed to systems of moral values. Following Bell and Marcuse, he further calls attention to the incapacity of art to assume this role. He then mentions the increasingly important roles of technology and science, before asking how the role of philosophy has changed.

Now continuing his earlier discussions of scientism, he maintains that the rise of technology and science as the veritable motor of the development of productive forces is linked with the victory of positivism. In this connection, he correlates forms of positivism with the Marxism of the Second International and with contemporary analytic philosophy, and then briefly identifies three typical counterreactions. These include the attempt to rescue an extra-scientific domain in philosophies of existence; the effort to renew foundationalist thought [Ursprungsphilosophie] and ontology, the latter of which he associates above all with Heidegger; and the Stalinist form of Soviet Marxism, or dialectical materialism. He then examines the relationship of these alternatives to his favorite theme: science.

Although prolegomenal, the discussion so far serves to establish the centrality of science in the contemporary world. This point reflects his belief, discussed above all in *Knowledge and Human Interests,* that since Kant philosophy has no longer understood science. Habermas, who holds that the understanding of science is a central philosophical task, now turns to the analysis of the recent role of philosophy in Marxism and in general, beginning with yet another attempt to clarify the relation of historical materialism to philosophy.

According to Habermas, if we understand philosophy as the most radical form of self-reflection at a given time, then Marxism is philosophy. But he denies that it is now possible to attempt to think the unity of the world from a position either prior to, or apart from, science in favor of the claim that philosophy arises out of the self-reflection of the sciences. He believes that at present the philosophical task can only be undertaken within the context of the self-reflection of the sciences. This claim represents an inversion of the well-known, Platonic view of philosophy as the science of sciences, which still survives in the positions of Kant, Hegel, and Husserl. From Habermas' perspective, philosophy has lost the autonomy it once claimed with respect to the sciences, which have become prior to it and on which it now depends. But he is unwilling to adopt the scientistic view that philosophy has no further reason for being. He ends his essay by illustrating his view of the role of philosophy today in the form of three theses.

First, he insists that from a philosophical vantage point the unity of nature and of history must be understood on the basis of general theories of nature and society. Adopting a Hegelian understanding of the nature of philosophy, he maintains that philosophy expresses the irreplaceable demand for unity and universality,[17] which can only be fulfilled scientifically and which is valuable in itself.[18] In this regard, he holds that historical materialism has a meaningful program for a future theory of social evolution, as distinguished from its present status. Second, he stresses the so-called self-interpretation and self-defense of reason as the task of philosophy. Finally, he sees as the deepest philosophical function the appeal to the power of radical self-reflection against every form of objectivism [Objektivismus], that is, against the ideological comprehension of thought and institutions.

This view of the role of philosophy carries forward Habermas' previous insistence on critical reflection as the still valid aspect of philosophy. The identification of objectivism with ideology points to the importance of historical materialism as the source of a materialistic critique. At this point, however, Habermas widens his understanding of the struggle against ideology in a manner that blurs the distinction between historical materialism understood as materialistic critique and critical self-reflection in general.

According to Habermas, who here recalls a number of familiar themes, radical self-reflection is directed against the absolution of foundationalism and pure theory, scientism, the scientistic self-understanding of the sciences, and the technocratic consciousness of political theory unrelated to the social basis. Although some of these themes are standard Marxist concerns, others, for instance, the problem of scientistic objectivism derived from Husserl, are only distantly related to historical materialism.

Habermas is less interested here in historical materialism than in a form of reason which preserves a valid function for philosophy. By implication, his claim for radical self-reflection, under which he also includes Marxism, is that this form of reason can resolve tasks common to historical materialism and to more traditional philosophy. Such tasks include the unification of theoretical and practical reason and the establishment of an identity between society and its citizens.

He now generalizes his claim in the statement that without philosophy and in the absence of so-called high religion [Hochreligion] he sees no way other than through reason to construct the identity in question. In a word, philosophical reason, namely, the radical self-reflection supposedly also characteristic of Marxism, is today propelled into the space left by the demise of religion as the source of unity in a fragmented world.

With respect to historical materialism, this essay reaffirms a conviction first voiced in the inaugural lecture for the positive connection of reason with interest. Habermas there argued that the unexamined claim for the practical utility of pure theory was itself a form of objectivism. In the historical redevelopment of the themes of this lecture, he further argued for the relevance of reason, and specifically insisted on the value of the materialistic critique of ideology. Now qualifying the view of the relevance of reason, he argues that radical self-reflection, which is presumably common to critical Marxism and to nonmetaphysical kinds of philosophy, is specifically relevant for the practical problems of daily life. More generally, the function of the appeal to reason as a unifying force is to restore the unity lacking in contemporary life and in reason itself. In sum, in this revised view the still valid portions of philosophy and of historical materialism come together in a concept of self-reflection which, he believes, combines both reason and interest.

Habermas' response to the question of the role of philosophy in historical materialism lies in the description of a form of reason that is practically relevant and common to both. Philosophical reason appears here as a productive force, that is, as a force which can produce a rational unity that is a conceptual analogue of the social unity at which Marxism aims. Rather than ideology, philosophy is the genus to which Marxism belongs and whose task it carries out.

Now, although interesting, this analysis is eccentric to the announced task of the reconstruction of historical materialism. Habermas has so far called for, and even offered a metatheoretical description of, the reconstruction of the theory; but he has not yet undertaken to carry it out. It is only finally in the long title essay of the book, "Towards a Reconstruction of Historical Materialism," that he undertakes to provide a more satisfactory version of the theory he has often interpreted and criticized, and which increasingly, as the essay on the role of philosophy in Marxism shows, he has begun to leave behind.

In the German original, but not in the English translation, the essay is preceded by a one-sentence statement indicating its occasional nature.[19] Habermas begins his discussion with a series of remarks concerning the classical understanding of historical materialism and its more recent redescription within Marxism. These comments are intended to situate his effort to reconstruct the theory within the context of the ongoing discussion.

He states that Marx, who preferred to apply the materialistic conception of history, only twice reflected upon the nature of the theory. This statement is a variant of his repeated criticism of historical materialism as lacking a reflective dimension necessary to justify its epistemological claims. He further maintains that recent discussion on the role of philosophy within Marxism has shown that the theory possesses the type of radical self-reflection that is descriptive of philosophy. In a word, Marx's supposed inattention to the quasi-Kantian problem of the nature of his conception of history is an indication of the incomplete, and by inference pre-critical, or dogmatic, nature of his philosophical position.

After his brief restatement of the theory's epistemological deficit, Habermas next describes Marx's position as a theory of social evolution and not as a heuristic. This description is puzzling unless it is realized that he has in mind the rejection of a possible misinterpretation of Marx's thought due to the influence of Engels on the reading of Marx's view. According to Habermas, who here refers to Krader's well-known studies of Marxian enthnology and anthropology,[20] Engels's description of the theory as a central thread [Leitfaden] and a method might mistakenly suggest that it is a heuristic which helps to structure a narrative exposition of history. On the contrary, Habermas claims that since Marx and Engels, historical materialism has always been understood as a theory.

The distinction between a theory and a heuristic, which Habermas does not explain, presumably means that historical materialism goes beyond an informal type of explanation in being a scientifically formulated and testable theory. This way of reading the position correlates well with his repeated insistence on the empirically testable dimension of the Marxian theory of history. With respect to previous discussions, the difference, upon which he now insists, lies in his reading of historical materialism as a theory of social evolution which, in virtue of its reflexive status, is informative for the aims of political action and, under certain circumstances, can be linked to theories of revolution and of strategy.[21]

His description here of historical materialism as a socially useful theory of history echoes his characterization of it in earlier texts, especially in the study of Marxism as critique. But he now opens the way to its reconstruction by linking its description to a theory of social evolution that surpasses the analysis of capitalism. Habermas, who has implied this conclusion in the introduction to the volume, now renders it explicit when he states that the theory of capitalist development elaborated by Marx in the *Grundrisse* and in *Capital* is merely a part of historical materialism.

Since we know that Habermas' intention here is to reconstruct the theory, he needs to interpret, criticize, and revise it. Surprisingly he fails at this point to take up the classical form of the theory, either in Marx's writings, or in those of Engels, the first Marxist. He turns rather to Stalin's supposedly consequential [folgenreicher] formulation of the theory.[22] According to Habermas, the theoretical formulation provided by Stalin requires a reconstruction. He suggests that the proposed reconstruction will be useful for the conceptual mastery [kritische Verarbeitung] of competing viewpoints, such as social scientific neoevolutionism and structuralism.

Left unclear in this statement is the crucial issue of whether the problem is limited to Stalin's reading of historical materialism, or whether it extends beyond Stalin's admittedly rudimentary grasp of the theory to the theory it-

self. Although Habermas here associates the problem with Stalin's approach
to Marx and Marxism, the very generality of the lengthy discussion, in which
Stalin's name only recurs once, strongly suggests that the allusion to the
latter's form of Marxism is simply tactical; it further implies that, in the
twilight of his effort to take historical materialism seriously as a potentially
viable theory, Habermas has decided to focus squarely on its origins in
Marx's position.

The discussion at this point concerns what Habermas describes as fundamental concepts [Grundkonzepte] and fundamental assumptions [Grundan-
nehmen] of the theory. He does not clarify the distinction between a concept
and an assumption, but turns immediately to such concepts as social labor
[gesellschaftliche Arbeit] and the history of the species [historische Gat-
tungsgeschichte] prior to further discussion of three so-called basic assumptions of historical materialism.

The concept of social labor is a leading theme in Marx's writings as early
as the *Paris Manuscripts* and remains so even in *Capital*. The concept of the history of the species has a more complex background. In the famous discussion
of alienation in the first of the *Paris Manuscripts,* Marx differentiates four subspecies, of which the third is the alienation from species being [Gattungs-
leben].[23] This idea is controversial, since it has sometimes been held that Marx
later abandoned this notion in the sixth of the "Theses on Feuerbach." In the
latter text he criticized the idea of an abstract human essence—which he attributed to Feuerbach—and substituted the notion of the ensemble of social relations.[24] In the *German Ideology,* as noted, he further elaborated the idea of a
historically variable form of social relations under the heading of the history
of the species.

Habermas approaches the concept of social labor from the perspective of
his own earlier series of distinctions concerning work and interaction. His
characterization of labor mainly follows the discussion in the *German Ideology*.
After describing human labor as the specific way in which individuals reproduce their lives, he redescribes it from his own vantage point as the goal-
directed transformation of material according to rules of instrumental action.
Production contrasts with distribution which, he maintains, requires rules of
interaction located on the level of intersubjective, linguistic understanding.
These rules can be separated from individual cases as recognized norms, or
rules of communicative action. According to Habermas, an economy is
merely a system which regulates both production and distribution.

This account of social labor prolongs Habermas' earlier effort to understand
Marx's position from a dichotomous perspective. The new elements here include the rapid attempt to demonstrate that the Marxian theory of economy
must presuppose a duality through the reconstruction of the concept of (political) economy in general, and the further accentuation of the linguistically-
based, quasi-Kantian dimension of the concept of communication, now restated in the terminology of analytic philosophy.

In his interpretation there is a direct analogy between Kant's view of the categories of the understanding as universal rules for the production of objects of possible experience and Habermas' reading of economic distribution as intersubjectively governed by rules, or norms; this analogy is only obscured, but not diminished, by the fact that he here locates these rules, perhaps in virtue of his interest in analytic philosophy of language or in transformational linguistics, on the level of language.

After this brief mention of social labor Habermas raises the question of the extent to which it accurately characterizes the forms of reproduction of human life. For an understanding of the human mode of existence he turns briefly to anthropology. According to Habermas, the Marxian concept of social labor is adequate to differentiate the modes of life of the hominids and the primates, but insufficient to capture the specifically human reproduction of life. He further states that the reproduction of human life occurs only when the economy of the hunt is supplemented by a familial social structure. This line of reasoning leads him to the conclusion that labor and language are older than man and society.[25]

Habermas notes that the two passages in which Marx discusses the concept of historical materialism are at the beginning of the *German Ideology* and in the famous preface to the *Critique of Political Economy*, that is, in texts later than the *Paris Manuscripts* and earlier than *Capital*. Now, adopting the perspective of the Marxian middle period, he states that Marx related the notion of social labor to the idea of the history of the species. In Habermas' interpretation, the concept of the mode of production [Produktionsweise] includes the forms of production and the relations of production. Noting that Marx distinguished five, or perhaps six, chronologically distinct modes of production, he opposes a weaker interpretation to what he calls the stronger, or dogmatic, view.

According to Habermas, the so-called weaker version is able to dispense with the species subject [Gattungssubjekt] that undergoes evolution since the bearers of evolution are the societies and the subjects integrated within them.[26] In the context of the controversy surrounding this topic, by implication he supports the claim that Marx abandoned the concept of species being as early as the *German Ideology*.[27] With respect to the theory of history, he locates the relative advantage of the weaker interpretation in its ability to separate social development from an intrinsic logic, and hence to dispense with linearity and necessity as well as continuity and irreversibility. He affirms his identification with this weaker version of historical materialism by stating his desire to defend its criteria for social progress.

At this point in the course of his attempted reconstruction of historical materialism Habermas is still committed, if not to the validity of the theory as a whole in its present form, at least to the intrinsic worth of certain of its essential elements. He specifically mentions his desire to defend the criteria of progress identified by the theory, that is, the development of the productive forces and relations of production which together constitute a given mode of production.[28]

After his accounts of social labor and of the history of the species, he next considers two so-called basic assumptions of historical materialism: what he calls the superstructure theorem [Überbautheorem], and the dialectic of the forces and relations of production. With respect to his previous inquiries into Marx and Marxism, this phase of the discussion breaks important new ground. Although Habermas has on occasion referred in passing to political economy, especially in the study of Marxism as critique, this marks the first systematic investigation in his writings of historical materialism from this perspective. As such, it represents a shift in the identification of the nature of the theory that will quickly open the way to a rejection of historical materialism in terms of a critical reading of Marxian political economy.

For a statement of the superstructure theorem, Habermas now abandons his recent reliance on the *German Ideology* and turns instead to a celebrated passage in the famous preface to the *Critique of Political Economy,* a work that clearly belongs to the later, more economic side of the theory. He distinguishes between so-called economistic and weaker versions of the theory. In the former interpretation, which is a form of economic reductionism, higher processes are causally determined by lower processes; in the weaker version of the thesis, the lower subsystems are limited [bestimmt werden] by the higher ones.

These two interpretations of the superstructure theorem are widely represented in a voluminous secondary discussion. Perhaps influenced by Kuhn's view of scientific revolutions, Habermas now argues in favor of a third alternative which combines features of the two forms of interpretation just distinguished. According to Habermas, the context in which Marx advanced his theorem makes it clear that the dependency of the superstructure on the economic base was intended to obtain only when society passed from one stage to another. Habermas believes that for Marx, economic determination is restricted to the transitional phase of social development, but does not otherwise hold.[29]

In the present context this suggestion has a triple function of combining the rival readings of the superstructure theorem, demonstrating the compatibility of his view of communication with Marx's theory, and of reinforcing his approach to historical materialism as a theory of social evolution. It is intended to combine both interpretations by acknowledging a real, but restricted, dependency of the superstructure on the base. In this manner he in effect reconciles two arguably incompatible readings of the superstructure theorem. He further shows the compatibility of his own view of communication with the Marxian theory since in his own terms interaction is independent of work except in the period of transition between social stages. He finally supports his approach to historical materialism as a theory of social evolution since, from his particular viewpoint, the economic determinism central to Marx's position is only intended as an explanation of social change.

Habermas' effort to restrict the range of application of the economic base is intended to avoid a form of reductionism prevalent within Marxism. Habermas immediately takes steps to limit even further the tendency to provide an economic interpretation of social phenomena, which he will later reject as concerns Marx's theory and as such. He suggests that the equation in the superstructure theorem of the base with the economic structure of society is true only in capitalism before briefly examining the mechanism of crisis.

In this connection, he rejects the allegedly technologistic reading of the dialectic of the forces and the relations of production as failing to differentiate the levels of work and interaction, an argument he has often made before. Now taking up the theme of the relevance of learning, mentioned in the introduction, he argues that the introduction of new forms of social integration depends on moral-practical knowledge available only on the plane of communication.[30] According to Habermas, although such knowledge is related to the domain of instrumental and strategic action, or the sphere of labor, it develops according to its own intrinsic logic.[31]

After these remarks on the history of the species, Habermas next focuses on Marx's attempt to comprehend the developmental sequence of society as a series of modes of production. He believes that although the Marxian model is insufficiently developed, it is more useful than competing alternatives. According to Habermas, the concept of a mode of production is unable to capture the universals of social development.[32]

He further holds that the need for stronger generalization can be satisfied through the search for highly abstract principles of social generalization made possible through innovations in the learning process.[33] The utility of such principles would be to classify, according to evolutionary features, the form of social integration of different stages. Habermas sketches, and then, relying on the work of Klaus Eder, illustrates his view. His key point is that we can only explain the solution of so-called steering problems in terms of learning mechanisms.[34]

This argument raises in different form the issue of the relation between his own position in this book and Marx's thought. Habermas reasserts his claim, frequently urged in this collection of texts, for the importance of the learning process as a force of social change and the related claim for the need to understand this process as located, beyond the domain of labor, on the plane of interaction. At the very least he holds that this view of education is broadly consistent with his way of reading Marx.

Now, in this volume, and especially in this essay, he is ostensibly engaged in a reconstruction of historical materialism. But in his concern with social universals he arguably transcends the spirit and certainly the letter of Marx's position, which is mainly concerned to specify the social characteristics intrinsic to a particular form of society. His tendency to pass beyond, and not merely to reconstruct, the Marxian perspective is further evident in his speculative remark, in a comment on progress and exploitation, that various forms of bureaucracy could outlive the economic form of class domination.[35] In effect, he here raises the possibility of the persistence of a rigid social structure in a future form of society which would no longer be determined by economic factors.

The essay so far has been directed to the examination of various facets of the Marxian approach to the explanation of social phenomena. Habermas, who has earlier stated his willingness to defend this approach, now undertakes this task through a rapid review of possible alternatives. As alternative forms of evolutionary theory he singles out three possibilities: structuralism, neoevolutionism, and sociological foundationalism. After brief remarks on each of these theories from the angle of vision of his own view, he ends with a comment on the normative foundations of communicative action and historical materialism.

This comment is intended to support the relative priority of interaction over work and to defend the validity of historical materialism. Now, again anticipating the theory of communicative action he will shortly develop in detail, he maintains that all communication necessarily presupposes the conditions of possible consensus. He interprets this statement to mean that the basis for the validity of speech-claims lies in universal and, hence, transcendental presuppositions, which cannot be rejected without deciding against reason.

Since for Habermas communication underlies other forms of action, the force of this claim is to argue for the rules of communicative action as the foundation of historical materialism. Although in quasi-Sartrian fashion he affirms the relative priority of his own theory, Habermas is not yet willing to abandon Marx's view. Drawing a connection between reason and the expansion of reason, he now interprets the latter from the vantage point of historical materialism, as the development of productive forces and the maturity of social integration. In this way, he makes good on his promise, as noted, to defend the validity of historical materialism.

We can conclude our consideration of Habermas' effort to reconstruct historical materialism by again evoking the difficult cohabitation in this volume between the views of Habermas and Marx. There is an ambivalence at the end of Habermas' discussion in this essay which runs throughout and typifies this book. It is as if, after much prior interpretation and criticism, when at this point he finally calls for and describes the metatheoretical conditions of the reconstruction of historical materialism, he is no longer convinced that this undertaking is really possible.

Now, the announced purpose of this essay is to reconstruct the theory. Yet, perhaps because of the concern to develop the theory of communicative action, he seems here to be arguing simultaneously for the priority of his own view and the viability of a reading of Marx's thought. What we are left with, then, is less a reconstruction of historical materialism than the further development of the premises of another position, which, while related to Marx's theory, presumably surpasses it in various ways, such as in its capacity to resist Habermas' critique of Marx's thought. As a result, like the later Sartre, now Habermas appears to cast his own theory in the role of a necessary supplement to, and finally more adequate replacement for, historical materialism.

This remark can be sharpened, since it concerns the success of the announced effort undertaken here, after earlier interpretation and criticism, to reconstruct historical materialism. Habermas describes his intention as the desire to reconstruct Stalin's influential, but misguided, version of the theory; but he focuses almost exclusively on Marx's writings and the problems of their interpretation. Now, in order to comprehend the results of Habermas' study, following his own practice we must distinguish "interpretation" and "criticism" from "reconstruction." From his own metatheoretical perspective, the latter term means "to provide a version of the same theory which is better able to attain its intrinsic goal."

In practice, Habermas' effort to reconstruct the theory takes the form of a review of its fundamental concepts and assumptions, including both interpretation and criticism of aspects of historical materialism and the further elaboration of parts of his own theory. As concerns historical materialism, with the exception of the account of the modes of production, he confines himself to interpretation and criticism. As concerns the modes of production, he goes beyond Marx in an effort to specify social universals which, he maintains, Marx failed to identify.

If this description of Habermas' discussion is correct, then the latter consists mainly of the interpretation and criticism of Marx's theory and the further elaboration of his own, rival view. The promised reconstruction can only lie in two aspects of the discussion: the extension of the Marxian notion of modes of production under the heading of social universals, and the theory of communicative action. Now, since Habermas never clarifies the relation between the modes of production and social universals, we need not accept the former as a reconstruction of the latter, more precisely as a further development of the theory according to its intrinsic goal.

We can further note that Habermas never claims that his own theory, which is obviously related in his mind to Marx's, is continuous with historical materialism. But he would have to make and to justify this claim for the elaboration of communicative action to count as the reconstruction of historical materialism. Accordingly, we can conclude that Habermas here issues a promissory note for the reconstruction of historical materialism which he does not finally redeem.

VI

THE REJECTION OF
HISTORICAL MATERIALISM

The critical remarks at the end of the previous chapter were intended less to question the idea of a reconstruction of historical materialism than to question Habermas' success in this endeavor. We can suppose that this problem has not escaped his attention. An indication of his preoccupation with this issue is the cryptic remark, noted previously, that it is no accident that in the composition of the essays in his book on the reconstruction of historical materialism he was concerned as well to elaborate his own theory. It is, then, significant that in later writings he quickly drops the very idea of a reconstruction of historical materialism. He further advances reasons why such an attempt is in principle misguided, which in effect may be read as an implicit self-criticism of his own earlier efforts to carry out that task.

We can usefully relate this attempted reconstruction to his reading of historical materialism in general. In previous writings he has interpreted, criticized, and attempted to reconstruct the theory. The latest, in fact conceptually final, phase of his discussion of historical materialism occurs in a recent work, *The Theory of Communicative Action (Theorie des kommunikativen Handelns)*.[1] In this book Habermas once again takes up and further develops numerous themes from his many other writings. The result, a sort of giant fresco which some have seen as his masterpiece, contains more than 1,100 pages and is not far from surpassing the practical limits of a single study.[2] In view of its dimensions and the relatively slight attention to historical materialism, whose interest here recedes before the emergence of Habermas' theory, it is neither practical nor necessary to describe the entire work, even in outline. For present purposes it will be sufficient to restrict our remarks to some main themes in the treatise which form the background of his account here of Marx and Marxism.

In this phase of the present study, it will be necessary to devote more attention than before to unraveling the intricacies of Habermas' discussion. His remarks on historical materialism at this point are on occasion overly complex and insufficiently clarified. It is as if, after many years of meditation, he no longer believed that careful discussion of Marx and Marxism could produce useful insight and, accordingly, he was in a hurry to turn to other issues. Now, whether or not this is even an approximate description of his state of mind when he composed this work, we can at least be aware of the need to clarify the remarks on historical materialism that close his lengthy attention to the topic if they are to be understood and accorded the weight they deserve.

The unusual complexity of this book concerns the discussion as a whole, and is not merely restricted to the remarks on Marx and Marxism. In his reading of historical materialism, there are a series of shifts in Habermas' orientation as concerns his approach to the theory, his criticism of it, and his attitude toward his own theory. In general terms, we can say that now he draws the conclusions which follow from his remarks on the labor theory of value as early as the discussion of Marxism as critique in order to refute historical materialism through a decisive criticism of its economic dimension.

We have already outlined a series of changes in his approach to historical materialism after the initial focus on the early Marxian texts from the dual perspectives of philosophical anthropology and nonfoundationalist, nonmetaphysical philosophy. These changes include his redescription of the theory as an empirically falsifiable theory of history with practical intent, his insistence on materialist critique centered in the *German Ideology*, and his further redescription of Marx's position as a theory of social evolution in the volume on the reconstruction of historical materialism. The title essay of that volume continues the tendency to concentrate on Marx to the relative exclusion of Marxism already evident in *Knowledge and Human Interests*.

In the latter book Habermas opened the way to an economic reading of historical materialism widely present in the Marxist discussion, but largely absent in his prior writings. In his attention to the passages on historical materialism in the *German Ideology* and in the preface to the *Critique of Political Economy*, he maintained his interest in the former text at the same time as he made a first, timid step toward the economic reading of the theory to be reconstructed. In his treatise on communicative action, we find a significant revision of this approach, which now has fully shifted toward an economic interpretation of historical materialism, firmly centered in Marx's later writings. From this perspective Marx's position, or historical materialism, must stand or fall on the validity of his economic theory. In the same way, Habermas' rejection of the theory is squarely based on his effort to provide a decisive critique of Marxian economics.

The change in Habermas' approach to historical materialism is correlated with a revision of his critique of the theory. In prior writings he has advanced two main criticisms of historical materialism. On the one hand, he has objected, from a quasi-Kantian stance, that Marx fails to raise the question of the condition of the possibility of knowledge. In *Knowledge and Human Interests*, he pursued this line of criticism in order to show how, following Hegel, Marx precedes Nietzsche down the road which leads to modern positivism. On the other hand, he has constantly objected in different ways, in a long series of texts, to Marx's supposed inability, because of his commitment to the

model of production, to maintain the necessary separation of work and interaction. Now, these two criticisms are obviously related since the function of
communication in Habermas' view is to guarantee the possibility of the unfettered reflection which he finds lacking in Marx's theory.

Interestingly, Habermas no longer insists at this point on the absence of a
critical dimension in Marx's position; he concentrates rather on the latter's
supposed inability to make out the distinction between work and interaction,
which he here renames as the levels of life-world and system. Two reasons
can be advanced for this change in Habermas' attitude toward the theory.
First, he now simply gives up the idea, clearly prominent in *Knowledge and
Human Interests*, of continuing the attempt to resolve the traditional problem
of knowledge. If the epistemological problem is not a central concern, then
there is no reason to criticize Marx for his possible failure in that regard. Second, it would be inconsistent to continue to scrutinize Marx's view as the necessary source of a theory of knowledge in the Kantian sense since Habermas
is here mainly concerned to criticize historical materialism as an economic
theory.

The changes in the interpretation and critique of historical materialism are
matched by a further shift in Habermas' understanding of the relation of his
own theory to Marx's. The theory of communicative action, which was not
present at the outset of his concern with Marx and Marxism, becomes progressively more important over time, especially in the present work. As early
as his attempt to reconstruct historical materialism, Habermas' theory had assumed roughly equal status in his mind with Marx's position. We have noted
the analogy between Habermas' comprehension at that point of the relation
of his own position to Marx's to Sartre's conviction that he can found Marxism through existentialism.

In his discussion of communicative action, Habermas' understanding of the
link between his theory and historical materialism changes significantly. Perhaps because he no longer believes that any form of the latter theory is viable,
he is no longer concerned to speculate on the relation between his view and
Marx's. As concerns the latter, beyond the criticism he raises, his main interest
now is to demonstrate that communicative action can in fact carry out the
tasks which historical materialism only intended to perform.

It follows that his fundamental commitment toward the goals of historical
materialism has not changed. What has changed is his earlier conviction that
it is in principle possible to attain them through a revised form of the theory.
At this point he continues to strive toward the realization of goals he regards
as intrinsic to the views of Marx and Marxism; but he no longer does so
through the framework of historical materialism, which supposedly can no
longer be revised. Rather, he undertakes to realize the theory's goals through
the means of another, perhaps incompatible theoretical paradigm, his own
theory of communicative action.

In the short (5 pages) forward to his enormous discussion, Habermas states
that his immediate aim is to propose the beginning of a theory of communica-

tive action already evoked in the forward to his discussion of the logic of the social sciences.[3] According to Habermas, his social theory [Gesellschafts-theorie] is not a metatheory, although it is concerned to specify its own critical standards [kritische Maßstäbe]. He further indicates that he does not understand the analysis of general structures of action oriented toward the understanding [verständigungsorientiertes Handeln] as a prolongation of the theory of knowledge [Erkenntnistheorie] by other means.

This statement of intentions is doubly interesting. First, it is obvious that since Habermas is still intellectually active his theory will change over time in later writings. That is the case with any author not content simply to repeat ideas arrived at earlier. But in view of the sheer dimensions of this book, it is difficult to imagine what it could possibly precede as a mere introduction. Perhaps Habermas has in mind a prolegomenal status similar to that of the *Critique of Pure Reason* to the future metaphysics that Kant never wrote.

It is further difficult to see why Habermas feels that he is still entitled to claim provisional status for a theory he began so many years ago and has since developed in many writings, above all in the present book.[4] Although he evidently believes that this form of the theory of communicative action is merely provisional, it seems probable that this text will be, and correctly should be, regarded as a major source of the mature view.

Second, we can note that Habermas now breaks with his earlier, epistemological approach to historical materialism. His statement in the preface to *Knowledge and Human Interests* that a radical critique of knowledge is possible only as social theory casts historical materialism in this role. Now, with the prominent exception of the early Lukács,[5] most writers in this field decline to interpret Marx and Marxism from an epistemological perspective.

Habermas later came to doubt the wisdom of his distinctively epistemological approach to Marx and Marxism. He comments on this change in his understanding of epistemology in a recent interview after he had completed his study of communicative action. Here he states that he still believes in the correctness of the argument developed in *Knowledge and Human Interests* although he no longer believes in the theory of knowledge as a *via regia*.[6] In a word, he has now abandoned the epistemological approach to historical materialism in particular and to theory in general which was earlier a prominent feature of his discussion.

In order to discuss Habermas' remarks in this context on historical materialism, we need to situate them in relation to his wider account of communicative action. The forbidding size and sprawling style of this book render it difficult even to state its main themes coherently. Since our present purpose is not to consider the theory of communicative action other than in relation to Habermas' reading of historial materialism, it will be sufficient to rely on a hint offered in another recent interview. Here Habermas offers a useful summary of his discussion of communicative action, apparently in part in order to provide an overview of his intentions in the book.[7]

After describing his work as a monstrosity [Monstrum], he distinguishes four main themes, namely rationality, communicative action, the dialectic of social rationalization, and the critique of functionalist reason. According to Habermas, the search for a theory of rationality is at present rendered particularly difficult by the popularity of the relativism which stems from Nietzsche. This is a theme which he has already discussed in some detail in *Knowledge and Human Interests*, and which he will later take up again in a work on the concept of modernity.

It is significant, in view of the title of his treatise, that he regards the theory of communicative action as merely one of the four main themes of his study. His modest assessment of the role of his theory in the present work is coupled with an extremely wide-ranging claim for its potential utility. He emphasizes that his theory of communicative action needs to be made fruitful for the discussion of a varied series of problems, including the theory of argumentation, the beginning point for social theory, and the interpretations of Mead's theory of symbolic interaction and Weber's dialectic of social rationalization.

Third, there is a dialectic of social rationalization [Rationalisierung], which was already a central theme in the work by Horkheimer and Adorno entitled *Dialectic of the Enlightenment*. In this connection, Habermas wants to demonstrate that the concepts of communicative action can be developed into a theory of modernity with the capacity to discriminate among sociopathological phenomena which, for the Marxist tradition, fall under the notion of *Verdinglichung*. Although Habermas identifies this aim with his study of communicative action, it seems fair to say that it is at best a minor theme in this work; it only becomes a major concern in the later effort to elaborate a theory of modernity.

Fourth, he describes his interest in a concept of society which brings together [zusammenfährt] systems theory and action theory in order to develop a critique of functionalist reason, intended to continue with other means the old critique of instrumental reason offered by the critical theory. Habermas hence indicates that, despite the criticisms of critical theory offered in this volume, he regards his own view as a later form of it. He further suggests that the dualistic approach he defends here, as a further version of his consistent attachment to a separation of work and interaction, can be understood as a later development of critical theory. Since the critical theory is a form of Marxism, we can say that Habermas comprehends his own critique of Marx as providing a Marxist corrective to the original formulation of historical materialism in Marx's writings.

This rapid series of remarks neither provides, nor is intended to provide, an adequate description of Habermas' book in general. It is unnecessary here to describe this study in further detail, since it mainly lies beyond the scope of this essay. It will be useful now to bring out a further theme in the account of communicative action which basically alters Habermas' approach to historical materialism. His list of four main themes in this book, especially his comment on the need to update the critique of reason begun by the critical theory, might suggest that he retains the sympathetic, but critical, attitude toward historical materialism in evidence in his earlier writings. Despite the suggestion of a continuity between his own view and Marxism, the fifth theme in this work, which he does not mention in his brief description of it, is a basic change in his grasp of the intrinsic resources of historical materialism.

We can bring out this change through a remark on his earlier effort to reconstruct historical materialism. Here and in previous criticism, Habermas made the silent assumption that the theory possessed a theoretical potential which could still be utilized. It would clearly be idle to undertake to reconstruct a theory which did not in some sense have a future, or more precisely, in whose future one did not believe. Now obviously all theories are not capable of such reconstruction. But in his writings up to this point, Habermas has always been careful to indicate his continuing attachment to historical materialism.

The difference is that he now explicitly denies this unacknowledged, but implicit and necessary, presupposition of his earlier writings on historical materialism. In the work on modernity, he will offer a reading of the history of philosophy intended to show that historical materialism belongs, not to the future, but to the past; it relies on the paradigm of consciousness whose capacity for further elaboration has been exhausted. At present, he does not offer any attempt to justify his turn away from historical materialism other than the mere assertion that the theory can no longer be defended. Toward the end of the second volume, in a long passage which sums up much of the discussion and hence needs to be cited in extenso, he writes:

> With the preceding investigation I want to introduce a theory of communicative action, which clarifies the normative foundations of social theory. The theory of communicative action should offer an alternative for the no longer defensible philosophy of history [die unhaltbar gewordene Geschichtsphilosophie] to which the older critical theory was still bound. It puts itself forward as the framework within which the interdisciplinary study of the precise model of capitalist modernisation can again be taken up [wieder aufgenommen werden kann].[8]

Two consequences follow immediately from this statement. First, it is clear that with this declaration Habermas has arrived at the end of his active concern with Marx and Marxism as an even potentially viable theoretical approach, although not at the end of his discussion of their views, which continues in his writings to date. The importance of this shift in his attitude is worth stressing. In previous texts, the many criticisms Habermas raised against historical materialism were always combined with a basic commitment to the theory. His objections were always directed to the present form of the view, its appearance, never to its essence, its very heart.

But if it is no longer possible to believe that the theory can be reconstructed in satisfactory form, then the distinction between the theory's essence and its appearance disappears. For this reason, for the first time, Habermas' criticisms of historical materialism are not intended to discern weaknesses to be overcome in a better form of the theory; they are intended rather to identify rea-

sons to consign it to history, reasons to abandon the theory to the historians
of philosophy. In sum, Habermas' critique is now intended to justify his rejection of historical materialism.

His discussion of historical materialism in this and later writings is never
intended to accord it consideration as an even possibly viable position; it is
rather invariably directed to situating this theory within the wider class of
philosophical positions, in practice the whole of post-Kantian modern philosophy, which Habermas in principle regards as an exhausted terrain, which is
not susceptible of further development. But it would be hasty to terminate
our consideration of his study of Marx and Marxism at this point, or to turn
directly to criticism of it, without further exposition of his reading of the theory. Even if he has now abandoned his earlier commitment, if not to the letter,
at least to the spirit of historical materialism in the form of a reconstruction
that would meet his objections to it, his continued effort to situate it within
the wider German philosophical tradition remains interesting.

Second, there is a change in Habermas' mind in the status of his own position. If historical materialism is no longer even a potentially viable option,
then communicative action can no longer come to its aid or pretend to provide
the final, but indispensable, element for a theory in need. As Habermas now
realizes, his view must henceforth stand on its own or must fly with its own
wings if it is to fly at all. But although he tacitly abandons Marx and Marxism,
he is unwilling to forego the project for which he believes historical materialism was formulated. The solution, since the latter theory is no longer apt for
the task, is for the theory of communicative action to take its place. For this
reason, Habermas now intends his view, not to complete, but rather to replace
historical materialism.

At this point, even as he moves beyond historical materialism, Habermas
retains a relation to the theory. The continued presence of Marx and Marxism
in Habermas' thought at a period when they are officially supposed to be absent is clearly a result of the extensive discussion Habermas has devoted over
a period of years to their views. The relation to Marx is mediated in several
ways, through a continued interest in a widened version of the Marxian problematic, for instance through an interpretation of historical materialism as a
theory of social evolution, which earlier figured prominently in the effort to
reconstruct it; the concern to take up themes prominent in Marxism, such as
the concept of reification and the critique of instrumental reason; and through
renewed attention to Max Weber, who was himself arguably influenced by
Marx.

If the old philosophy of history is irreparably defective, its inadequacies cannot be remedied through its reconstruction or in other ways. Habermas argues
for this conclusion in the second volume in his account, "Marx and the Thesis
of Inner Colonisation [innerer Kolonisierung]." This is a long chapter which
forms the second section of a three-part "Final Consideration: From Parsons
over Weber to Marx." In order to understand his criticisms of historical mater-

ialism at this point, we need to view them in the context of his analysis of the Weberian problem of inner colonization.

We can begin with a remark on Habermas' strategy in order to clarify the complicated argument he develops here. There is a complex relation between his constant concern with rationality, which continues the emphasis of earlier texts, and the critique at this point of historical materialism from a perspective dependent on the reception of Marx's theory. Habermas is concerned at present to stress the relation between the positions of Marx and Weber. Although Weber is a highly original thinker, his thought reflects Marx's influence in many ways. An example is the concept of rationalization, which can be described as a theory of social reason mediated by the constraints of the capitalist economy. Habermas' concern now is with the problem of inner colonization, which he sees as arising out of Weber's theory of rationalization.

According to Habermas, this problem has previously been studied from the Marxist perspectives by Lukács and Merleau-Ponty. But there is a clear difference between the approaches of previous Marxists and Habermas. Whereas previous Marxists tried to incorporate the Weberian problem within the Marxist angle of vision, Habermas utilizes it to reject that perspective, from which it arguably follows and to which it remains related, by going beyond historical materialism.

After this clarification of Habermas' strategy, we can describe the problem of inner colonization he discerns in Weber's thought. Briefly stated, the thesis in question asserts that "as a result of capitalist growth the subsystems of trade [Wirtschaft] and state grow ever more complex and penetrate ever more deeply in the symbolic reproduction of the life-world."[9] According to Habermas, neither Weber's position nor Marx's has the theoretical resources necessary to analyze this situation.

Habermas' critique of Weber's position is in part an extension to it of an objection he has often raised against Marx. He now maintains that the thesis in question requires a distinction between the concepts of system and life-world not present in that form in Weber's writings. Since the required distinction is central to Habermas' view, the criticism tacitly suggests that communicative action can come to the aid of Weber's theory.

Now using the *Verdinglichung*, which is another form of Lukács's term for alienation [Reifikation], he further objects that the problem-complex of inner colonization cannot be satisfactorily analyzed through a theory of objectification. In a clear reference to his own view, which he now offers as a replacement for the old philosophy of history, or historical materialism, he writes: "The theory of late capitalist objectification [Verdinglichung] reformulated in the system/life-world perspective requires therefore completion through an analysis of the culturally modern which takes the place of a revised theory of class consciousness."[10]

The significance of this comment for Habermas' view of historical materialism becomes apparent if we differentiate various attitudes to historical materialism in his writings. He initially favored the so-called phenomenological approach, which he associated above all with Marcuse. In later writings, beginning with *Knowledge and Human Interests*, he gives qualified endorsement to a form of what, in the discussion of modernity, he will call the Weber/Hegel approach to Marx. The latter is perhaps best exemplified by Lukács, who admittedly determined Habermas' initial reading of Marx and Marxism. We can note that Lukács always regarded the problem of alienation as central to the views of Hegel and Marx.[11] He believed that the difference in their respective analyses of this problem reflected a distinction in kind between idealism and materialism.

In previous writings, Habermas has called for the reconstruction of historical materialism in order to develop further its line of thought. Since at this crucial point in the argument he fails to renew this call, it can only mean that he has given up his belief that the theory can ever be reconstructed in a satisfactory manner. He now tacitly makes this admission in the suggestion that we cannot come to grips with the phenomenon of inner colonization from the vantage point of the old theory of history; we can only take up this problem from the perspective of another theory which is intended not to develop further, nor to complete, but simply to replace its predecessor.

We can restate the same point in relation to the idea of the growth of the history of philosophy. Above we have distinguished between incompatible views of theory replacement and theory growth. We have noted that Kant held that later theories supplant earlier ones, whereas Hegel believed that it was both possible and necessary to build upon prior theories. From this perspective, Habermas' decision not to develop, but to replace, historical materialism implies an alteration in his attitude toward the comprehension of the growth of the history of philosophy. He has now obviously abandoned the quasi-Hegelian notion—tacitly supposed in his earlier writings as the basis of his effort to reconstruct historical materialism—in which later positions build upon and complete earlier ones; in its place he has adopted another view, closer to Kant, in which later views simply replace their inadequate predecessors.

Habermas' analysis of historical materialism once more calls to mind Sartre's relation to Marxism. It is sometimes overlooked that this relation did not arise instantaneously at a point in time; it has its own history, a series of phases through which it passed. Scholars who concentrate on such later writings as *Search for a Method* and the *Critique of Dialectical Reason* often neglect the relevant earlier writings, especially "Marxism and Revolution."[12] If we compare Sartre's various accounts of Marxism, we perceive an evolution from a more textually centered attitude in the earlier writings to a later, more general reading, that he analyzes in discussions increasingly distant from the texts.

We can note a similar evolution in Habermas' writings on historical materialism. As an author, one of his distinctive traits is an apparently encyclopedic grasp of the available background material. In his numerous discussions of Marx and Marxism, he routinely refers to numerous primary and secondary sources. In the present context, he breaks sharply with his prior practice. Interestingly, in a chapter almost sixty pages in length directly devoted to Marx, none (!) of the seventy-seven footnotes contains a direct reference to Marx's writings. On the contrary, his effort here to refute Marx is based squarely on his own prior writings on historical materialism and on the secondary literature.

In general terms, we can say that in the twilight of his interest in historical materialism, Habermas closes the circle by returning to the sources of his concern, which he further elaborates by conjoining different strands in a complex conceptual matrix. As concerns his reading of what he now calls the old philosophy of history, we have already noted the importance of such varied themes as Lukács, French existentialism, and a rejection of an economic reading of historical materialism. These and other themes now recur in a series of remarks which, however, is not simply repetitive, or even merely derivative, of Habermas' earlier discussions.

In comparison to his prior writings on historical materialism, at this point there are two major changes: a detailed critique of the theory from an economic angle of vision and a resolute turn towards Weber. On the one hand, Habermas now justifies his earlier decision to distance himself from an economic reading of historical materialism through a sustained attack on the Marxian value theory. Obviously he regards it as central to the wider Marxian position, which he now interprets as an economic theory. The result is a significant shift in his reading of historical materialism that brings out a tendency that began to appear in the volume on the reconstruction of historical materialism, especially in the title essay.

As early as that discussion we noted a dual attitude toward historical materialism deriving from the perspectives of the *German Ideology* and the *Critique of Political Economy*, interpreting it as the materialist critique of ideology and as the related economic theory. Now, the latter reading was potentially available in the early, more anthropological writings, especially the *Paris Manuscripts*. Marx here prepares the way for his own distinctively economic approach to the analysis of social phenomena by building upon Engels's slightly earlier discussion of political economy.[13] Like many other students of Marx, Habermas ignores the presence of an important economic dimension in Marx's early thought in favor of its reformulation in later writings.

On the other hand, Habermas strives here to fuse together various facets of his approach to historical materialism in reference to Weber's thought. The effort to combine the attitudes of Weber, Lukács and French phenomenology in a single approach to a Hegelian philosophy of history emerges from a creative rethinking of a thesis originally proposed by Merleau-Ponty. According to the latter, Lukács's approach to Marx, which Merleau-Ponty describes as the origin of Western Marxism,[14] arose in reaction to Weber. He believed that Weber's theory of ideal types was intended to solve the problem of the understanding [entendement];[15] and he further believed that Lukács's aim was contained in a related question: how is it possible to recover an absolute in the flux of history?[16] Habermas here accepts the suggestion that Lukács's

Hegelianized Marxism is crucially dependent on Weber, although he rethinks the relation of Lucács to Weber in a new way.

Habermas' discussion of this complex point remains unclear. He acknowledges that Marx and Weber began from different concerns: Marx from the problems of system and Weber from problems of integration.[17] Nonetheless, he maintains that since Weber's reception prepared the way for Western Marxism, it is appropriate to interpret Marx from this angle of vision.[18] In a word, despite the fundamental differences separating the views of Marx and Weber, at this point Habermas believes that the latter's position offers a perspective appropriate for the critique of Marx's thought.

Habermas finds the specific link in Lukács's effort to bring together the Weberian theory of rationalization with the Marxian view of political economy. His interpretation presents a double advantage in the present context. First, it enables him to criticize such widely divergent views as those of Weber, Lukács, and the representatives of critical theory in a single conceptual breath, so to speak, in terms of their supposed relation. He rejects, for instance, Lukács's supposedly objectivistic distortion of subjectivity in the well-known views of class consciousness and reification [Verdinglichung]. He brings a more complex criticism against the critical theory. Despite the rejection by Adorno and Horkheimer of the concept of class consciousness, Habermas maintains that critical theory in general still suffers, because of its dependence on Lukács, from all the inadequacies of Weber's view.

Second, Habermas now feels justified in criticizing Marxian political economy. In a passage suggesting that his main concern is to appropriate for his own purposes certain concepts borrowed from historical materialism, he writes: " . . . I will now work out what the Marxian theory of value performs for a theory of reification translated into systems and life-world concepts and where its weaknesses lie . . ."[19]

If we reflect on Habermas' discussion so far, we can see that it is at best prolegomenal to a critique of historical materialism. Even after the remarks on the link between Marx, Weber, Lukács, and Merleau-Ponty, it remains unclear how the proposed retrospective reconstruction of the origins of Western Marxism concerns the supposed *aporia* of Marxian political economy. It is clear, however, that Habermas here intentionally formulates his critique of historical materialism from his own intended post-Marxian perspective, as an indication of the fact that he has now moved beyond Marxism. Significantly, the problem is no longer whether the theory, more precisely Marxian political economy, is valid, or even whether it can be reconstructed in a better way. The issue rather is how this view can be useful for another position, that is, for the theory of communicative action.

Here as elsewhere, Habermas' remarks on Marx are filtered through a wide, on occasion even bewildering, awareness of various thinkers and problems, which he typically endeavors to combine within the framework of a single analysis. In comparison with previous stages of his discussion of historical materialism, we can note changes of terminology which reflect his concern at this point with Weber, Parsons, and phenomenology, in whose views he finds analogies for different aspects of the theory.

Weber's thesis of inner colonization is held to correspond roughly to the distinction between superstructure and base, which he earlier discussed in his remarks on the so-called superstructure theorem. In the positions of Husserl and Schutz, he finds analyses of the symbolic reproduction of life-world, which he sees as analogous to ideology, or false consciousness of the economic base. The labor theory of value [Werttheorie] is supposedly similar to Parson's action-theoretical introduction of a steering mechanism [Steerungsmedien].[20] He further presupposes, as he notes, Parson's linkage of the paradigms of action/life-world and system.[21] In view of the complexity of Habermas' approach, it is not surprising that it is sometimes difficult even to discern the outlines of the main threads in the discussion.

As concerns historical materialism, the critique Habermas proposes here is a reformulation, in terms of current concerns and new terminology, of earlier objections, above all as concerns Marx's monism. Habermas, as noted, calls attention to Weber through remarks on the problem of inner colonization. Although, as noted, Habermas is here officially concerned with the Weberian problem of inner colonization, it is perhaps Parson's problematic which at this point mainly determines his comments on historical materialism.

According to Habermas, Marx's value theory formulates rules for the basic relation of exchange [fundamentale Austaushbeziehung] between the economic system and the life-world, which in turn enable the discussion of system integration.[22] The result is a theory that possesses two distinct, but related levels, including, in the terminology Habermas employs here, class language, concerning action-theoretical concepts such as concrete work, class interest, etc., and value language [Verwertungssprache], concerning such system-theoretical, basic concepts as abstract work, value, etc.[23]

Habermas' proposed linguistic reinterpretation of historical materialism further develops an interest already manifest in his earlier effort to reconstruct the theory. Now, this dualistic reading of the Marxian position is problematic since he has consistently objected that Marx fails to separate the dimensions in question, although it is permissible as a description of Parson's theory. At this point Habermas utilizes his dualistic reading of Marx's thought to identify three proposed weaknesses in the Marxian value theory. The first weakness is ascribed to Marx's relation to Hegel, which accounts for his failure properly to distinguish the concepts of system and life-world. This point is the latest formulation of Habermas' frequent objection, in terms borrowed here from other thinkers, that Marx fails to differentiate the levels of work and interaction.

He now develops this criticism in a manner that recalls his earlier discussion of Hegel's thought from the perspective of a distinction he finds lacking in Marx's position. According to Habermas, Marx follows the young Hegel in differentiating system and life-world as a sundered ethical totality [eine zerrissene sittliche Totalität]. He interprets this similarity as implying a basic commitment to totality, and hence to monism, that arguably impedes Marx from consciously drawing a distinction that Hegel employed. Habermas writes: "Marx in fact operates on the two analytical levels of 'system' and 'life-world'; but their separation is not really presupposed in the basic politico-economic concepts, which remain dependent on the Hegelian logic."[24]

Habermas regards Marx's monism as entailing far-reaching consequences for the latter's position, especially for his view of revolution. He detects a basic tension in Marx's insistence on the progressive pauperization of the proletariat through the growth of capital and a basically contrary analysis of practical-political action. Now reiterating in other words a point already made in *Knowledge and Human Interests*, he maintains that, although Marx cannot justify their separation, system and life-world appear in the Marxian position under the twin headings of the realms of necessity and of freedom. In a word, he believes that like Hegel Marx presupposed the interpretation of system and life-world against the background concept of totality which effectively precluded their satisfactory differentiation. In contrast, according to Habermas, in his discussion of social evolution Weber has shown that we must distinguish the level of the differentiation of system and the class-specific forms of its institutionalization.

The complex formulation of this criticism should not be allowed to hide its familiar nature. Habermas' main point is that an economic approach to the interpretation of social reality is inadequate to illuminate the situation of late capitalism. It is precisely this reason which will later impel him to advance his own theory of modernity. At this point, the new element in this objection is an implicit shift from the question of the proper reading of Marx's view to the related problem of the identification of its intrinsic limitations.

The difficulty is no longer that Marx has been interpreted too narrowly in an economic sense, since Habermas now accepts this interpretation as the correct approach;[25] the difficulty is rather that since Marx supposedly failed to free himself from Hegel's influence, he cannot fairly be understood in a different manner. The result is a basic change in Habermas' reading of the relation of historical materialism to the surrounding philosophical tradition.

Whereas in previous writings he consistently sought to find an acceptable way to grasp the difference between idealism and materialism, he now appears to abandon that attempt. He tacitly admits that beyond the obvious differences separating the two positions of Marx and Hegel there is an underlying continuity. In this way he adumbrates his later effort in the discussion of modernity to reject Marx because of a failure to break with Hegel. Here he suggests that Marx's alleged incapacity to differentiate the economic and cultural dimensions of society is linked to another weakness of the Marxian value theory, which he states as follows: "Marx lacks criteria in terms of which to distinguish the destruction of traditional forms of life from the objectification of post-traditional life-worlds."[26]

A note on terminology will be useful to understand this criticism. "Objectification" and "alienation" are alternative translations for "Verdinglichung."

The latter term is the etymologically exact synonym for Lukács's term, "Reifikation"; "Ding" is the precise German equivalent of the Latin word "res." Now, as Lukács later realized, his term conceals a distinction crucial to Marx's theory between alienation and objectification, and he attributed the conflation to Hegel.[27]

In contemporary terminology, in Marx's theory objectification is a necessary, but not a sufficient, condition of alienation. That this is so is the basis of Marx's occasional speculation on a nonalienating form of human activity, possible in a post-capitalist phase of society when the individual will supposedly be able to develop through the objectification of person-specific capacities. Habermas, who is certainly aware of these distinctions, does not respect them since he employs the term "Verdinglichung" to refer to Marx's general treatment of alienation. The result is an interesting tension in Habermas' view, which we can express through his relation to Lukács. In Habermas' discussion of historical materialism since the "Literaturbericht," he has consistently been critical of Lukács; but even here he continues to defend the perspective of the early Lukács, which the latter later abandoned, in not distinguishing alienation and objectification.[28]

Habermas observes that for Marx and the Marxist tradition, the concept of alienation refers above all to wage labor. He suggests that in the early writings, this concept is modeled on the expressivist notion of creative activity; but Marx supposedly later frees himself from this analogy through the value theory which relates work-power to commodity-form. As a result of the alleged change of the concept of concrete work into one of abstract work, he believes that the notion of alienation loses its specificity. According to Habermas, there is no historical index, or concrete historical reference, since Marx cannot distinguish between objectification and the structural differentiation of the life-world. For this reason, he believes that the Marxian theory of value cannot serve as the basis of a concept of alienation which identifies other than economic forms of rationalization. But this is merely another way of saying, as Habermas has already argued, that an economic perspective is insufficient to provide a full analysis of the late capitalist forms of life.

The first two criticisms are both formulated from the perspective of a dualistic reading of Marx's position, and each is directed against Marx's putative failure to respect the distinction between the different levels of system and life-world. These two criticisms are further symmetrical: the first concerns Marx's supposed incapacity to separate the levels Habermas desires to differentiate, and the second concerns the consequences of that alleged incapacity.

This critique carries further a well-known way of comprehending Marx's relation to the philosophic background. Since Lukács and Korsch developed a thoroughly Hegelian form of Marxism, it has been customary to locate the genesis of Marx's philosophic thought in his reaction against basic Hegelian ideas. Many students of Marx, including Habermas, have described Marx's rethinking of idealistic precepts as the source of historical materialism. In his earlier writings on historical materialism, Habermas consistently argued for the importance of Marx's criticism of Hegel's view. Now extending this view-point, he suggests that the limitations of historical materialism are due to Marx's inability completely to transcend Hegel, especially in his acceptance of the latter's monism.

In his objection to Marx's Hegelian monism, Habermas' intent is to argue for what, following current usage in analytic philosophy of science, he de-scribes as a paradigm change. His claim is that it is not an accident that the monistic model of social theory has proven unsatisfactory, since we require a dualistic model to provide an analysis of modern capitalism. An immediate consequence of this statement is to render explicit what has been implicit ever since Habermas began to criticize Marx. The various criticisms may seem to be, or even are, immanent to historical materialism; but they are formulated from the perspective of a different idea of the nature of social theory.

Since this point is important, but by no means obvious, it will be useful to develop it further. Like many writers on historical materialism, especially Marxists, at least initially Habermas did not reflect on the different conceptual models inherent in Marx and Marxism, or their relation to his own developing view. But he later began to do so, as witness his silent shift to the analysis of Marx's position, especially in writings beginning with *Knowledge and Human Interests*, his rapid discussion of different ideas of the evolution of the-ory from a metatheoretical perspective in his effort to reconstruct historical materialism, and his brief mention there of the relation of his own theory to Marx's. The result of this slow development is to clarify the difference be-tween the respective concepts of theory which finally becomes fully apparent in Habermas' rejection of Marxian monism in favor of his own dualistic per-spective. This perspective was implicit in his objection to the supposed lack of a reflective dimension in Marx's view, even if Habermas may not have been fully aware of the consequences of his criticism. It follows that, perhaps as early as the initial phase of his discussion of Marx and Marxism, and certainly in writings later than the analysis of Marxism as critique, Habermas has con-sistently presupposed a different concept of theory, at least in part incompati-ble with the concept intrinsic in Marx's position.

Habermas' suggestion of the need for a paradigm change is both a rejection of Marx's monistic model and a plea *pro domo* for Habermas' own dualistic form of social theory. The latter commitment has been consistently in evi-dence throughout his prior discussion of historical materialism in his constant adherence to the separation of the twin levels of work and interaction; this commitment remains equally important here under the heading of the distinc-tion of life-world and system.

Habermas' stress on dualism in social theory is the basis of his third criti-cism of historical materialism. We can infer that the first two objections are preliminary, since he describes the third one as decisive [entscheidend]. This criticism provides a more general statement of his rejection of monism in the context of the now familiar requirement to differentiate life-world and system. He writes: "The third and deciding weakness of value theory I see in the over generalization of a special case of the subsumption of the life-world under system imperatives."[29]

Habermas argues for this criticism in a series of rapid comments. He points out that the process of objectification is not necessarily confined to the sphere in which it arises. Recurring to a point already apparent in the title essay of the book on the reconstruction of historical materialism, he notes that a form of economy dependent on monetary imperatives is not self-contained; it requires supplementation through an administrative system that functions according to power. He concludes that so-called communicative life-relations can take up into themselves both money and power. It follows that from Habermas' angle of vision, Marx's concept of objectification is too narrow, since he restricts it to the financial dimension of social reality.

Habermas regards this objection as decisive; but it is not significantly different from the other criticisms he raises. What is different is the conclusion concerning the notion of subjectivity which he draws from this analysis. In previous writings on historical materialism, he has argued that Marx's concept of subjectivity presupposes a notion of goal-directed activity concerned with production. Communicative action, the topic of Habermas' theory, supposedly occurs on a separate level, unconstrained by goal-oriented concerns. In his conclusion, he acknowledges a tension between his own view of subjectivity and Marx's which, he believes, shares the action-theoretical vantage point of Weber and Parsons. In each case, the problem is that, as he writes, "the model of goal-directed activity [das Modell der Zwecktätigkeit] is regarded as fundamental for social action."[30]

This statement is significant as a clear acknowledgment that his dualistic critique of Marxian monism requires Habermas to defend a relevantly different view of human subjectivity and of human activity. He is consistent and insightful in calling attention to this important consequence. Surprisingly, at this point he seems to shrink back from this obvious conclusion in his summary statement, which also marks the outer limits of his discussion of historical materialism.

Habermas' summary eschews any mention of the radical consequences which derive from his critique of historical materialism. Instead, he restricts himself to a restatement of his familiar assertion that the Marxian value theory can only result in an economically foreshortened interpretation, unsatisfactory as an analysis of late capitalism. He maintains that Marx correctly pointed to the evolutionary primacy of trade; but the latter's superstructure/base model is too narrow to do justice to its topic. He further maintains that at present we require a more complex explanatory model which, he suggests, will enable us to see that objectification results from bureaucratic and monetary factors in both the public and the private spheres.

The most startling aspect of this discussion is his description of the concept of the relation of superstructure and base as trivial. This statement is unexpected in view of his earlier, patient effort to reconstruct this relation in acceptable form. But it is not unexpected in terms of the intrinsic logic of the

development of his reading of historical materialism, which he now regards
as an exhausted form of theory. From that particular vantage point, the characterization of the superstructure/base distinction as trivial has at least autobi-
ographical value in respect to the evolution of Habermas' discussion of Marx
and Marxism. It tacitly concedes that his own earlier effort to reconstruct the
so-called superstructure theorem was not only in vain, but misguided. It is
obviously pointless to devote serious consideration to the reformulation of a
merely trivial notion. In a lengthy passage, which must be quoted in full as
the final word on his lengthy effort directly to interpret and to criticize historical materialism, and which clearly records the basic change in his attitude toward Marx and Marxism, he writes:

> The three analyzed weaknesses of the value theory explain why the critique
> of political economy, despite its two stage social concept combining system and
> life-world cannot offer a satisfactory explanation of late capitalism. The Marx-
> ian approach [Ansatz] requires an economically foreshortened interpretation of
> the developed capitalist societies. For this Marx correctly asserted an evolution-
> ary primacy of trade: it is the problems of this subsystem which determine the
> developmental path of society in general. However, this primacy should not
> mislead in causing to coincide [zuschneiden] the complementary relation of
> economy and state apparatus through a trivial concept of superstructure and
> base. Against the monetarism of the value theory we must deal with two steer-
> ing mechanisms and four levels, through whose two mutually supplementing
> subsystems the life-world subordinates its imperatives. The effects of objectifi-
> cation can arise equally from bureaucratisation and from the monetarisation of
> public as well as private areas of life.[31]

This brief statement is more appropriate within the framework of the critique of historical materialism than as the close of an extended discussion of
the theory over more than three decades. We can find a more satisfactory statement in a recent work on the structure of modern philosophy. *The Philosophical Discourse of Modernity* (*Der philosophische Diskurs der Moderne*, 1985). This
book, which does not require a general description at present, has already been
mentioned in passing throughout the prior discussion. Suffice it to say that
in the course of a detailed reading of philosophy since Hegel, Habermas here
puts forward the theory of modernity he regards as a necessary alternative
to historical materialism.

His remarks on the post-Kantian philosophical tradition build upon his
prior account in *Knowledge and Human Interests*, above all his remarks on
Nietzsche. At this point he carries that analysis further by relating a large number
of later views to Nietzsche's. He here describes the latter's view, in distinction
to his earlier account, not as continuous with, but rather in opposition to,
Hegel's thought. We need now to complete this description of Habermas' discussion of historical materialism by briefly considering his most recent and
apparently final estimate of Marx's place within the wider context of his reading of post-Kantian philosophy.

It is apparent in this text that Habermas has now moved beyond the point at which historical materialism is a main concern. As a result of his critique of the theory in his treatise on communicative action, it loses its former luster, which is decisively tarnished; historical materialism is henceforth demoted to a supporting role, at most a secondary interest, eccentric to his primary pursuit, which is the further elaboration of his own theory. Nonetheless, although Habermas has now abandoned any hope he once cherished for the viability of the tradition emanating from Marx, he continues to reflect upon it.

The passage in which Habermas takes up this problem is brief, but doubly helpful: in respect to his final view of historical materialism, as a kind of closing of the books dealing with this topic, and as an indication of the extent to which his attitude toward the theory has changed in the course of the discussion. The passage, whose title is difficult to render into English, is called "Excursus on the Obsolescence [Veralten] of the Production Paradigm."[32]

In the writings on historical materialism prior to his work on communicative action, Habermas was deeply concerned with its grasp of reason. Examples include his defense of critical theory, itself a form of neo-Marxism, against Husserl in the inaugural lecture, and his repeated attention to the problem of reflection in various contexts. In the treatise on communicative action Habermas puts forward his own concept of communicative reflection, but restricts his critique of historical materialism to its intrinsic monism. Although monism is linked to a type of reason, in that text he does not dwell on this connection. More generally, in writings after the systematic and historical accounts of the relation of knowledge and interest he has bracketed further consideration of this issue within historical materialism.

At this point Habermas returns to this theme with an observation on the relation between theory and reason. He begins with the remark that any theory of modernity which derives from the philosophy of reflection [Reflexionsphilosophie] necessarily preserves an interior relation to the concept of reason [Vernunft] or rationality [Rationalität]; and he further remarks that this is not the case without qualification [ohne weiteres] for fundamental concepts of the philosophy of praxis [Praxisphilosophie] like action, self-creation, and work.[33]

This comment is double suggestive: for an understanding of Habermas' views at this point of reason in general and within historical materialism. Habermas is clearly not concerned to differentiate reason from rationality, which he seems to equate. By implication, any view of social rationality—for instance, Weber's—counts as a theory of reason. We can further note that the term "philosophy of praxis" is widely employed within Marxism to designate the so-called Marxist humanism associated with a group of Yugoslav thinkers, loosely clustered around the journal *Praxis*.

In the essay on the role of philosophy in Marxism, Habermas described Marxism as philosophy in virtue of its supposed concern with radical reflection; but he now seems to modify this interpretation. With respect to historical materialism, his statement can be construed in two ways, each of which leads to the same conclusion, that is: as the assertion that the philosophy of praxis, which derives from reflection, has perhaps lost its attachment to reason; or as the contrary assertion that the philosophy of praxis is perhaps unrelated to reason since it does not derive from reflection. In a word, whatever the proper interpretation of the relation of historical materialism to reflection, Habermas here raises the question of whether the theory has lost its link to reason and, accordingly, its claim to be rational.

Habermas now turns to the issue of the relation of Marxism to Marx. In connection with his view of communicative action, we have noted his elaboration of Merleau-Ponty's thesis on the origins of Western Marxism. He here takes up this theme again in the attempted differentiation of two main approaches within Western Marxism, which he associates respectively with the sociologist Max Weber on the one hand and the phenomenologists Husserl and Heidegger on the other.

Now, under the influence of Weber, he suggests that Lukács and the representatives of critical theory understood objectification as rationalization. In this way, they supposedly arrived at a materialistic appropriation of Hegel and a critical concept of rationality independent of the paradigm of production. In contrast, according to Habermas, Marcuse and the later Sartre tried to renew the paradigm of production by reading Marx's early writings from a Husserlian perspective which led to a normative concept of praxis without a concept of rationality.

This analysis casts light on Habermas' previous writings on historical materialism and on his present understanding of the theory's connection to communicative action. In his discussion of communicative action, he identified with critical theory; and in several texts, especially *Knowledge and Human Interests*, he criticized a phenomenological form of Marxism. The justification for his earlier defense of critical theory lies in a partial denial of the continuity between this form of Marxism and Marx. In its alleged independence of the paradigm of production critical theory supposedly remains open to the effort to provide a dualistic social theory. Conversely, we now see that the attack on the phenomenological strain of Marxism was motivated by its putative adoption of a concept of praxis unrelated to a normative view of rationality; this is a form of the criticism Habermas has often brought earlier against Marx.

Both points depend on the relation of forms of historical materialism to reason. What is at stake now is less the possibility of an adequate form of the theory—although that theme is still lurking in the background—than a social theory with an adequate concept of rationality. As Habermas reads so-called Western Marxism, obviously both strands he distinguishes are incomplete. The Weberian strand, although independent of the exhausted paradigm, by implication has no theory of praxis of its own; the phenomenological strand, which depends on the paradigm in question, has no theory of rationality. Clearly, it is the latter form of Marxism, and not Marxism in general, which Habermas had in mind in his remark that historical materialism is not without qualification related to a concept of reason.

Since for Habermas the virtues and defects of the Weberian and phenomeno-logical forms of Marxism are complementary, he needs to bring them together in a synthesis. He sees the realization of this possibility as requiring a paradigm change from productive activity to communicative action. He writes: "That is to say, the theory of communicative action establishes an internal relation between practice [Praxis] and rationality."[34]

His argument here in favor of a change to a new paradigm depends on the demonstration of the inadequacy of the old paradigm. Now, he believes that he has already shown the *aporia* of the Weberian form of Marxism; this was a main aim of his remarks on historical materialism in the treatise on commu-nicative action. Accordingly, he concentrates at present on a rapid critique of the effort, which he associates with the Hungarian Marxists Agnes Heller and György Markus, and the phenomenologists Peter Berger and Thomas Luckmann, to renew the paradigm of production from a phenomenological perspective.

In his critique, he identifies three problems as following from the old para-digm, namely, reductionism, naturalism, and empiricism. He then ends his discussion with two general points that concern his final intentions toward his-torical materialism. On the one hand, in reference to the traditional Marxist problem of human emancipation, he states that "the emancipatory perspective proceeds precisely not from the production paradigm, but from the paradigm of action oriented towards mutual understanding."[35] This is a clear suggestion that historical materialism cannot lead to human emancipation which, how-ever, follows from communicative action. In his mind his own theory is a source of the revolutionary potential historical materialism claimed but never possessed. In other words, communicative action goes beyond historical ma-terialism in achieving the latter's goals by other means.

On the other hand, he reaffirms his frequently voiced claim, which derives from the alleged Marxian commitment to the paradigm of production, that reason has no role to play in historical materialism. In a passage which is diffi-cult to translate, he insists, as concerns reason, on the practical superiority of communicative action over the paradigm of production: "As to how this idea of reason as something that is in fact built into communicative relations, and that can in practice be seized upon, could be grounded—about this a theory committed to the paradigm of production can say nothing."[36]

The result of this "Excursus" is to reveal the paradoxical nature of what ap-pears to be Habermas' final attitude toward historical materialism. After hav-ing interpreted, criticized, and reconstructed the theory, he has now identified what he regards as uncurable defects intrinsic to it. Although he is convinced that historical materialism has irreparably failed as a theory, he has no inten-tion of renouncing it. Since he rejects the very idea that the theory can be re-constructed in viable form, one might expect him to decline to endorse any-thing more than its intrinsic goals. Until recently, however, Habermas was still concerned to register his identification, or perhaps even his solidarity, with historical materialism. For instance, in an interview in 1979 he stated without qualification that it is not possible to save the Marxian theory of value,[37] but he is proud to consider himself a Marxist.[38]

Now there is no question that, whatever 'orthodoxy' means, Habermas has never made this or an analogous claim for his relation to historical materialism. What appears paradoxical is how Habermas can claim to be a Marxist at all, while declining to accept the overall theory of historical materialism as he comprehends it. We can focus this issue by calling attention to an analogy between Habermas' most recent, arguably final view of historical materialism and Lukács's understanding of so-called bourgeois philosophy. Habermas has often indicated, as noted, that his initial approach to Marx was mediated through Lukács's brilliant early work, *History and Class Consciousness*.

This is not the place to provide a general discussion of that fascinating book, whose influence on later Marxism has not yet even started to diminish. It will be sufficient to recall Lukács's conviction that the problems of bourgeois philosophy were real; they could not be resolved within it; they could be resolved on the level of Marxism.[39] Now he also held, in a discussion of Marxist orthodoxy, that it is possible to dismiss all of Marx's views and still remain an orthodox Marxist.[40]

There is a clear, but limited, analogy between Lukács's early view of the relation of bourgeois philosophy to Marxism and Habermas' seemingly final view of the relation of historical materialism to communicative ethics. Like Lukács's reading of bourgeois philosophy, Habermas holds that historical materialism concerns real problems, which it is incapable of resolving, but which can be resolved on the plane of communicative action. Like Lukács, he further believes that it is possible to deny elements of the theory, in fact the general validity of Marx's version of it, and yet remain a Marxist.

The difference is that Lukács maintains that it is possible to deny specific Marxist concepts since Marxism is a method. Habermas, on the contrary, seems to be making a more controversial claim. His view seems to be that it is necessary to deny the validity of historical materialism, which is inherently unable to realize its goals; but it is possible to reach the intrinsic aims of the theory in a different way, namely by accepting another paradigm exemplied in his own theory. If one is committed to the intentions of historical materialism, then, Habermas tacitly suggests, one can be a Marxist who denies the validity of the theory. In a word, at this moment, when he has left historical materialism behind, when he has interpreted, failed to reconstruct, and decisively criticized Marx's theory, Habermas has never been more committed to its intrinsic goals.

VII

THE CONCEPT OF IDEOLOGY
AND THE CRISIS THEORY

The discussion so far has been limited to the presentation of Habermas' reading of historical materialism in four phases, including interpretation, critique, reconstruction, and rejection. In order to aid the comprehension of his reading, it seemed useful to focus on description prior to the evaluation of his approach to Marx and Marxism. With the exception of brief remarks on obvious difficulties in Habermas' proposed reconstruction of historical materialism—necessary to understand why he quickly abandons the attempted reconstruction and subsequently rejects a theory to which he has previously been committed—criticism has so far mainly been restricted to comments on his grasp of thinkers outside the orbit of historical materialism.

After this description of Habermas' approach to historical materialism, we need now to evaluate it as an interpretation of Marx and Marxism. Now, this task is doubly complicated. There is little in the burgeoning literature on Habermas which speaks directly to this issue; but the literature concerning Marx and Marxism is overly abundant and offers a wide, often confusing variety of approaches. In the discussion of historical materialism, there is probably no single fixed point in the flux of interpretation. In that sense, it resembles the question of how to understand the history of philosophy. It is significant that after some two-and-a-half thousand years, there is still no agreement on how this is to be done or even on the related question of the extent to which the prior philosophical tradition remains relevant to present concerns.

Now, there are different ways to evaluate Habermas' reading of historical materialism, for instance by comparison with other readings against the broader background of available discussion. The difficulty of this kind of evaluation is that it presupposes a detailed account of the entire Marxist tradition which, even if it were possible at this late date, would overstep the limits of the present study.[1] We can further note that a comparative evaluation enabling us to situate Habermas' approach to Marx and Marxism within the secondary literature would not necessarily cast light on its truth.

Although there are indeed other possibilities, it is always preferable to evaluate a discussion or a theory in terms of its intrinsic intention. Habermas, who employs this standard for his attempted reconstruction of historical materialism, further indicates his intent with respect to the theory at several places. For instance, in his metatheoretical remarks on theory reconstruction, as noted, he remarks that his concern with Marx and Marxism is neither dogmatic nor directed at historical-philological issues. And in a recent interview, he states that his fundamental project has always been to renew the theory of society grounded in the theoretical and sociological problems which arise out of the movement of thought from Kant to Marx.[2]

Habermas' self-described intention in respect to Marx and Marxism corresponds to the aim of this essay. At present, we are not concerned merely to describe another interpretation of historical materialism as a view in the history of social philosophy that is still of interest; we are concerned rather to determine the truth, wherever it may lie. Accordingly, it is appropriate to evaluate Habermas' reading of historical materialism in terms of a goal he explicitly embraces, that is, as part of the continuing effort to achieve viable social theory.

Although Habermas indicates that he is not concerned with historical-philological issues, they are relevant to his goal; these issues arise in the course of his attempt to pursue viable social theory through the discussion of historical materialism. Since he approaches this aim through a critical reading of historical materialism, we can evaluate his concern with viable social theory through his discussion of Marx and Marxism.

It is obviously neither necessary nor even possible to give equally detailed consideration to each of the many aspects of historical materialism Habermas takes up in the course of his inquiry. Accordingly, it will be useful to find a way to focus our study. Now, we have already noted that a central issue in the discussion of Marx and Marxism is the identification of the nature of historical materialism. Since the theory appears differently from dissimilar angles of vision, it seems appropriate to begin by reflecting on Habermas' basic insight into its nature.

In general terms, with the possible exception of his initial interpretation in the "Literaturbericht," Habermas has always regarded historical materialism from the perspective of the so-called superstructure theorem, that is, as an economic interpretation of social phenomena. This insight into the nature of historical materialism is present almost from the beginning of his discussion of the theory; but it is obscured in his attention to special problems of interpretation, such as the relation of the theory to philosophy of science. Although the discussion of historical materialism in relation to contemporary philosophy of science provides an interesting perspective from which to assess its strengths and weaknesses, it does not contribute to the rather different problem of the identification of the nature of the theory. In fact, it is fair to say that to the extent that Habermas attempts to define the theory's essence through a comparative evaluation of its capacities, he is guilty of a methodological error.

The main lines of his interpretation of historical materialism from the angle of vision of the so-called superstructure theorem are in place as early as his account of the theory as critique. At this point he stresses the economic interpretation of historical materialism in comments on the theory of economic crises and the labor theory of value; and he relies on a generally economic interpretation of social phenomena as the background for his critique of the epistemological dimension of the theory. Later writings only further develop the consequences of his acceptance of an economic understanding of historical materialism. It is only afterward that Habermas uses the term "superstructure theorem" and comments in detail on the Marxian value theory; but, as noted, the later economic refutation was already called for by the tacit identification of historical materialism as an economic explanation of social phenomena.

An evaluation of Habermas' reading of historical materialism on its own terms must focus on his search for a viable social theory through an analysis of the superstructure theorem. In this respect, we need to differentiate his decision to adopt a rival view, namely his own, from his critique of historical materialism; the former is justified only in terms of the latter. Hence, we can evaluate the success of his effort to pursue the goal of a viable social theory in terms the discussion of historical materialism both through his criticism of that theory and through his effort to surpass it within his own view.

Habermas' critique of historical materialism is an attack on Marxian political economy, and, more generally, on the economic explanation of social phenomena. In order to evaluate his success in this endeavor, we need to review his interpretation of Marxian political economy. We will review his reading of this aspect of the theory on several levels, beginning with a brief sketch of the role of political economy in his discussion of Marx and Marxism.

The chronological record of Habermas' interest in Marxian political economy, particularly the labor theory of value, is not a simple linear progression. Like the discussion of historical materialism in general, whose complicated form reflects occasional situations and the evolution of his understanding of Marx, his comprehension of the nature and importance of Marxian political economy evolves greatly in the course of his writings. In general terms, we can say that Habermas' concern with Marxian political economy is almost absent, or at best present as a merely secondary theme, at the inception of his reading of Marx and Marxism. It only later emerges into full view, then recedes into the background, where it remains present as a constant, but muted concern, before its reemergence as a principal topic in the concluding phase of the discussion. Here it assumes form, already implicit in his initial attention to it, as the central part of a position, whose fate as an actually, or even potentially, viable theoretical entity supposedly must be decided through an inquiry into the Marxian analysis of political economy.

The interest in Marxian political economy is almost absent in the early "Literaturbericht." At this point, it is present most prominently, but still in marginal fashion, in the brief remarks on materialistic dialectic. Here Habermas considers Adorno's attack on philosophical foundationalism [Ursprungsphilosophie] in relation to the traditional Marxist problem of the unity of theory and practice. After commenting that the resolution of this problem entails the rejection of the idea of philosophical foundationalism, he mentions, but does not further discuss, several aspects of Marxian political economy, such as the contradiction between the forces and the relations of production, and the realm of freedom beyond the realm of necessity. In part because of his emphasis on Marx's early writings and their concern with philosophical anthropology, in this context he does not make political economy a main theme of his discussion.

In a sense, Habermas' relative deemphasis of political economy in the consideration of Marx's early writings is consistent with their content. Although these problems were already important to Marx's thought in the *Paris Manuscripts*, especially in the first and second parts, they become even more visible in subsequent writings; here the overtly philosophical discussion present in the *Critique of Hegel's Philosophy of Right* and the third and fourth parts of the *Paris Manuscripts* recedes before the emergence of economic themes.

The theme of political economy is not entirely absent in Habermas' treatment of the early writings; but it is not a main concern. It only becomes one, and accordingly only emerges into full view, as a consequence of a shift in Habermas' attention, in the account of Marx's position as critique, to later writings from the *German Ideology* onward, with special attention to the *Grundrisse* and *Capital*. In discussion after this point, Habermas' focus remains fixed on Marx's later, supposedly more mature writings and never loses sight of the economic problems with which Marx was increasingly preoccupied.

Habermas' concern with Marxian political economy appears in varying degrees in the writings after the "Literaturbericht." In his discussion of Marx's position as critique, it is present in the background, especially in his remarks on the doctrine of ideology and the crisis theory. It is present, although not a prominent element, in *Knowledge and Human Interests*. His interest in economic themes is most evident in the account of the materialist concept of synthesis through social labor. Here he repeats a number of points from the preceding critique of the crisis theory, such as the identification of social knowledge as a source of value,[3] a point he again reinforces through attention to the supposed differences he perceives between the *Grundrisse* and *Capital*. He further criticizes what he regards as Marx's failure to differentiate work and interaction. And he relates the phenomenon of the fetishism of commodities to the problem of the experience of reflection.

At this point in his reading of historical materialism, political economy is still a peripheral concern. His main aim is not to demonstrate that Marxian political economy is mistaken; it is rather to point out that Marx did not sufficiently develop his flawed suggestions about a future science of man, which, in positivistic fashion, equated critique with natural science.[4] This discussion combines themes from earlier writings, including an interest in philosophical anthropology and critique, but does not yet directly address problems of political economy.

The theme of political economy still remains peripheral to the discussion in the volume of essays concerning the reconstruction of historical materialism. Habermas' attention to political economy, which is severely restricted here, mainly touches on the superstructure theorem, with some mention of the development of modes of production. In the introduction to the volume, he asserts that Marx focuses mainly on forces of production to the neglect of this theorem, which remains foreshortened. He develops this point in the long title essay, which contains a brief analysis of the theorem in question and some discussion of the difficulties that arise in the attempt to correlate social evolution with changes in the modes of production.

It is not Habermas' intent to provide a full, or even reasonably complete, treatment of Marxian political economy at this point. In this specific context, his reading of historical materialism leaves him open to the charge that he is guilty of a *proteron histeron*. His announced aim to reconstruct the Marxian theory presupposes that it is ineffective in attaining Marx's goals for it. But Habermas fails here to provide the direct criticism of Marxian political economy obviously required if, as he maintains, it is a central element of the position. If, as Habermas believes, political economy is the nucleus of Marx's theory, then any attempt to reconstruct the position in general must be preceded by a demonstration of the weakness of Marxian political economy.

The failure to provide a critique of Marxian political economy is only made good, insofar as it ever is, in Habermas' lengthy study of communicative action. It is finally only here, at the moment that he consigns Marx's theory, but not its goal, to the historical oblivion of positions which can no longer speak to us, that he again takes up in more completely, although still insufficiently, developed form, the critique of selected aspects of Marxian political economy.

His critique of the economic dimension of historical materialism is in effect a clear rejection of what most Marxists have always regarded as a central dimension of the theory. Lukács, for instance, regards the Marxian analysis of commodity-structure as potentially central to the solution of all problems.[5] In his writings on historical materialism, Habermas criticizes the economic approach to the explanation of social phenomena on several levels, including the concept of ideology, the theory of economic crises, and the labor theory of value. In order to evaluate his critique of the economic approach to social explanation, we will consider his objections to these three aspects of Marxian political economy.

In Marx's position there is a clear link between ideology and the economic approach to social phenomena. The notion of ideology functions to explain the source of a false consciousness of social reality, especially the economic base, through the relation of consciousness to the form of distribution of the means of production. This concept, which is not explicit in Marx's early writings, does not assume explicit form before the *German Ideology*. Despite extensive discussion in the secondary literature on Marx and Marxism, the idea of ideology remains unclear.[6] But its intrinsic unclarity has not prevented generations of Marxists from employing it as a weapon to reject non-Marxist thought, which they routinely and uninsightfully describe as mere ideology.

Habermas' opposition to the economic interpretation of social phenomena directly conflicts with the conception of ideology. Interestingly, he does not devote much attention to this topic. In his writings on historical materialism, he comments on the problem of ideology in two places: in a passage in the early "Literaturbericht," where he considers the relation of the doctrines of ideology and revolution, and in the discussion of Marxism as critique, where he attends to the question of the critical appropriation of traditional ideas.

The early discussion of ideology in the "Literaturbericht" is mainly an exposition of the concept in the context of an account of the philosophical discussion of Marx. Following remarks on the critique of philosophical foundationalism [Ursprungsphilosophie], Habermas comments that a philosophical discussion of the Marxian conception of ideology would lead to a consideration of the presuppositions of the philosophy. He then offers a general description of the concept of ideology, which ends in the assertion that the notions of ideology and revolution comprise a single conceptual whole.

Habermas insists in various ways on his critical perspective throughout his discussion of historical materialism; but his account here of the concept of ideology is basically expository and derivative. He focuses on ideology from two perspectives: as a critique of the concept of orthodox philosophy, following Korsch's rejection of the so-called bourgeois concern with presuppositionless philosophical theory,[7] and with respect to the concept of revolution, following Lukács's interest in the revolutionary power of self-consciousness.[8]

For Habermas' criticism of ideology, we need to turn to his later remarks on this concept in the context of his discussion of Marxism as critique. The criticism here reflects Habermas' claim, which will later form the basis of his objection to the Marxian value theory, that Marxian monism does not permit an adequate grasp of reason; it is directed to the supposed dependence, in historical materialism, of political actions on economic interests. Habermas here anticipates a point he will later expand in the course of his discussion of communicative action, namely, that the economic sphere of society is insufficient to provide an explanatory model.

At this point he uses the pretended relation of politics to economics as a test case for the economic approach to the interpretation of social phenomena. His argument turns on the presence of an intrinsic tension in the Marxian position between an alleged dependency of political action on economic interests and the converse claim that the political efficacy of political groups demands at least the partial independence of the owners of the means of production.

His discussion at this point, as noted, is complex. In this complicated analysis, we can detect two main arguments against the concept of ideology: the claim that Marx must be able to derive politics from economics, although the later development of capitalism has broken this link,[9] and the further claim that Marx's theory harbors a scientistic self-misunderstanding which in practice leads to the reliance on a realistic theory of epistemology.[10]

The first argument relates more closely to some of the more extreme forms of Marxism than to Marx's theory, even as Habermas reads it. As noted, in his discussion of the superstructure theorem, he rejects the so-called economistic reading as a general interpretation on the grounds that it is inconsistent with Marx's intention. He maintains that it is valid only for the critical phase in which a society passes to a new developmental level.[11]

Now if we accept Habermas' reading of the superstructure theorem, we immediately perceive that his criticism applies only to its so-called economistic version, which he precisely rejects as its correct interpretation. For it is only if the base in all cases causally determines the superstructure than we can even talk of the general need to derive politics from economics. In Habermas' interpretation, it is perfectly possible to accept his observation that the development of capitalism has broken the link of politics to economics. In other words, there is no contradiction between Habermas' interpretation and the acknowledged fact that weaker parties utilize the political process as a means of defense, or the further fact that the state intervenes in the economic process, or even the conclusion that we are no longer in the grip of blind economic law. In sum, even if Habermas' criticism is valid against a so-called economistic version of the superstructure theorem, it does not count against his own interpretation of this theorem.

In order to respond to the second criticism—or the claim that in practice historical materialism is guilty of a scientistic self-misunderstanding leading to a reliance on a realistic theory of epistemology—we will need to introduce distinctions between issues of scientism and realist epistemology, and between philosophy as science and as related to science. From this angle of vision, we will see that Habermas' latter criticism is at most valid against some forms of Marxism, but not against Marx's position.

Habermas' observation that both Marx and the Marxists often refer to their views, including the concept of ideology, as science is not necessarily significant. Since the term "science" is not univocal, the question arises as to how it is to be understood. At this point Habermas does not attempt to elucidate this complex term; he merely refers to a passage in *Knowledge and Human Interests* where he comments on Marx's allusions to his position as a science of man and its proposed comparison to physics.

These allusions do not demonstrate the objection Habermas makes here. In contemporary terminology, Marx's references to his thought as a science of man are consistent with its reading as philosophical anthropology, an interpretation Habermas now rejects; but they do not support the further charge of scientism. Marx's comparison of his position to physics merely echoes Kant's similar comparison.[12] When Marx compares his thought to science, he usually has in mind a notion of rigorous philosophy, as understood by philosophers since Plato, especially in nineteenth century Germany, in their fascination with the idea that philosophy could literally become science.

In the idealist tradition and afterward, a whole series of thinkers, including Fichte and Hegel, referred to their views as science.[13] This same concern was later continued by Husserlian phenomenology[14] and the positivists of the Vienna circle.[15] In contrast, when Marxists since Engels make a similar reference, they usually have in mind an opposition between philosophy and science. Althusser's recent attempt to distinguish sharply between chronologically and conceptually distinct phases in Marx's position, in his reading an early philosophical and a later scientific period, is only the latest example in a long series of Marxist interpretations which continue to understand science and philosophy as exclusive alternatives.[16]

Habermas is correct to point out that Marxism since Engels has always relied on a realistic theory of knowledge; but he is mistaken in his extension of this description to Marx's position. Curiously, Habermas uses the verb "abbilden" (from "Bild" or picture, literally meaning "to picture, to copy") to refer to Marxist epistemology. The more usual term is "wiederspiegeln," (from "Spiegel," or mirror, as in "spiegeln," literally meaning "to mirror, to reflect"), since the theory is commonly referred to as a "Wiederspiegelungs-theorie," or theory of reflection.

Now, as Habermas must be aware, the reliance on a realistic approach to knowledge is not confined to Marxism. A similar view is frequent outside Marxism, for instance in Wittgenstein's early thought.[17] Hence, it would be interesting to know if Habermas maintains that an automatic link exists between realistic epistemology and scientism, or whether this is only the case for historical materialism.

Since Marx holds a radically different view of epistemology, we must resist the attempt to link it to the Marxist approach. For purposes of his argument, Habermas claims that Marx invokes a causal, or realistic, theory of knowledge in the preface to the *Critique of Political Economy*. Now, there are three reasons to reject this claim. First, since Habermas makes no effort to support his reading through textual interpretation, but merely asserts his view, there is no reason we should accept it as valid. Second, as noted, Habermas himself rejects his proposed reading in a later essay, which casts doubt on his acceptance of it here without further discussion.

The third, most important reason, follows from Marx's texts. As for other philosophers, Marx's own writings have always been, are still, and must remain the only reliable source of his position. As he does not often reflect on his view of knowledge, its interpretation requires a difficult, retrospective reconstruction from a variety of hints. Now, these hints are of unequal value and occasionally even misleading, as witness the famous remark, in the second afterword to *Capital*, that his view is the inversion of Hegel's.

As concerns epistemology, the single most helpful passage occurs in the introduction to the *Grundrisse*. Here, in a text Habermas does not mention, Marx insists with unusual clarity on a dialectical analysis of the relation between thought and being, closely similar to Hegel's view.[18] This passage not only contradicts a realistic interpretation of Marx's theory of knowledge; it further contradicts Habermas' explicit conclusion that, in virtue of Marx's realistic epistemology, Marxian political economy lacks an awareness of the conditions of theory. Clearly Marx is aware of the conditions of theory, which he analyzes in this passage, but in a manner that reveals his hostility to the kind of quasi-Kantian angle of vision which continues to determine Habermas' approach to epistemological questions.

This rapid review of Habermas' critique reveals that it does not successfully refute the concept of ideology. In fact, of the two criticisms only one, namely Marx's alleged reduction of politics to economics, even concerns the idea of ideology either in Marx's corpus or in Habermas' earlier exposition of it. Now, it is not an accident that this criticism fails, since it rests on a conflation of ideology and the so-called superstructure theorem. Since these views, although linked, are distinct, their separation must be maintained.

The link between these views is that both concern the relation of forms of consciousness to the economic level of society. Habermas correctly notes that the superstructure theorem asserts the subordination of various subsystems in the superstructure, such as art, religion, law, and philosophy, to the economic substructure of society. The doctrine of ideology says that when the society in which we live impedes the social development of human beings for essentially economic reasons related to the maximization of profit, our understanding of the society is distorted, above all with respect to its economic base. Accordingly, both views are connected to Marx's overall interest in the economic explanation of social phenomena.

Although the concepts of ideology and superstructure overlap, the two theories are different and in fact independent of each other. The difference between the two theories is clear: ideology concerns the distortion of consciousness, whereas the superstructure theorem describes an inherent limitation on consciousness which is not, for that reason, false. There is an equally clear independence of the two views: the sphere of culture could be largely emancipated from the economic process, as Habermas pretends, although we misunderstand the nature of our society, especially its distribution of the means of production; and conversely, culture could be largely determined by economic motives, as, for instance, in an economistic interpretation of the theorem, and we could be aware of the fact.

Habermas' criticism of the doctrine of ideology fails because it is insufficiently sensitive to the doctrine's separation from the superstructure theorem. Even if the attempted empirical refutation of the alleged reduction of politics to economics were correct, it would not count against the concept in question. In order to make out his argument, Habermas would further need to demonstrate that the political dimension is undistorted by its relation to the economic substructure. In effect, this criticism, which rests on a conflation of ideology and the superstructure theorem, must fail since it substitutes for an attack on the former a complaint about the latter.

After this discussion of Habermas' critique of the doctrine of ideology, we turn now to the second phase of his critique of Marx's economic explanation of social phenomena in his analysis of the Marxian theory of economic crises. Like ideology, the theory of crises is located within the superstructure as a facet of mental life. It differs from ideology as truth from falsity. Whereas ideology occults the true nature of the social context, especially the economic basis of society, the crisis theory offers an account of the intrinsic instability which Marx believes is characteristic of capitalism. More precisely, it represents an effort to apply the theory of the economic substructure of society to the analysis of problems specific to the private ownership of the means of production.

Since the formulation of Marx's theory, his understanding of economic crises has received much attention. It was quickly recognized that the ability of his theory to explain the crises which occur within capitalism is an index of the wider success of the position as an explanatory model. This part of the theory has been often studied within the massive secondary literature.[19] In the present context, the crisis theory is double important: as a specific test of Marx's attempt to lay bare the anatomy of capitalism, and as a general indication of the utility of the economic explanation of social phenomena.

Habermas considers the problem of economic crises in two places in his corpus: in his work *Legitimation Crisis*, which is only incidentally related to Marx's thought,[20] and in the essay on Marxism as critique. The former discussion offers an interesting effort to develop a viable theory of crisis on the supposed ruins of previous thought. It falls, however, outside the scope of this essay, which is limited to Habermas' reading of historical materialism. Habermas' effort to develop an alternative view of economic crisis further presupposes the failure of the Marxian crisis theory, whereas that alleged failure remains to be shown.

We can restrict ourselves here to the evaluation of Habermas' critical, but rapid, discussion of Marx's crisis theory in his discussion of Marxism as critique. At this point, Habermas studies two forms of crisis: the relation between critique and crisis, and the approach to the economic substructure of society as a crisis complex. Since this is the only detailed passage on this aspect of Marx's position in Habermas' published writings on historical materialism to date, it is significant that he is only indirectly concerned in this text with the crisis theory; he is directly concerned rather with the viability of Marxian political economy, which he approaches through critical comments on one of its important themes.

In Marx's corpus, there are numerous appeals to the crisis theory to explain various functional problems of capitalist society; but there is no direct exposition or general discussion of the theory itself. Marx's approach to the crisis theory determines Habermas' discussion of it. Since Marx fails to provide a general account of the crisis theory, it must be identified in at least recognizable form before it can be criticized. In general terms, Habermas' critique unfolds in two phases: an initial, but controversial, description of the crisis theory; and a later effort, in which he analyzes a series of related phenomena, to link the defects in the theory with the Marxian theory of value.

In this discussion of the Marxian crisis theory, Habermas presupposes that historical materialism is critique. He further follows Koselleck in drawing attention to a link between critique and crisis, in an account of the so-called mythological origins and scientific status of an empirical philosophy of history with practical intent, similar to his related effort to link ideology to mythology. According to Habermas, critique is the practical intent to resolve a crisis. By implication, as critique historical materialism is intended to overcome the crises it discerns.

This assignment of a curative, or practically therapeutic value, to historical materialism is exceedingly general. Habermas now relates it to political economy by ascribing a particular intention to Marx. He maintains that unlike religion, or philosophy influenced by it, Marx understood the crisis complex materialistically, that is, in terms of the dialectic of social labor, in the form of a critique of political economy. This line of reasoning allows him to conclude that "the critique of Political Economy is a theory of crisis in the genuine sense [im genuinen Verstande]."[21]

Habermas' description is a crucial element in his critique of Marx's crisis theory; but it is doubly problematic as a general interpretation of historical materialism and as a specific account of the crisis theory. In the context of his discussion of Marxism as critique, we can understand him to be saying that Marx's empirically falsifiable philosophy of history is in fact a critique of political economy, or a genuine theory of crisis. This clarification is, however, puzzling for reasons related to the differences in the ways that philosophy and science are falsifiable.

Even if a theory of political economy can be empirically falsified or falsifiable, it is unclear how this could be the case for philosophy. In fact, that philosophy is empirically unfalsifiable, whereas science is empirically falsifiable, has been advanced as a way to distinguish between them. Presumably philosophical status precludes empirical falsifiability; and, conversely, a theory which is empirically falsifiable is not philosophy, but something else, such as social or natural science.[22] That does not mean, of course, that philosophy is immune to falsification, which routinely occurs through criticism, discovery of counterexamples for generalizations, detection of logical flaws in arguments, etc. It only means that the falsification of philosophical theories is not to be carried on in an empirical fashion. Hence, merely to suggest that Marx's position is both philosophy and social science in the form of political economy does not resolve the problem of how it can be simultaneously philosophy and empirically falsifiable.

In insisting on the supposed falsifiability of historical materialism, Habermas is continuing a concern with empirical falsification of philosophical theory deeply imbedded in the history of Marxism, beginning with Engels's misguided effort, as noted, to refute Kant through practice. This attempt is not only in error; it further tends to obscure a significant, but clearly empirically unfalsifiable component of the Marxian position, namely its philosophical anthropology, or concept of human being. This concept, which arguably underlies the wider Marxian theory, cannot be falsified by any empirical observation since it is the basis of the Marxian interpretation of social reality. More precisely, since the Marxian concept of human being precedes and makes possible the understanding of the empirical data, with respect to which it is relatively and unavoidably a priori, no a posteriori observation can cast doubt on it. Although this idea can indeed be criticized and even rejected on such grounds as its general utility with respect to other forms of theory, that is not the same as an empirical refutation.

This remark concerning Habermas' view of the nature of historical material-ism should not be confused with his controversial description of Marxian po-litical economy as a genuine theory of crisis. This identification, which is use-ful in the context of an emerging attempt to refute historical materialism through a critique of its economic dimension, should be resisted for several reasons. Clearly the suggested equation of the crisis theory and political econ-omy tends to restrict consideration of Marx's view of political economy to the latter only. Obviously, Marx's analysis of this domain is an important part of the wider theory in general; but the theory of political economy is wider than the crisis theory, as Habermas realizes in his subsequent critique of the Marxian theory of value; and the entire theory of historical materialism in-cludes the critique of political economy as one of its parts.

Now, perhaps when Habermas wrote this passage, he believed, as others have argued, that Marx's later economic thought decisively breaks with his earlier view.[23] But this line of argument will not suffice, since Marxian political economy is not self-contained, as it would need to be. Rather, it is precisely dependent on Marxian philosophical anthropology. One way to make this point is to demonstrate that the labor theory of value presupposes the concepts of alienation and objectification, in a word the entire theory of alienation, which is not strictly economic at all, but philosophical.

Indeed, the identification of the Marxian critique of political economy with either a crisis theory or a so-called genuine crisis theory is controversial. It is significant that Marx does not make a similar claim. Rather, he stresses the need to study the anatomy of bourgeois society from the angle of political economy[24] and insists on the necessity to examine the modes and the condi-tions of production and exchange within capitalism.[25] Hence, it is unclear what justification, other than simple assertion, Habermas can provide for his pro-posed equation between the analysis of capitalism in general and the crisis theory.

Perhaps what he means is that Marx regards the stage of capitalism as a tran-sitory phenomenon, with special attention to the occurrence of the economic crises which supposedly shape and ultimately transform it. It is certainly im-portant to bring out Marx's belief in the inherent instability of capitalism as a phase of social evolution. But Habermas goes too far in equating the theory of crises with the overall analysis of capitalism, or even with its central insight. The basic element in the Marxian analysis of capitalism is not the economic crises that tend to occur; it is the private ownership of the means of production which defines capitalism as an economic stage, and which gives rise to eco-nomic crises.

If Habermas believes that the theory of political economy is a theory of crisis, it is unclear why he would further insist that the latter is a genuine example, in contemporary terminology a genuine token of the type. In order for the implicit distinction to have an objective correlative, we need to be able to point to a false example of the theory of crisis. Now, since we know that Habermas holds that Marx's crisis theory is false, it is difficult to understand why he also believes it to be genuine. What, then, is an example of that kind of theory which is not genuine, if genuineness and falsity are to be distinguished? In any case, from his angle of vision it would be more accurate to describe Marx's view as a genuine example of a false theory.

We have so far been concerned only with Habermas' identification of the nature of the crisis theory through a suggested equation of a genuine crisis theory with political economy. Through an attempted differentiation of forms of economic crisis, Habermas further attempts to link his understanding of that theory with the concept of ideology and with problems in Marxian political economy. Concerning the crises of capitalism, he differentiates two related theses: the thesis that the crises depend on the utilization of capital, and, hence, on the appropriation of surplus value; and the related thesis that, as he writes: "the basis of the world as a crisis complex is exclusively the economy, that is inextricably involved in these economic crises and is resolvable together with them."[26]

The effect of this stage of discussion is to reinforce the significance in Habermas' eyes of his incipient critique of Marxian political economy, here pursued in relation to the Marxian crisis theory. According to Habermas, the former thesis, which is developed in historical materialism as the doctrine of ideology, depends on the latter, which arises within political economy as the crisis theory.[27] This is another way of saying that this aspect of historical materialism must stand on the underlying economic analysis. Habermas only reinforces his insistence on the importance of political economy in the second thesis. Unfortunately, he states this thesis in cumbersome fashion. But its meaning can be paraphrased as the claim that since the nature of the crises of capitalism is economic, they must be resolved in economic terms.

Habermas' insistence on the relation of the crisis theory to Marxian political economy opens the way to an analytical discussion of difficulties in the theory. We have already noted his desire to equate the theory of political economy with a genuine theory of crisis. Since he does not differentiate the crisis theory from the view of political economy, in fact conflates them, he utilizes his discussion of the former to point to difficulties in the latter. At this point, his attention is officially directed to the crisis theory; in fact his critique of it is a means to a further end. For he here begins to formulate the critique of the labor theory of value which, in the discussion of communicative action, will lead him to reject historical materialism in general.

We can say, then, that for both Marx and Habermas, the crisis theory is a means to another end: for Marx, it provides a test of the adequacy of his overall understanding of the anatomy of capitalism from the perspective of political economy; for Habermas it offers an occasion to question that understanding and, by implication, to question the economic approach to the explanation of social phenomena in general.

Habermas' analytical discussion of the crisis theory is divided into three parts. These include an examination of the law of the falling rate of profit in connection with the labor theory of value and the increase in mechanization, a reconstruction of the labor theory of value, and a brief discussion of the real possibility of democratic socialism. Since we are at present concerned with his critique of the crisis theory, at this point it will not be necessary to pursue his proposed alternative to the labor theory of value or his view of democratic socialism.

As noted, Habermas' critique here of the crisis theory is made through remarks on the law of the falling rate of profit. We can understand the logic of his critique by a remark on the relation of the law of the falling rate of profit to the crisis theory.[28] In that connection, we can distinguish different forms of crisis, including the partial crises and business cycles which are a recurring feature of capitalism, and the general crisis which hypothetically leads to a collapse of the economic system. We can further distinguish possible and necessary crises. Under the former heading we can include those crises that derive from underconsumption or stagnation, as distinguished from the necessary crisis, which follows from a falling rate of profit.

Now Marx was above all concerned to identify reasons for the intrinsic instability of capitalism on economic grounds, such as the falling rate of profit which, he believed, necessarily leads to a general economic crisis. Habermas' strategy is to argue for the real possibility of democratic socialism while denying the necessity of the general economic collapse of capitalism. In that sense, his critique, which depends on a two-fold analysis of the law of the falling rate of profit, is distantly related to Bernstein's classic discussion.[29] Habermas' argument is an effort to deny that the rate of profit must, or in fact does, fall, and hence to deny the very idea of the intrinsically necessary economic collapse of a form of society based on the private ownership of the means of production.

His argument against the necessary fall in the rate of profit turns on the relation of this law to the theory of surplus value. He begins by pointing out that the crises within capitalism are situated in a recurrent cycle due both to a fall in the rate of profit and a decrease in the opportunity for profitable investment. He next observes that, according to Marx, the fall in the rate of profit leads to the introduction of labor-saving machinery, a progressive mechanization of the productive process, a tendential fall of the rate of profit, and a repetition of the crisis. He then briefly reviews aspects of the controversy surrounding the law of the tendential fall of the rate of profit which, he suggests, leads to the range of problems concerning the productivity of labor.

Habermas' response is based on his rival view of the productivity of labor. According to Habermas, Marx ignores "the rising rate of surplus value" which results from increasing mechanization in his official view. In the

Grundrisse he considered "the scientific development of the technical forces of production" and other means as "a source of the increase in value,"[30] but he did not include them in his official formulation of the labor theory of value.

This argument is interesting, although not necessarily decisive. It indicates that Marx's theory is potentially more successful than it is in the form in which he presented it in his later writings. As he did in *Knowledge and Human Interests*, Habermas here maintains that there are ideas in Marx's writings which the latter does not always follow up, but which, if developed, would result in a theory of more explanatory power. That the theory could have been better than it is is an indirect argument for the concept of theory reconstruction.

This objection further suggests that Marx tended to ignore ideas or information that ran contrary to his own view.[31] From the Marxian perspective, obviously the increase in surplus value due to the introduction of labor-saving machinery would in part explain the surprising resilience of capitalism at the cost of undermining Marx's conviction that use-value is created through labor-power only.[32]

In the second part, Habermas bolsters his argument against the necessary occurrence of a fundamental economic crisis through an examination of the law regarding the tendency of the rate of profit to fall with the increase in mechanization. His complex empirical argument is intended as a refutation of the law in question. He maintains that recent history fails to confirm a fall in the rate of profit; and he further maintains that the law is valid for a given social stage only, since the cost of the reproduction of labor-power is a historical variable. According to Habermas, Marx noted this fact, but did not systematically incorporate it into his theory.

In the framework of an article on Marx's position as a scientifically falsifiable philosophy of history, the observation that part of the position is out of step with our empirical knowledge of society amounts to a claim that it has been refuted. In effect, Habermas asserts that the law of the fall in the rate of profit has been empirically falsified by the course of history. In that case, either we need to abandon the theory or endeavor to 'fix' or otherwise reconstruct it. At this point Habermas, who is not yet ready to abandon the labor theory of value, undertakes to provide an acceptable reconstruction of it.

We can prescind from the consideration of Habermas' new form of the labor theory of value in order to concentrate here on the success of his objection against the Marxian crisis theory. The two arguments against the necessary occurrence of a deep-seated economic crisis are in fact variations on a single theme. In comments on the significance of technological innovation, Habermas contends that as a result of such innovation productivity tends to rise and profit tends not to fall. In this way, he concludes that Marx is wrong to argue for the necessary occurrence of a deep crisis threatening to capitalism itself; according to Habermas, an inspection of Marx's own writings reveals reasons to hold that the free enterprise system is intrinsically stable.

If this statement of his argument is correct, then the objection is only partially successful. His argument is interesting as an attempt to maintain much

of the framework of Marxian political economy—including the acknowledgment of the existence of economic crises linked to the form of organization
of the means of production—while utilizing Marxian insights to demonstrate
the relative stability of capitalism itself. This is important, since there is reason
to believe that capitalism was perhaps more complex than Marx's theoretical
model recognized, and, in any case, his theory must now be revised to account
for changes in the free enterprise system over the last hundred years.

The deeper problem concerns Habermas' success in refuting the crisis theory. In this regard, we need to separate two kinds of questions. On the one
hand, there are complicated empirical issues concerning the supposed tendencies of profits not to fall and of productivity to increase. It is sufficient to note
that these issues are susceptible to empirical analysis; but Habermas, who
makes claims about them, does not attempt to demonstrate his view empirically. To take a single example, although he states that in capitalist countries
the rate of profit has shown no unambiguous tendency towards decline in the
last eighty years,[33] he offers no data to support this belief. But from an empirical perspective, as he must realize, this kind of unsupported statement is so
broad as to be nearly meaningless.

On the other hand, there is a set of theoretical issues concerning the success
of his response to Marx's theory. Here there are two points to be made. First,
it is apparent that Habermas' discussion is overly selective, even as an analysis
of Marx's view of the likelihood of the economic instability of capitalism. Obviously there are different types of crisis. As he himself points out, he considers only crises linked to the fall in the rate of profit.[34] He omits, for instance,
the equally important crises, prevalent in both Western Europe and North
America at present, related to so-called realization, that is, the problem of the
production of surplus value through the circulation of capital.[35] Hence, his argument against the crisis theory counts at most as an objection to the Marxian
analysis of the supposed tendency of profit to diminish.

Second, it is arguable that in his selective consideration of crises related to
a fall in the rate of profit Habermas has overlooked a crucial dimension of
Marx's view. Habermas' analysis is formulated solely in relation to profit, that
is, in economic terms. This angle of vision totally neglects the relation of
human beings to an understanding of the long-term prospects for the free market system. Certainly, Marx's attention to this dimension is a factor which
continues to separate his view of political economy from others, formulated
in more exclusively economic ways, such as the recently fashionable views of
so-called supply side economics and monetarism.

Emphasis on the relation of human beings to capitalism as a factor in the
understanding of its long-term viability yields at least two grounds for dissatisfaction with Habermas' critique of the ability of the Marxian crisis theory
to deal with crises due to a fall in the rate of profit. On the one hand, even
if wages may seem to be rising in the Western industrialized nations, the enormous disparity with wages in Eastern industrialized and third world nations
obviously reflects on the rate of profit in Western society. Habermas' discus-

sion is too simplistic, since it fails to consider this and other relevant factors.

On the other hand, it may turn out that crises in the rate of profit are inseparable from crises of realization. Habermas implicitly recognizes this linkage in his account of what he sees as the present possibility of democratic socialism, in which human beings would be freed from further dependence on capital accumulation.[36] It is at least conceivable that in the future the free enterprise system will be undercut by the widespread desire for another kind of life.

This possibility provides another reason for thinking that Habermas in part misses a central issue in relation to the Marxian crisis theory, that is, a reason based on self-consciousness for holding that a revised form of the theory is valid in a way which escapes his objection. The problem of profit may finally not be the most important factor since there could be a decisive crisis in capitalism on grounds connected less with the health of the economic dimension of society than with a desire for independence from that dimension.

After his rapid critique of the crisis theory, Habermas turns to the exposition of an alternative to the Marxian labor theory of value and, as noted, to consideration of the current possibility of democratic socialism. According to Habermas, this possibility has become real through the development of techniques of crisis management, such as those associated with Keynesian economics. His discussion now loses any pretense of a relation to the crisis theory, presumably—but certainly contrary to fact—because we have now entered a historical period in which serious economic crises will no longer occur.

We can end this review of Habermas' critique of the Marxian crisis theory with a general remark. Perhaps because he identifies Marxian political economy with the crisis theory, his discussion of the latter is overly selective. He considers only one of the two forms of crisis he distinguishes, and he fails even to provide a statement of the nature and role of the theory in historical materialism in general. In effect, he dismisses the crisis theory, whose importance he does not recognize in his eagerness to criticize and to reformulate the economic theory, which he mistakenly conflates with it.

The crisis theory cannot merely be discarded as an outmoded feature of Marx's thought. Even on Habermas' controversial reading of historical materialism as a theory of social evolution, it is necessary in order to explain the allegedly intrinsic instability of capitalism. Indeed, there is a tension in Habermas' reading of historical materialism: for he holds that it is a theory of social evolution, but he denies the existence of the economic crises which are Marx's main reason for the belief in the transitory nature of capitalism. Since economic crises continue to occur, if there were no crisis theory the resultant inability to explain such phenomena would seriously undermine Marx's position; it would deprive his position of the capacity to account for an important feature of capitalist society, whose recurrent crises cannot simply be ignored. To ignore such crises would be to abandon any pretense that the position is practically relevant; and it would further render implausible the belief, to which Habermas subscribes, that capitalism is a transitory phase in the development of human society.

VIII

THE LABOR THEORY
OF VALUE AND
HISTORICAL MATERIALISM

The previous chapter began the task of the evaluation of Habermas' critical reading of historical materialism as an economic interpretation of social phenomena. From the perspective of the so-called superstructure theorem, we have so far reviewed two features of his critique of historical materialism: his criticisms of the notion of ideology and of the crisis theory. The present chapter will take up a third feature of his critique under the heading of the labor theory of value, which he also calls Marx's value theory.

In comparison with the discussions of ideology and the crisis theory, Habermas' critique of the labor theory of value is better developed and more focused. The critical remarks on ideology and the crisis theory were intended to discern defects in parts of historical materialism which could presumably be remedied through its reconstruction. In contrast, the critique of the value theory is intended as a rejection, not of a part of the theory, or even of an essential element thereof, but of the theory in general.

At this point, the general critique of Marxian monism, deriving from Marx's supposed inability to separate the concepts of superstructure and base, and Habermas' further objections to facets of the wider position, come together in a specific series of criticisms. The latter are intended to demonstrate the failure of historical materialism as a theory and, by extension, the failure of the economic approach to the explanation of social phenomena. Since for Habermas the success or failure of historical materialism turns finally on the Marxian theory of value, it is appropriate to consider his critique of the value theory in detail.

In Habermas' writings on historical materialism, there are two critical discussions of the labor theory of value: a brief mention in the context of his interpretation of Marxism as critique, and a more detailed account embedded in the elaboration of his theory of communicative action. Since there is no statement of the nature and role of the labor theory of value in his corpus, it will be helpful to make a few general remarks about it and its relation to historical materialism in order to provide a background for an evaluation of his critique of it.

The labor theory of value is only implicitly present in the early Marxian writings, even in those largely concerned with economic questions, such as the *Paris Manuscripts*. It is still not explicit in the *German Ideology*, which Althusser and his disciples regard as Marx's first mature, scientific work. But it is clearly explicit in the *Grundrisse*, where Marx distinguishes forms of value related to use and exchange, and links them to surplus value and capital accumulation, and in all later economic writings.

A value theory is already present in the tradition in early Greek thought, for instance in Aristotle's writings. Forms of the labor theory of value are present in the views of Marx's predecessors, particularly Smith and Ricardo. In his economic writings, Marx built upon and modified earlier views in the process of arriving at his own conception. Not surprisingly, since the labor theory of value is perhaps the most controversial element in historical materialism, there is no agreement about its proper interpretation. The best known and most developed form of the theory occurs in a strategic place in Marx's acknowledged masterpiece, in the initial chapter of the first book of *Capital*. Here, in a discussion entitled "Commodities," Marx provides a detailed account of his view of value from various angles of vision. The central and arguably most difficult point of his analysis is the assertion that, as noted, the value of an article, that is, a commodity intended for sale or exchange, is a function of the labor-time socially necessary for its production.

We can further mention some among the many approaches to the labor theory of value. A brief survey is sufficient to demonstrate that agreement is lacking on the validity and even the nature of the theory itself. At the end of the nineteenth century, Böhm-Bawerk maintained in opposition to Marx, that (1) value cannot be measured quantitatively in Marx's sense; (2) prices do not depend only on value, but on other factors as well; (3) the statement that value governs the movement of prices is both arbitrary and scientifically useless.[1]

This attack was quickly answered by Hilferding.[2] More recently, Howard and King have argued that Marx's labor theory of value is superior to that of any classical economist. They further maintain that the traditional, neoclassical criticism is ineffective against a theory which, however, has a restricted application in respect to the more successful neo-Keynesian theory.[3]

The disagreement between Böhm-Bawerk on the one hand and Howard and King on the other concerns the economic usefulness of the labor theory of value to measure price. Even this idea, which most writers have always regarded as the main point of the theory, has recently been contested. According to Heilbroner,[4] Marx is more interested in the problem, which classical economics failed to note, of how to use labor as a means for establishing ratios of exchange.

As a result of his critique of the labor theory of value Habermas rejects historical materialism as even a potentially viable theory. The relative importance of the value theory for the overall position, and hence the importance of its criticism, depends on the reading of the wider position. An obvious lesson of the discussion of historical materialism in an immense literature is the fact that there are many ways to understand Marx's position. Since we are concerned with an economic aspect of the view, at present it will suffice to distinguish roughly between opposing conceptions of the relation of political economy to historical materialism.

The Marxian view of political economy can be regarded from varying angles of vision as either centrally, or only incidentally, related to the wider position. In the former case, in which Marx's theory is regarded as a theory of political economy, there is a tendency to argue for the independence of his later, more obviously economic writings from his earlier, apparently more philosophical discussion; and there is a further tendency to regard effective criticism of the labor theory of value as fatal to the Marxian view in general. This is the approach Habermas must take if his critique of the labor theory of value is to lead to a rejection of historical materialism.

In the latter case, there is an opposing tendency to believe that the earlier and later writings, despite their apparent difference in perspective, are related as integral parts of a single theoretical vision. As concerns the labor theory of value, a typical form of this view consists in the argument that the theory is not self-subsistent, but dependent on earlier concepts, such as those of alienation and objectification.

From this perspective, since Marx's position is only partly economic in nature, even the most decisive criticism of the labor theory of value is not fatal for Marx's position as a whole. At most the refutation of the Marxian value theory means that a part of the edifice, a dimension that Marx regarded as important, must be abandoned; but the edifice as such will remain standing. If, on the contrary, Marx's position is wholly, or even mainly, political economy, then the refutation of the labor theory of value is enough to cause the collapse of the entire edifice.

These brief remarks will provide a background for our evaluation of Habermas' critique of the labor theory of value. We can begin with a glance at his rapid reference to this topic in the discussion of Marxism as critique, before proceeding to a more careful review of his later complex refutation in the account of communicative action. His allusion to the Marxian value theory occurs here in the context of a critique of the crisis theory.

The first two parts of the discussion of the crisis theory concern problems related to the law of the declining rate of profit, which are respectively due to the exclusion of other forms of value-formation and the neglect of empirical factors. In the third part of the discussion, Habermas proposes an alternative view of value-formation, meant to be more inclusive than the labor theory of value. Now turning from crises linked to the fall in the rate of profit to those connected with problems of realization [Realisationskrise], he proposes to replace the Marxian labor theory of value, which he has not so far directly examined or even stated, by his own view. According to Habermas, if value follows from productivity as such, then, under certain conditions, it is possible both to raise profit and real wages.[5]

Habermas' argument in favor of his new, rival value theory can be paraphrased as follows: The law of surplus value is valid only for a given level of the technical forces of production. For example, the cost of reproducing labor-power depends on the cultural standard of life, as Marx himself realized. Accordingly, it is rational to suppose that in contemporary society the standard has increased so that it can no longer be measured in terms of English workers of the middle of the last century. A revision [Revision] of the work-theoretical foundations is important for crises related to the fall in the rate of profit and to those connected to problems of realization. In this context, Habermas cites a passage in which Marx connects production to consumption, before proposing a revised theory of value intended to be useful for the introduction of democratic principles, including the better distribution of the profits in order to encourage consumption.

Suffice it to say that if this statement of Habermas' argument is accurate, there is an important confusion between the theoretical issue of how value is to be comprehended and such significant, but essentially practical, issues as the introduction of democratic measures into political economy or the resolution of economic crises due either to the fall in the rate of profit or the lag of consumption behind production. A revision of the view of value is a theoretical problem, obviously important for an understanding of what takes place; any interpretation of the social context is informed by a theoretical perspective. But a revision of the theory has no consequences whatsoever for the resolution of such practical questions as economic crises or the possibility of democratic socialism.

The proposed revision raises interesting questions concerning its relation to historical materialism. Here he has not yet formulated the metatheoretical justification of theory reconstruction which is the basis of his attempt, as noted, to improve a theory by taking it apart and putting it back together in order better to attain its intrinsic goals. Hence, there is an interesting ambiguity in the term "revision" which masks Habermas' precise intention at this point. In later writings on historical materialism, as we have seen, he will successively undertake to reconstruct and to replace the theory by his own view.

Whatever Habermas' intention, clearly his revised theory of value is meant as an improvement over Marx's view. Now, we have already noted that the proposed revision is not adequate to resolve the practical problems to which Habermas points. We must now determine if it is theoretically more adequate than the Marxian model. For this purpose it will be useful to provide a slightly fuller, but still incomplete, description of the Marxian value theory, beginning with the difference between labor and labor power.

The Marxian value theory depends on a fundamental distinction between labor and labor power.[6] If useful work adds value to commodities, it is labor power which the workers sell to capitalists for a money wage. Labor power relates in general to labor as potency to act, since the worker, who cannot sell the results of his labor, can indeed sell the power to labor, that is, the potential which is manifested in the actual manifestation of human productive capacities. It is in the course of this manifestation, in which use values are transformed and increase their exchange value, that surplus value is created. The latter is defined as the difference between what the capitalist pays for the labor power and the value which the manifestation of such labor power adds to the value of the commodities.

According to the Marxian theory of value, abstract labor produces commodities. Value is defined as the 'objectification' or 'materialization' of abstract labor. In other words, value is measured in units of time necessary on the average to produce a commodity. From this angle of vision value is intrinsic to the commodity and exchange value is a necessary form of the appearance of value. It follows that there is a relation between the labor-time furnished by the worker in the production of the commodity and the price for which the commodity can be sold. Even if, as Marx points out, the relation between labor time and price is not direct, and in fact is mediated through different products and different industries across a given national economy, in the final analysis price is indeed a function of labor time.

In the present context, it is not possible to propose a general theory of value, surely an enormous task, or even to demonstrate the relative advantage of one view. Now, it is difficult to characterize Habermas' suggestion as more than that, since he does not develop it into a full-fledged theory. It will be sufficient here to note an important difference between the Marxian view of value and Habermas' proposed revision of it as concerns the relation of political economy to such standard Marxian themes as alienation, objectification, and the stability of capitalism.

Marx's value theory is oriented toward an understanding of the long-range viability of capitalism in terms of the effect on the workers of the drive toward the continual augmentation of production and the accumulation of value. He believes that in the long run the resultant increase in misery due to the increase in surplus value and to the desire to maximize capital accumulation is dangerous for the stability of the capitalist economy.

Habermas' suggestion has the advantage of linking value to production. It thus provides a way to understand the utility of technology and increasing mechanization. But its price is to render it impossible to relate the stability of capitalism to the workers' welfare. Now, this may be desirable for various reasons, but it is certainly different from, and clearly incompatible with, Marx's project. In a word, Marx links value to objectification and alienation, whereas Habermas, on the contrary, uncouples value from alienation while retaining the link to objectification.

Habermas' initial approach to the value theory is intended as a revision in the context of a wide-ranging interpretation and critique of historical materialism leading up to his effort to reconstruct it. At this point, he regards the value theory as merely one of the aspects of a wider position to which he remains committed. When he returns to the value theory in the wake of his arguably unsuccessful reconstruction of historical materialism, his attitude toward Marx and Marxism has basically changed in at least three ways. First, he no longer believes that historical materialism is even potentially viable; he thus abandons the attempt to reconstruct it. Second, his criticism is no longer directed toward discerning problems that can be alleviated through another, better form of the original theory; his criticism is rather aimed at identifying reasons for a rejection of the theory in favor of another.

Third, there is a significant shift in the strategy of his critique. He continues to regard historical materialism as an economic theory, although he has now abandoned his identification of political economy with a so-called genuine crisis theory. Obviously, the labor theory of value is an economic view. If its decisive critique is sufficient to refute historical materialism, then by implication the latter is a theory of political economy and the value theory is either identical with or essential to it. This claim, which is never actually articulated, is an unstated premise of his effort to refute historical materialism in terms of Marxian value theory.

In comparison with the earlier, brief allusion to the Marxian value theory, the discussion in the context of the theory of communicative action is obviously more detailed. It further differs in a number of other ways, in that it includes a noneconomic approach to the critique of the value theory, a general reliance on the phenomenological concept of the life-world, and a specific effort to provide a quasi-linguistic reading of the Marxian labor theory of value. Since each of these aspects is arguably unusual, but ingredient in Habermas' critique, it will be useful to mention them prior to an evaluation of his proposed refutation.

It is not surprising, since the labor theory of value is an economic view, that it is usually criticized from the economic perspective which Habermas himself adopted in the earlier attempt to revise the theory. Curiously, although his refutation of historical materialism depends on an economic reading of it, his critique of the Marxian value theory here is only incidentally economic in nature. In fact, it is fair to say that his focus is not on the idea of value within political economy on either a practical or a theoretical level at all. As we shall see below in a review of the specific criticisms, his aim seems to be to object to the very idea of an economic approach to social theory.

If this is a correct description of Habermas' approach, its ability to refute the labor theory of value is questionable, even apart from the power of his particular criticisms, for an obvious reason. It is unclear how an economic theory can be refuted on noneconomic grounds. Now this observation is only potentially damaging to Habermas' discussion if his intention was in fact to refute Marx's value theory. A refutation might be carried out in various ways, such as by showing that another value theory is superior to Marx's, as Habermas tried to do in the context of his discussion of Marxism as critique;

or that it is inadequate with respect to its self-assigned task, the criterion he suggests in his brief metatheoretical remarks on theory reconstruction; or even that it fails to meet the criteria for scientific theory.[7]

Now, although Habermas criticizes the labor theory of value, there are indications that refutation is not his aim at all. These include the fact that his critique occurs in a sub-chapter headed "Marx and the Thesis of Inner Colonisation;" and his complex statement of his intention here to respond to Adorno's and Horkheimer's supposed inability to appropriate part of Weber's position by rendering explicit "what Marx's theory of value provides for a theory of objectification [Verdinglichung] translated into system/life-world concepts and where its weaknesses lie."[8]

As a description of intent, the latter statement is unambiguous. It tells us that Habermas in only interested in the labor theory of value, and by implication in Marx's position, for what it can offer to another type of theory. It follows that his critique is not meant to be immediate, or internal to the theory, since it is mediated through another theoretical model which he has already adopted as a replacement for the Marxian model. It further follows that if we are to evaluate his critique of Marx's value theory, we need to understand his proposed critique from an implicitly post-Marxian perspective, which declines the Marxian approach to social theory, but not the aim of social theory.

To put this point in other words, in criticizing the labor theory of value Habermas does not intend, or does not only intend, to object to a particular form of economic theory. If that were his intention, or his main intention, then presumably he would have formulated his critique in specifically economic terms so that it would count directly against a specific kind of economic theory. Rather, his goal, which is apparently more general, seems to be to criticize an approach to social theory from what he regards as an exaggeratedly economic perspective, that is, an approach which over-emphasizes the economic component of social reality.

If we read his critique as presupposing another theoretical model of social reality, then we can understand why he attacks an economic theory on non-economic grounds, through the specifically phenomenological concept of the life-world. In Husserl's writings, the theme of the life-world is most prominent, although in still undeveloped form, in his last, unfinished book.[9] Husserl here criticizes Kant's alleged failure to make explicit the presupposition of the world as revealed in the natural attitude, in effect as taken for granted. With empirical psychology, in the Crisis Husserl regarded the life-world as one of the two themes whose study leads to transcendental phenomenology.

It has been suggested that the life-world is a concept which opens the way for a phenomenological approach to history,[10] in a sense as a quasi-phenomenological alternative to the Marxian theory of praxis. Hence, it is significant that Habermas understands the writings of Schutz, the phenomenologist influenced by Husserl who has probably done the most to develop the concept of the life-world, as an effort to work out a theory of daily life with pragmatic overtones.[11]

When Habermas speaks of the life-world, he is apparently less interested in the phenomenological background of the term than in the general problem of the comprehension of the social world as revealed in experience. His critique of the labor theory of value here is not meant to propose an alternative, phenomenological form of economic analysis. Rather, it is intended to reveal the limitations of an economically centered understanding of advanced capitalism. Although the Marxian form of social theory may have been useful in an earlier period, the later development of capitalism, or the object of the theory, has made it imperative to revise our approach to social reality.

In terms of his understanding of the function of the concept of the life-world in Habermas' critique, we can comprehend why he believes that his objections provide a sufficient basis for the rejection of the Marxian position. The reason is not that the Marxian value theory is a central element of the position as a whole which, accordingly, collapses when its foundation is refuted. This kind of argument is suggested by the approach to Marx's position in terms of the fundamental distinction between superstructure and economic base. But Habermas must employ another strategy since he does not criticize Marxian political economy as such.

In fact, he could not argue in this fashion and remain consistent since elsewhere, as noted, he has maintained that Marx's position is a theory of social evolution and not basically a theory of political economy at all. Rather, his strategy seems to be to demonstrate that a social theory which, like Marx's, accords explanatory primacy to political economy does not and cannot provide an adequate description of social reality.

We can clarify this point by some additional comments on his description of his critical discussion of the Marxian value theory. We have noted his indication that he adopts a different theoretical model for purposes of his discussion. Now, one of the tasks of his critique must be to show that the decision to abandon the Marxian model of theory in favor of another alternative is not merely arbitrary, but justified by the inherent limitations of the general Marxian approach to social theory. The difficulty with Marx's explanatory model cannot simply be that it was insufficiently developed in his position or in those of his followers.

If that were the case, then in principle it would be possible to reconstruct the Marxian view, as Habermas in fact tried to do in an earlier phase of his dialogue with Marx and Marxism. If an attempt of this kind were possible, there would then be no reason to abandon a Marxian form of social theory in general, and perhaps even no reason to abandon Marx's own position. The decision to opt for a rival type of social explanation is justified only if he can demonstrate that Marx's position has significant intrinsic weaknesses, which cannot be overcome through its reconstruction, and that there is another, better alternative available.

We can regard his critique of the labor theory of value as a concerted effort to demonstrate the intrinsic limitations of Marx's position, or any position like it, for the comprehension of advanced capitalism. Here we need to distinguish between his descriptions of the Marxian position and of the Marxian value theory, and to distinguish them both from the specific criticisms he addresses to the latter. Habermas follows other commentators, especially Lukács, in suggesting that, with respect to other alternatives, the superiority of Marx's position lies in its view of commodity analysis.[12]

This economic vantage point allows Marx to describe the development of capitalist society as a crisis-laden process of the self-accumulation of capital and the conflictive interaction of social classes. According to Habermas, wage labor neutralizes the results of producers with respect to the life-world context of their actions. The result is the 'thingification' [Versachlichung] of socially interpreted action relations, coordinated, not in terms of norms and values, or a process of agreement, but through the medium of exchange-value.

Habermas supplements his economic interpretation of Marx's position, more precisely his approach to it as a pioneering form of commodity analysis, with a reading of the value theory as providing rules for the basic relation of exchange [fundamentale Austauschbeziehung] between the economic system and the life-world. In his interpretation of the Marxian value theory, he adopts the perspective, or at least the language, of analytic philosophy of science, apparently related to recent work in translation theory.

Following E.M. Lange and H. Brunkhorst, he differentiates two pairs of theory and observation languages, as concerns the life-world of capitalists and wage laborers on the one hand and as concerns the systematic interrelations of capital accumulation on the other. According to Habermas, the labor theory can be understood as the attempt to render explicit the rules of translation between observations formulated in the respective languages of theory and observation.[13] In other words, the value theory provides rules for the market-regulated appropriation of labor power [Arbeitskraft], according to which, in Habermas' terminology, so-called systematic statements [Aussagen] can be translated, through the mediation of anonymous relations of value, into historical statements, expressed as relations of interaction between social classes.[14] From this angle of vision, the value theory is an effort, as Habermas states, to specify the rules for the translation in question.[15]

Habermas' characterization of the labor theory of value, from the vantage point of analytic philosophy of science, as an effort at translation theory is both novel and controversial. The novelty does not lie in the effort to link Marx's position with the philosophy of science, or even with science. This interest is widespread in the literature on Marx; in practice it has led to some catastrophic results, of which the genetic theories of Lyssenko are only the best known example.[16]

Rather, the novelty resides in the specific description, perhaps unprecedented in the discussion on Marx, of the labor theory of value as an attempt to specify rules of translation. Although it is well known that toward the end of his life Stalin tried to develop a specifically Marxist analysis of language, Habermas seems to go even further in attributing something like a linguistic theory to Marx.

There may be a relation between Marx's thought and linguistic theory; but it is obviously controversial to regard the labor theory of value in any literal sense either as a theory of translation, or as providing rules for one, or even as a theory in the philosophy of science. In general terms, the labor theory proposes an understanding of the relation between prices and values mediated through the manifestation of the labor power of individual workers, or, in Habermas' terminology, between economic values and the actions of individuals in the life-world. Marx's value theory is arguably unrelated to questions of translation, which is accordingly a mistake in descriptive terms; but it is rather centrally concerned with how to understand the basic relations of modern social life from a fundamentally economic perspective. For a variety of reasons, including the fact that Marx never provided a single synthetic statement of the labor theory of value, which he preferred to apply, there is ample room for disagreement about its precise interpretation or possible validity. What cannot be denied, but which Habermas in fact seems to deny, is that Marx's theory is what its name says it is, that is, a theory of economic value as a function of labor-time.

The perspective of analytic philosophy of science, which informs Habermas' characterization of the labor theory of value as an effort to specify rules of translation, further determines his critique of the theory. His critique of the labor theory of value is not directly concerned with the Marxian problem of the expression of price as a function of value, for which the theory is arguably intended. Rather, it is oriented toward Habermas' own focus, determined by his interest in analytic philosophy of science, on the connection between theory and observation, as provided in the lived experience of life-world. In other words, Habermas scrutinizes the labor theory of value not as the economic view it purports to be, but as an attempt to provide an account of the link between the two levels of observation and theory, roughly comparable to the Marxian distinction between base and superstructure.

His specific objections to the labor theory of value do not reflect its intended economic role as much as its controversial reading as an attempt to specify rules for translation, judged against a phenomenological background, between observation language and theoretical language. Briefly stated, Habermas' three objections concern Marx's supposed inability to distinguish between system and life-world, his understanding of the latter notion, and his grasp of its relation to the concept of system. Habermas sees Marx's major failure as an inability to grasp the idea of the life-world and, accordingly, its relation to other basic ideas necessary for an adequate form of social theory.

Habermas' first criticism is that Marx operates with the distinction between system and life-world, but, because of his dependence on Hegel's *Logic*, he does not really presuppose their separation.[17] According to Habermas, the relation between theoretical statements of both types can only be clarified through a semantical explanation presupposing a logical relation, in the Hegelian sense, between the development of system and a structural change in the life-world. Marx supposedly attempted to carry out this task through a semantically postulated value theory, on pain of being obliged to recur to empirical research on the transformation of concrete into abstract forms of work.

We can clarify this objection by calling attention to its background in Lenin's thought. It is well known that in his *Philosophical Notebooks* Lenin claimed that thorough mastery of the entirety of Hegel's *Science of Logic* is a necessary precondition for the comprehension of Marx's *Capital*.[18] It follows the *Capital* is relevantly similar to the *Logic* and, in virtue of that similarity, may well have similar defects. What Habermas does here is to adapt this line of argument to identify a specific weakness in *Capital* which he attributes to its dependence on the *Logic*.

To avoid confusion, we must distinguish between the objection Habermas brings against the labor theory of value and the series of issues he raises in this connection. It is doubtless interesting to reflect on the relation between Marx and Hegel. The suggestion that *Capital* depends in some crucial way on the *Logic* provides an interesting way to focus on this connection.

Habermas implicitly suggests that he will use this link as a means to demonstrate that Marx's value theory is unsuccessful as an attempted specification of the rules for translation between observation and theoretical languages. But his argument is doubly flawed since it does not prove that this weakness in Marx's value theory derives from its relation to Hegel's position, nor does it prove that Marx even intended his theory to carry out the task that Habermas assigns to it. It fails, therefore, even to demonstrate the existence of the problem which Habermas claims to discern.

In part following Lukács, Habermas attributes Marx's supposed failure specifically to separate the concepts of system and life-world in his position to his acceptance of the Hegelian notion of the whole, or totality, in particular to his concern with concrete totality.[19] He sees Marx's interest in totality, which allegedly impelled him to construe system and life-world as a 'untrue' whole, as responsible for his failure to note the high degree of structural differentiation in every modern society. He believes that this oversight is related to a second weakness in the value theory, that is, the lack of criteria necessary to distinguish between the destruction of traditional forms of life and the objectification [Verdinglichung] of so-called post-traditional life-worlds.[20]

Habermas clarifies his objection through a remark on a change in Marx's concept of alienation [Entfremdung] in later writings. In part following Taylor's recent emphasis of the romantic concept of expressivism, or fulfillment through creative activity, he differentiates two stages in Marx's view of alienation.[21] He believes that in the *Paris Manuscripts*, Marx proposes an expressivist model of creative activity, influenced by Herder and the Romantics; but Marx supposedly later freed himself from this idea through the adoption of the labor theory of value.

Habermas argues that the introduction of the second form of the theory, which stresses the transformation of concrete into abstract work, causes the concept of alienation to lose its specificity, or historical index. He maintains that as a result Marx is unable to distinguish between objectification [Verdinglichung] and the structural differentiation of the life-world. According to Habermas, Marx is no longer concerned with the distance from an ideal form of practice; rather, he is concerned with what Habermas calls the "instrumentalization," or realization, of a form of life accepted as an intrinsic goal [Selbstzweck].

The description of the proposed evolution of the Marxian view of alienation is useful in the context of the debate about this concept; but it does not demonstrate his criticism of the Marxian value theory. In the attempt to make out a distinction in kind between Marx's early and late writings, it has sometimes been argued that the concept of alienation is absent in his mature period.[22] Habermas here comes down on the side of those who believe that, despite change, there is a basic continuity in the evolution of Marx's thought, in which the concept of alienation remains a constant feature.[23]

His claim that in the later writings Marx employs a different concept of alienation dependent on the labor theory of value must be resisted; for Marx's theory that value is constituted through labor-power presupposes the notions of alienation and objectification, and not conversely. It is only because labor-power assumes objective form in the commodity, which can be bought and sold, that workers are alienated and surplus value is constituted. Habermas' argument makes alienation, which he conflates with objectification, dependent on the labor theory of value, which in Marx's thought in fact derives from these concepts.

For the reasons mentioned, Habermas' reading of the purported evolution of the concept of alienation, at least in its present form, does not demonstrate his objection to the labor theory of value. Even if his reading could be successfully reconstructed, it would not show a weakness in the Marxian value theory. In fact here, somewhat surprisingly in view of his basic objections to the labor theory of value and his rejection of historical materialism because of the putative weakness of its central element, Habermas does not claim that the value theory is incorrect; rather, he maintains that its introduction transformed the concept of alienation, and, hence, altered the wider position in a way that made it inadequate to comprehend modern society.

His second objection, which is independent of his general characterization of the labor theory from the vantage point of analytic philosophy of science, features an effort to link the value theory to the concepts of alienation and objectification. Habermas here suggests that the initial version of Marx's concept of alienation is connected to a theory of practice, or *Praxisphilosophie*, although this connection is later broken through the turn to a value theory. Now, a theory of practice presupposes an understanding of human activity. Habermas focuses on the Marxian view of human activity in his third, supposedly decisive, objection to the Marxian labor theory as "an overgeneralization of a special case of the subsumption of the life-world under system imperatives."[24]

Habermas justifies this criticism in a complex argument directed against Marx as well as Max Weber, Western Marxism, and Parsons, all of whom are allegedly guilty of the same error due to their supposed misunderstanding of human being in terms of the concept of goal-directed activity. Since we are concerned here with Habermas' critique of the Marxian value theory, we do not need to pursue the proposed connection between its purported defects and those of other views.

As concerns Marx, Habermas' argument is designed to establish that he casts his conceptual net too narrowly; more precisely, he is obliged to employ a reductive approach to connect elements which in fact are independent of each other. Habermas makes this argument through an implicit appeal to the distinction between work and interaction which, in various forms, has continually appeared in his writings since his early article on Hegel.

At this point, Habermas abandons any pretense of an immanent critique of the Marxian value theory. His final criticism derives from the introduction of his own, rival social theory, to which he appeals in order to object to Marx's view. He now proposes a dualistic model of society, consisting of the work world, which turns on money, and the administrative system, which concerns power. In his rival model, these two domains are linked through communicative relations over, that is, above, money and power. This alternative social theory provides a dualistic standard for the critique of the Marxian value theory.

According to Habermas, the labor theory of value concerns money only, although alienation is broader than that sphere. He maintains that Marx's error is to overgeneralize from a special case because he based his discussion on a model of goal-directed activity. In a single complex sentence, Habermas writes: "The value theory is developed in action-theoretical concepts which oblige the genesis of objectification to begin below the level of interaction and (further) oblige the handling of the distortion of relations of interaction themselves, therefore the loss of wordliness [Entweltlichung] of communicative actions transformed into communicative media, as well as the technicization [Technisierung] of the life-world which arises as derived [abgeleitete] phenomena."[25]

This criticism brings together a number of issues around the theme of the labor theory of value, including goal-directed activity, the model of society to which it leads, Marx's possible overgeneralization of this explanatory model, and its relation to the Marxian value theory. Habermas maintains that he is taking aim at the value theory; but his discussion here, which is obviously unfocused, is no more than the occasion to raise issues which are mainly incidental to it.

Since he notes that the value theory is formulated in "action-theoretical concepts," whose adequacy he questions, the target of his criticism lies deeper than the value theory. In other words, his objection is not directed in the first instance against the labor theory of value, which is part of the chain of reasoning leading away from the adoption of a goal-oriented theory of activity; it is rather directed against the adequacy of this concept of activity as a basis for modern social theory.

An awareness that the labor theory of value merely provides the occasion at this point for his criticism of the action-theoretical basis of the Marxian explanatory model enables us to understand the logic of the two-stage argument Habermas proposes. As he reads Marx, the latter employs a goal-directed concept of activity, which in the first instance is economic in character, since economic needs are prior to all others. Habermas opposes this approach to human activity and to social theory through the introduction of different models of both. More precisely, he presupposes the separate and apparently primordial status of an element that Marx can supposedly only explain in a reductionist fashion.

Habermas justifies his introduction of another explanatory model through his interpretation of modern capitalism. He maintains that the Marxian social model combines system of life-world, or the imperatives of political economy and the resultant form of social relations, in a way which is simply not characteristic of modern society in general. He believes that a more accurate image of modern society which, however, does not neglect political economy, is provided by his own triple distinction between the levels of the work world, administration, and communication. But to accept Habermas' model is to acknowledge the primordial, or at least the equiprimordial, status of communication as a non-goal-directed form of activity.

There is a clear contrast between Habermas' interpretation of Marx and his own rival view. As he reads Marx, there is an unavoidable dependence of communicative activity on economic imperatives, and hence on goal-directed activity. This is merely another form of the familiar complaint that Marx fails to separate work and interaction because of his reliance on a model of production. In contrast, for Habermas communication is either at least equiprimordial with, or even, as he seems to suggest at various places in his discussion of historical materialism, prior to other, goal-directed forms of activity as their connecting link and foundation.

This criticism, as noted, does not directly impinge on the value theory; but through its objection to Marx's concept of activity, it is germane to the wider position. Since Marx's general view of activity is well represented elsewhere in the philosophical tradition, in virtue of his criticism of Marx on this point Habermas challenges a deeply-rooted and widespread approach to the understanding of human being. Since the importance of this challenge to Marx extends beyond his position, it will be useful to bring out the link of Marx's understanding of human being to the history of philosophy.

Marx's view of the person, as noted, cannot be fully understood apart from German idealism, especially Fichte's view of human activity as restricted by its products, whose manifestation produces the social context in which human fulfillment is to be sought. The proximal influence on the view of the person as active, not passive, lies in Fichte's understanding of the self; but this general approach is older than German idealism, and goes back in the philosophical tradition at least to the Aristotelian concept of *energeia*. There is accordingly a lengthy and important precedent for the general Marxian comprehension of human being as fundamentally active, even if the connection to Marx's thought is not often drawn.[26]

The view of human being as active is in tension with the traditional insistence on disinterested and objective thought as the source of incorrigible truth in the full sense, which is a staple of the philosophical tradition at least since Plato. This point is clearly seen by Descartes at the beginning of modern philosophy; it is the basis for his adoption of a spectator theory of knowledge in which the subject is depicted as a mere epistemological construct. His influential view was later followed for the same reason by such important thinkers as Kant and Husserl.

In general, the thrust of Marx's position, particularly his view of human being as intrinsically active, but rendered passive because of capitalism, is anti-Cartesian. Following important predecessors like Vico, Fichte, and Hegel, Marx stresses such factors as the relation to the social context, the connection between thought and time, and practice as the test of truth, factors which represent a turn away from the spectator view of subjectivity. At stake in the anti-Cartesian reaction is the idea of truth as the product of objective thought, which brings together such unlikely conceptual bedfellows in modern philosophy as Descartes and Kant, Husserl and even Heidegger.[27]

Habermas' criticism of Marx's reliance on a goal-directed form of activity is directed, beyond the problem of adequate social theory, toward the reestablishment of a viable form of the traditional philosophical claim to truth through the medium of wholly free communication. Now, a dispute about basic explanatory models is difficult to resolve. A disagreement concerning a choice prior to the theory which follows from it cannot be settled on a theoretical basis; it can only be resolved on pragmatic grounds, in terms of the comparative usefulness of different, competing forms of explanation. In the present context, Habermas argues in favor of his own model in two ways: through the claim that Marx is able to account of communication in a reductive way only, by deriving it from something else; and through the further claim that the Marxian model does not provide a satisfactory interpretation of the social context.

Neither of these lines of argument successfully tips the balance in favor of Habermas' rival explanatory model. If, for purposes of discussion, we grant his claim that Marx can only account for communication by making it dependent on another factor, it does not follow that we need to comprehend communication in Habermas' sense. It is possible that Marx is correct in his view of the relation of communication to other forms of activity. The mere fact that Marx's perspective leads to consequences in conflict with the view of communication Habermas wishes to defend is only significant if we have already accepted Habermas' view. It is further possible that both Marx and Habermas are incorrect. If Marx's view of communication were mistaken, we need not, therefore, accept Habermas' concept of communication unless he can demonstrate, which he does not even attempt to do, that there are no other plausible alternatives.

The other line of argument is more interesting, since it implicitly suggests a pragmatic standard to choose between the explanatory models of Marx and Habermas, namely their relative success in understanding modern society. Where Marx's position makes political economy central to social theory, Habermas tries to preserve this element, although he removes it from center stage. He believes that his own explanatory model provides a richer and more faithful image of advanced capitalism since it can account for more features of modern society than Marx's theory and does not overgeneralize.

Now, both these beliefs are questionable. Since Habermas' claim that Marx cannot understand alienation not directly related to the work process is unsupported by argument, there is no reason to believe that his view is richer than the Marxian model. As he only states, but does not actually show, that Marx overgeneralizes from a case uncharacteristic of modern society, there is no ground either to object to the Marxian model or to accept his rival view. Even if we grant that Marx's position is problematic, we need not concede without argument that there are areas of modern society which somehow completely escape the influence of the economic sector.

In fact, it seems premature even to argue the case of Habermas' interpretation of advanced capitalism on a pragmatic basis at all. Whereas Marx offers a lengthy discussion of modern society in great detail, with the exception of his critique of the supposed inadequacies of Marx's position, Habermas so far has only issued a promissory note for the description of modern society. This note must be redeemed before we can evaluate the comparative merits of his view in relation to other alternatives.

In particular—since this inference is important to his analysis—he needs to demonstrate how contemporary society differs from the form of capitalism that Marx discusses, in order to make a case for his claim that society has changed in a manner which makes Marx's theory either inadequate or less adequate than it once was. It is not unreasonable to believe that Marx's theory now must be updated in order to account for changes in capitalism; in fact, Marx specifically allowed for this possibility in his discussion of social categories. But the need to do so must be shown and not merely assumed.[28]

Our discussion of the objections that Habermas brings against the Marxian value theory has shown that his critique is directed less against it than against historical materialism in general. Of the three criticisms, only the first—which concerns Marx's supposed failure to root the separation between system and life-world in his view of political economy—even directly speaks to the labor theory of value. The other, broader criticisms utilize the occasion provided by mention of the Marxian value theory to present objections to the position as a whole, in particular, objections to the reliance on the economic dimension of social reality as a basic explanatory tool to comprehend other aspects of modern capitalism. Certainly, the second and third objections, which respectively address the effect of the introduction of value theory on the whole position and Marx's overgeneralization from a special case, are unrelated to the validity of the labor theory of value.

We can summarize this examination of the objections Habermas raises against the Marxian value theory by setting his critique in context. It is known that Marx intended his controversial theory as a central element of his analysis of political economy; it is further known that many writers have criticized this analysis, mainly on economic grounds. Since Habermas' critique is not formulated on an economic level, and is not mainly concerned with the theory other than as an excuse to criticize Marx's wider position, it is doubtful that his critique exposes basic weaknesses in the labor theory.

The belief that Habermas' critique does not present a serious challenge to the beleaguered Marxian value theory is supported by the conclusion he draws at the close of his examination of it. His statement, which does not mention the value theory, concerns the actual and possible success of the Marxian approach to social theory. According to Habermas, Marx's two-level distinction between system and life-world did not provide a satisfactory explanation of late capitalism since the Marxian approach [der Marxsche Ansatz], with its insistence on the evolutionary primacy of trade [Wirtschaft], demanded an economically foreshortened interpretation of developed capitalist society.[29]

Although he concedes that Marx correctly understood that problems of trade determine the evolution of society as a whole, Habermas now warns against any attempt to interpret the complementary relation of economy and the state apparatus in terms of what he describes as a trivial superstructure/base distinction (!); and he offers his own social model as a replacement for Marx's view.

In order to evaluate Habermas' conclusion, we need to separate the issues concerning the labor theory of value, as well as the actual and possible utility of Marx's position, from further issues linked to the Marxian emphasis on political economy. Habermas' critique of the value theory shows neither that the position as a whole must, nor that it in fact does, fail to explain contemporary capitalism.

With respect to the accomplishment of Marx's wider position, Habermas' conclusion can only result from his attempted refutation of the labor theory of value, or from the objections he brings against the view in general. But our review of his critique has shown that he does not expose new weaknesses in the Marxian value theory and that his objections to the position as a whole on this basis are not compelling.

Habermas' conclusion is problematic. His agreement with the view he attributes to Marx, according to which trade possesses an evolutionary primacy, betrays a possible confusion between trade and the conditions of capital accumulation. It is not the case that all forms of trade possess an evolutionary primacy. From the Marxian perspective trade as such, which, for instance, includes the exchange that was the dominant form of trade prior to the emergence of capitalism in world history, is not an effective agent of social change. Social change is set in motion by that form of trade associated with the so-called free market economy, in which, at the cost of the alienation which is the precondition of surplus value, capital is accumulated.

In terms of this clarification, we can restate Habermas' conclusion as the claim that Marx overgeneralizes the legitimate role of the economic aspect of society. The most interesting part of his conclusion is the claim that Marx's approach to social theory must fail. As was the case earlier, Habermas seems to be making a quasi-Kantian point, on methodological grounds—linked to the type of stress Marx places on the economic dimension of social reality—that Marx cannot develop a satisfactory comprehension of modern society. In effect, his claim is that in virtue of the nature of the Marxian theory, it is in principle inadequate to grasp its object, that is, the social context, which accordingly can be perceived as a kind of thing-in-itself, unknowable by thought. His argument turns on the distinction between the evolutionary primacy of trade which, he acknowledges, determines social development as a whole, and Marx's further insistence on the role of economic constraints within a given social stage.

Habermas' point has an obvious analogy with contemporary analytic philosophy of science. Kuhn's famous distinction between normal and revolutionary phases of science[30] reappears in Habermas' implicit separation of stable and unstable social stages. In regard to the former, political economy is only one of the relevant factors, whereas for the evolution between social stages economic constraints play a dominant role.

The assumption that within a given social stage political economy does not have primacy underlies Habermas' otherwise incomprehensible statement that the complementary relation between the economy and the state apparatus must not be adapted to a trivial superstructure/base analysis. If the economic dimension is not primary, then obviously the Marxian form of explanation is reductionistic and must result in an inadequate image of the social context.

The weakness of this conclusion is due to the fact that Habermas repeatedly asserts, but never demonstrates, his claim. If we are to grant that Marx extends his economic analysis beyond the range of its legitimate application, or the symmetrical claim that within a given social stage an interpretation based on the priority of the economic dimension of social reality necessarily leads to a distortion, then Habermas must show that non-economic factors enjoy co-equal status with economic ones. In the terms constitutive of his own analytical framework, he needs to demonstrate that the administrative apparatus is on the same plane as the economic structure of society; and he further needs to demonstrate—if this is his view—that both are founded in communication.

In the absence of the required demonstration, we are left with a choice, which cannot be favorable for Habermas, between his unsupported assertion on the one hand and Marx's detailed discussion of modern capitalism on the other. In other words, Habermas' effort here to argue that Marx's position is methodologically unsound suffers from a basic methodological flaw. For he assumes as the basis of his critique of Marx that his own alternative model must be accepted, although this remains to be shown. His critique fails to persuade since he does not demonstrate that Marx's analysis is incorrect, and he further does not prove that his own alternative need be adopted.

We can close our account of Habermas' critique of the labor theory of value with a final comment of his strategy. Our discussion has shown that he criticizes the Marxian value theory in order to undermine the position as a whole. If this is an accurate description of Habermas' intention, it is not an accident that his refutation of historical materialism fails. Marx's approach cannot be refuted through criticism of the labor theory of value. For his methodology, including his insistence on the explanatory significance of political economy associated with his distinction between superstructure and base, is completely independent of the validity of the value theory.

IX

THEORY, PRACTICE, AND THE RELEVANCE OF REASON

The two previous chapters were concerned with the evaluation of Habermas' approach to historical materialism from a philosophical perspective in terms of certain important economic issues and concepts. Now, in the proposed refutation of the labor theory of value, we saw that Habermas identifies problems leading him to renounce historical materialism as an even possibly viable theory; but he continues to identify with his interpretation of the theory's aim. In view of this identification, it is reasonable to regard his own position, especially the theory of communicative action, as an effort to achieve by other means what historical materialism only intended to reach.

This insight provides a clue toward a perspective useful for the further evaluation of Habermas' reading of historical materialism. Since Marx and Engels, one of its main themes has always been the relation of theory and practice [Praxis]. Habermas relies on this theme as a standard to differentiate historical materialism from other, more traditional forms of philosophical theory as early as the "Literaturbericht," and he raises this issue from another perspective in his investigations into the connection of knowledge and interest. Accordingly, the aim of this chapter is to evaluate his contribution to a basic Marxist theme: the problem of theory and practice.

At this point the evaluation goes beyond such issues as the interpretation and criticism of historical materialism to determine Habermas' success in his proposed effort to attain the ends of the theory with other means. His interpretation and criticism of Marx and Marxism are still relevant, but they are not the end in view. They play only a subordinate role as the means to a further end: the identification of unresolved problems within historical materialism. For the focus has shifted beyond the interpretation, criticism, and reconstruction of historical materialism, and in fact beyond the theory in any form, in order to consider proposed solutions for its traditional concerns in the form of Habermas' rival theory. His own position is clearly intended to provide solutions in a manner that does not fall prey to the difficulties already identified in historical materialism.[1]

In order to understand Habermas' contribution to the relation of theory and practice, it will be useful to describe the problem as understood within historical materialism, and then further to describe Habermas' reaction to it in a series of stages that includes his initial appeal to the concern with practice as a criterion to differentiate historical materialism from other forms of philosophical and social theory, his later critique of historical materialism in terms of its understanding of practice, and his still later effort to rethink the relation of theory and practice through a reformulation of the latter concept. The central notion which, from this perspective, links Habermas' reading of historical materialism with his effort to rethink the relation of theory and practice is an implicit appeal to a concept neither described in detail, or even named, which we can call the relevance of reason.

There is probably no issue in historical materialism which is more frequently mentioned than the issue of the relation of theory and practice. Surprisingly, it has rarely been studied in detail,[2] and even the precise meaning of the terms "theory" and "practice" is unclear. Within Marxist circles, we can further note an insufficient awareness of the link between their concern with the connection of theory and practice and the prior philosophical tradition, which in turn leads Marxists to exaggerate the novelty of their attention to this issue.[3]

The Marxist problem of the relation of theory to practice is only a recent form of a longstanding concern for the link between philosophy and politics, or life in the social context. This connection is already well developed in Greek philosophy, as witness the Socratic insistence on the inseparability of knowing and doing. Plato, who argued that the political community could not do without philosophy, raised the question of the extent to which it was in fact able to guide the state.[4] Aristotle, who did not contest the social utility of reason, argued that only the practical form of philosophy was practically relevant. According to Aristotle, pure reason, such as metaphysics, is useful for its own sake alone.[5] He further argued against Plato that ethics is an inexact, or approximative, science, unlike the pure, or theoretical, sciences.[6]

The theme of the relevance of philosophy for society reappeared in a new form in modern thought under the heading of the link between theory and practice. Now, although both Plato and Aristotle maintained the utility of philosophy in one or more forms for the social context, each was careful to maintain the separation of the realms of theory and practice. Plato, for instance, never confused the invisible realm of ideas with the world of visible appearances, what Merleau-Ponty called the visible and the invisible; Aristotle characteristically distinguished forms of theory as a function of different types of object, thereby opening the way for the Kantian differentiation of types of reason.

When Kant takes up the theme of the relation of philosophy and society, he adopts a more extreme position than either Plato or Aristotle. In fact, Kant proposes two divergent, incompatible analyses: the need to subordinate theory to practice, and the idea that theory entirely includes practice. On the one hand, he distinguishes forms of reason in order to argue for the dominance of practical reason over theory in a manner which is finally unsatisfactory.

On the other hand, he argues that practice never surpasses theory, which is completely adequate to resolve moral questions.

This latter belief is the source of the conviction underlying his ethical theory that any and all questions of how to act can be resolved on the plane of pure practical reason, that is, in the form of moral imperatives entirely devoid of content. This same belief further provides the basis for his view of philosophy, or philosophical reason, as intrinsically useful. According to Kant, the so-called cosmical concept of philosophy is a discipline which embodies the highest form of reason, but in which everyone, as he claims, necessarily has an interest. From this perspective he maintains that philosophy is not an abstract enterprise of no practical import; it is rather "the science of the relation of all knowledge to the essential ends of human reason [teleologia rationis humanae]" which makes of the philosopher "the lawgiver of human reason."[7]

Kant's unlimited faith in the practical utility of theoretical reason was arguably intended to dispel the doubts of Greek thinkers who regarded philosophy not as indispensable, but of limited worth. In the post-Kantian tradition, a more nuanced position, more restrictive than the Kantian view, was immediately sketched by Hegel. We can distinguish two stages in his understanding of the relation of philosophical reason to the social world. On the one hand, there is the early claim that philosophical concepts put themselves inexorably into practice, better known in Victor Hugo's memorable phrase that there is nothing so powerful in all the world as an idea whose time has come. On the other hand, several years later Hegel insists that philosophy cannot change the world since it only arrives after the fact.

These views have sometimes been seen as incompatible; in fact they are two aspects of a single underlying doctrine, namely, the belief that ideas precede their realization on the practical plane.[8] In this way, Hegel's more moderate view of the relevance of reason for social change represents a qualified return to the Greek view of reason as indispensable, but of limited utility for society.

This incomplete sketch of some main views of the relation of theory, especially philosophy, to the social context is not meant to take the place of a fuller account; it is rather meant to point to the considerable historical background that lies behind the distinctive rethinking of this problem in historical materialism. As an aid to comprehending the question of the relation of theory and practice in historical materialism, it will be useful to differentiate the views of practice associated with the positions of Marx and Engels, and to describe the general Marxian understanding of the problem of the relation of theory and practice.

Even before the rise of the Yugoslav form of Marxist humanism, a claim had been made for practice as the leading concept of Marx's thought.[9] Marx on occasion mentions practice, for instance in his sustained critique of the effects of capitalism, or in his analysis of the social role of absolute idealism. But with the exception of a brief statement in the so-called "Theses on Feuerbach," there is no sustained treatment of this concept in his writings and his view of it is unclear. The result is a paradoxical situation in which it is widely believed that practice is a crucial notion in Marx's theory, but there is considerable disagreement about its precise interpretation and, hence, about his position in general, in particular his analysis of the problem of theory and practice.

In the present context, there can be no pretense of discussing Marx's understanding of practice in general, even in outline. Suffice it to say that his view of this concept, which is incomplete as it stands, and is never 'thematized' in his writings, combines elements drawn from different sources ranging over themes as widely diverse as free activity in the social context, revolutionary activity which effects basic social change, a view of social life as essentially practical, and the pragmatic ascertainment of claims to truth.[10] In part Marx generalizes Aristotle's view of praxis as political activity of the citizen only, to apply to all human beings in a future form of society;[11] and he rejects Kant's claim that practical questions can be resolved on the theoretical level in favor of practice as the test of theory.[12]

The idea of practice is one of the most important differences separating the positions of Marx and Engels. In general terms, Marx's multifaceted understanding of practice is wider than Engels's well-known identification of the concept with industry in terms of a simple opposition of theory to practice, or the pragmatic, experiential determination of truth claims.[13] Engels's concern is never to formulate a general theory of human activity; his interest is mainly directed to understanding the relation of practice to philosophical theory as a test to unmask so-called idealist mythology, such as Kant's idea of the thing-in-itself.[14] Practice, for Engels, functions as a concept correlated with materialism, or science in general, as opposed to idealism, or ideology.

In comparison, Marx's view of practice is more often cited, but less well understood, more poorly delineated, and certainly less influential than Engels's concept on later Marxist thinkers. Now, it is not surprising, in view of the diverse ways in which "practice" is interpreted, that in the writings of Marx and Marxism there is no single text which provides a definitive overview of its relation to theory.

In Marx's writings, we can detect three general points, each of which is later elaborated in different ways in the Marxist analysis of the relation of theory and practice. These are the view that man is the root of man, which is the basis of his form of philosophical anthropology; the belief that for methodological reasons idealism is cut off from an adequate comprehension of practical life; and the assertion that a certain form of thought is distorted by its relation to a distorted kind of social context, which it reinforces instead of altering.

These insights form the bases for the differing, perhaps even incompatible, analyses of the relation of theory to practice associated respectively with the Frankfurt School; the classical Marxist view, represented by Engels and others in a form of neo-Kantian argument, that so-called bourgeois thought is incapable of understanding bourgeois reality and the equally widespread, classical Marxist assimilation of so-called bourgeois thought to mere ideology.

Habermas' contribution to the series of issues known collectively as the relation of theory to practice is a further development of the form of neo-
Marxism elaborated in the Frankfurt School approach. The latter derives from
Horkheimer's well-known distinction between what he called critical and traditional forms of theory. As concerns this problem, Habermas' effort is to
rethink the classical Frankfurt School distinction in a manner which combines
epistemologically and socially critical aspects within a single theory, or view
of reason in the full sense, as relevant.

In Habermas' writings on historical materialism we can differentiate three
phases in his discussion of this problem, including an initial description
of historical materialism in terms of a putative concern with the relation of
theory to practice, in tacit reference to the Frankfurt School dichotomy of
traditional and critical forms of theory; a later rethinking of the relation
of theory to practice which further elaborates the Frankfurt School dichotomy
in the form of a trichotomy featuring a distinction between work and interaction; and a final elaboration of the concept of interaction, or communication,
central both to his view of theory and to his revised analysis of its relation
to practice.

In the "Literaturbericht," Habermas' initial effort to describe the essential
features of historical materialism already presupposes the fundamental dichotomy which underlies critical theory. In a series of early essays from the 1930's,
especially in the discussion of "Traditional and Critical Theory," Horkheimer
established the basis for a so-called critical theory of society which runs
throughout the work of the Frankfurt School and continues to determine
Habermas' effort to contribute to the resolution of the problems of historical
materialism by other means.

In his seminal paper, Horkheimer opposed traditional and critical forms of
theory, as exemplified by Descartes's "Discourse on Method" and Marx's critique of political economy. According to Horkheimer, the former exhibits a
concern with universal, systematic science, and a tendency towards mathemat-
ization; the latter is a nontraditional conception in which human activity has
society itself for the object, there is an explicit awareness of the relation of
the individual to society, and stress is placed on the need to maintain a critical
attitude in order to strive for emancipation. He writes: "It is the task of the
critical theoretician to reduce the tension between his own insight and op-
pressed humanity in whose service he thinks."[15]

Among the members of the Frankfurt School, Habermas is arguably influenced more by Adorno and Marcuse than by Horkheimer, whom he rarely
mentions. Nevertheless, his effort in the early "Literaturbericht" to characterize historical materialism as a novel form of philosophy generally follows
Horkheimer's influential differentiation of critical theory from the philosophical background to which it continues to belong. Examples include stress on
the difference in kind between historical materialism and other forms of philosophy, an insistence that even in its critique of political economy historical

materialism remains philosophy, the conviction that the unity of theory and practice can only be grasped from the perspective of historical materialism, a basically antimetaphysical stance, and a concern with emancipation as a distinguishing feature of Marx and Marxism.

In subsequent writings, Habermas' repeated efforts to specify the particular nature of, and to criticize, historical materialism, continue to presuppose in various ways a difference in kind between historical materialism and traditional philosophy. But as early as his essay on Marxism as critique, his attitude toward the presumed dichotomy between historical materialism and traditional philosophy becomes seriously ambivalent. Here he continues the attempt he shares with Horkheimer and numerous other Marxists to describe historical materialism as relevantly different when he stresses that it is located between philosophy and science. But unlike Horkheimer and others, he now criticizes the theory for its specific difference with respect to the philosophical tradition, more precisely for an alleged failure to pose the Kantian epistemological question.

Horkheimer, of course, is clear that critical theory is superior to traditional theory as concerns the problem of human emancipation, which is his central concern. Hence, it is sufficient for his purposes to identify the ways in which so-called critical theory differs from its traditional predecessor. Habermas' hesitation arises from his attachment both to human emancipation and to epistemology from a Kantian perspective, as well as his desire to surrender neither in favor of the other. With respect to Horkheimer and other members of the first generation of the Frankfurt School, the ambivalence in Habermas' attitude toward the specific difference of historical materialism is evident in a more critical attitude toward Marx and Marxism, as well as toward the interpretation of their writings.

Horkheimer is no more than incidentally concerned with the Marxist discussion. Accordingly, one difference between Horkheimer and Habermas lies in the latter's interest in other interpretations of Marx and Marxism. In the "Literaturbericht" as well as in his other early texts on historical materialism, Habermas is initially occupied with writers on the theory and then with the theory itself, but not yet with the Marxist analysis of theory and practice. Significantly, at this point he is not critical of the issues concerning the relation of theory to practice. He seems content to insist on the link of historical materialism with human emancipation without raising the Kantian question of the possibility of the practical role that can be attributed to the theory.

In summary, it is clear that in the initial phase of his reading of historical materialism Habermas follows the Frankfurt School view of the theory, as exemplified in Horkheimer's classic statement, as different in kind from traditional theory. Although he is not uncritical with respect to the theory, which he evaluates from the standpoint of Kantian epistemology, he is not yet critical of its claim to provide a correct analysis of the relation of theory to practice. He only raises the Kantian question of the social utility of theory in the next phase of his study of the problem of theory and practice. This occurs in three texts: above all in the systematic discussion of the inaugural essay, in its restatement from a historical perspective, and, to a lesser extent, in the early article on Hegel.

These discussions, although interrelated, constitute elements of a general analysis of the relation of theory and practice, which he here rethinks under the heading of knowledge and interest, but which he never presents in the form of a single synthesis. In general terms, we can describe the development of his view of theory and practice as including an initial examination of the Frankfurt School dichotomy, in conjunction with a positive characterization of the relation of knowledge and interest through unconstrained dialogue; followed by a clarification of the concept of interest in German idealist and postidealist philosophy and psychoanalysis (Freud); and ending with a brief note on the link of dialogue and morality.

The different moments of this complex discussion comprise aspects of a single argument which progresses through a negative and then through a positive phase. Presupposing the dichotomy of critical and traditional theory, at first Habermas tries to rule out the claim for the relevance of reason in the traditional sense; later he constructs an analysis meant to show that critical reason in fact demonstrates its intrinsic relevance and, hence, provides the necessary unity of theory and practice.

In order to evaluate the second stage of the discussion of theory and practice, it will be useful to examine its component parts before commenting on it as a whole and in relation to the initial stage of the discussion. As concerns the second stage of the discussion, the systematic analysis of knowledge and interest is crucial. It is here that Habermas critically examines the relevance of historical materialism which he has earlier uncritically asserted as its defining characteristic. This text further contains the only argument he offers against the relevance of traditional theory as well as the general outline of the counterargument he proposes in favor of the relevance of a revised form of critical theory.

The argument against the relevance of traditional theory presupposes the well-known Frankfurt School dichotomy between traditional and critical theory—here exemplified by the opposition between the views of Husserl and Horkheimer—on which Habermas uncritically relied in his initial description of historical materialism. In noting the continuity between Husserl's insistence on the relevance of theory and Greek philosophy, Habermas tacitly suggests that the question of theory and practice has its roots in ancient thought; it is thus a continuing theme in modern and ancient philosophy, which historical materialism only prolongs from this perspective.

In this context he offers two objections to the traditional claim for the social utility of philosophy. First, he maintains that there is no disinterested reason; even in Greek philosophy this was at best a supposedly hollow pretense. Now, this criticism, if granted, does not help his argument, since it tends only to undercut the separation he desires to maintain between traditional and critical theory. Theory leads to knowledge; if all forms of knowledge are interested, and none is disinterested, then there can only be relative distinctions among forms of interest, since there are no radical separations, or distinctions in kind. In a word, the price of accepting this objection is to undercut the very distinction between traditional and critical theory which it presupposes.

Second, he attempts to turn Husserl's concept of objectivism against Husserl's own position which, according to Habermas, only uncritically assumes the relevance of reason. Above we have argued that Habermas misinterprets the concept of objectivism in his effort to turn it against Husserl. There is no need to repeat that argument here. At present it is sufficient to note the relation of his criticism of Husserl to the negative argument he makes against the relevance of traditional theory as represented by Husserl's position.

Now, the most this objection could prove is that Husserl does not go far enough in his examination of the relevance of theory which, following Plato especially, he merely posits. To show that the relevance of reason has not been demonstrated is not the same as showing that the required demonstration cannot be carried out. If the relevance of reason is uncritically assumed, but not established, it does not follow that traditional reason is unrelated to practice; it merely follows that the relation has not been demonstrated.

We can summarize our remarks on the negative phase of the argument as follows: Habermas does not show the traditional theory is irrelevant to practice. It remains to be seen if he can argue successfully for the relevance of critical theory. The positive phase of the argument, which is independent of the success of his effort to discredit noncritical, presumably traditional, forms of theory receives its first, general statement in this text and a later elaboration in succeeding writings.

The positive, or constructive, phase of the argument is meant to demonstrate the relation of knowledge to interest, or theory to practice. In that sense, his tacit intention is to bring to a close the controversy surrounding a theme which has been extensively discussed since the origins of the philosophical tradition. As concerns this particular problem, Habermas implicitly portrays historical materialism in a manner similar to the Young Hegelian view of Hegel, that is as in a sense ending the philosophical tradition.[16]

Habermas' analysis of the relation of knowledge to interest is not general, since he holds that so-called traditional theory, as exemplified in Husserl's position, is insufficiently critical and even unconsciously positivistic in its putative fall into objectivism. In his positive argument, he adopts the restricted perspective of a critical theory understood in terms of his own reformulation of Horkheimer's classic distinction.

Habermas' constructive analysis of the problem of theory and practice turns on a reinterpretation of the nature of dialogue in order to demonstrate what he regards as the inseparable connection of knowledge and interest. We can provide a retrospective reconstruction of his account in terms of two main elements: his revision here and elsewhere of Horkheimer's distinction in trichotomous form, and the series of theses that Habermas offers in his inaugural essay. The former speaks in general to the relation of a kind of knowledge and interest, and the latter refines that relation in a series of partial descriptions.

Habermas' revision of Horkheimer's distinction carries further the concern, which extends backward over Kant at least until Aristotle, to classify types of (philosophical) theory in terms of their objects and methods. The proposed reformulation supplements Horkheimer's differentiation of critical and non-critical theory through a further differentiation of the latter, modeled on Dilthey's well-known distinction between natural and social, or human sciences, [Geisteswissenschaften]. Dilthey's distinction apparently derives from Droysen's separation of speculative, physical, and historical methods, respectively intended to know, to explain, and to understand.[17]

In his elaboration of Horkheimer's view, Habermas, who does not mention Droysen, comes close to the latter's trichotomous distinction, in which the speculative method, interpreted as intrinsic to critical theory, differs in kind from the methods associated with traditional forms of theory. Apparently following Droysen, Habermas maintains that the two latter forms of theory are concerned with types of knowledge peculiar to their respective domains, that is, in his terminology, either, as in the case of natural, or empirical-analytic sciences, with technical-cognitive interests; or, in the case of the social, or historical-hermeneutic, sciences, with a practical interest.[18]

Habermas is consistent in his attempted correlation of forms of theory with forms of interest, since he denies that knowledge and interest are separable. In his view all types of knowledge are related to practice, but only critical theory is intrinsically linked to human emancipation. In the context of a comparative analysis of the positions of Husserl and Horkheimer, the intended correlation of human emancipation and critical theory is meant to uphold the latter's original distinction; but the argument is controversial.

Habermas maintains that critical theory is intrinsically linked with the interests of humanity in a different, or deeper, manner than is the case for other forms of theory.[19] His conviction is in tension with his argument elsewhere—ostensibly following an aspect of Marx's thought not taken up in the final version of the theory—that science and technology play a positive role in social development, the growth of human freedom, and the rendering possible of a transition to democratic socialism. The result is an obvious dilemma: either it is the case that noncritical kinds of thought contribute to human emancipation, which in turn undercuts the proposed correlation of forms of theory and forms of interest; or the proposed correlation stands, but only critical theory is linked to the emancipation of humanity.

The suggested correlation of critical theory only with human emancipation goes beyond Horkheimer's original view, which it is arguably meant to defend and to elaborate. The latter never maintained that the future of humanity depended on critical theory; he rather believed that it rested on the existence of a so-called critical attitude, not to be conflated with a single form of theory, which includes as well elements drawn from traditional theories and the supposedly dying culture.[20]

Habermas, who fails to notice the distinction between a critical attitude, which can be associated with any form of theory, and the so-called critical variation on theory in general, conflates the two halves of this distinction; it is perhaps for this reason that he wants to limit the correlation of human emancipation to critical theory only instead of attempting to determine if there is a particular, that is, relevantly different, kind of social utility associated with critical theory.

Habermas' trichotomous reformulation of Horkheimer's original distinction does not establish that only critical theory is connected to human emancipation. The more interesting issue, which is independent of any claim for exclusivity, is the positive argument in favor of a link between critical theory and human emancipation. In his inaugural lecture Habermas argues for this link in two stages, including an initial clarification of his understanding of critical theory, followed by a series of theses meant to demonstrate the claimed relation of knowledge and interest manifested in this form of theory.

In his clarification, Habermas follows Horkheimer's association of critical theory with the resistance to ideology. According to Horkheimer, the only advantage of critical theory for this task lies in its concern to abolish social injustice.[21] Habermas now broadens Horkheimer's view in two ways: by associating critical theory with other endeavors to pierce the veil of social illusion, and by linking the required effort to self-reflection.

Habermas maintains that the critique of ideology, which here functions as a pseudonym for both critical theory and historical materialism, shares with psychoanalysis the goal of reflection on ideologically frozen relations of dependence.[22] But if both critical theory and psychoanalysis aim at human autonomy through reflection, and if such reflection is a defining characteristic of critical social theory, then it cannot be the case that historical materialism is the only form of critical theory linked to human emancipation. Habermas now admits this point when he suggests that a form of philosophy which turns away from a presuppositionless analysis of ontology is also engaged in the same task.

If we bracket the many issues raised by a joint description of critical theory, psychoanalysis, and philosophy, we can paraphrase his main point as an assertion of the liberating power of self-reflection concerned with human being, or in Habermas' terminology, with an emancipatory cognitive interest. As noted, in this text he argues for the relation of knowledge and interest in a series of five theses. Since he interprets critical theory in a wide sense that allegedly goes beyond historical materialism, we cannot evaluate his argument from the traditional Marxist perspective; we need rather to evaluate his argument as an analysis of the allegedly intrinsic connection of knowledge with interest, that is, as a metatheory of the relation of theory and practice under the sign of human emancipation.

Habermas seems to think that he is staking out an alternative to a well-known position, widely represented in the history of philosophy. But it is unclear if anyone has actually held the view he desires to refute. His analysis apparently supposes what probably no one has ever denied, namely, that knowledge is intrinsically related to interest. It is true that in his ethical writings Kant suggested that there can be an interest which urges us to follow the ideas of morality; but he clearly meant a subjective, or personal, interest, since he insisted on the value, indeed the necessity, of acting according to the objective dictates determined by pure practical reason.[23] Even Aristotle, who distinguished pure and practical forms of theory, accepted the intrinsic relation of knowledge and interest. He only intended to deny the Platonic view that theory as such is useful, since according to Aristotle only some of its types have an end beyond the knowledge process itself.

The problem at hand, then, is not to establish the relation of knowledge to interest, but rather to arrive at a proper understanding of that relation. In his clarification Habermas does not need to demonstrate a relation of knowledge to interest either in general or as established through self-reflection; he does need to demonstrate that through critical self-reflection this relation furthers human emancipation. In other words, he must show that a particular form of the link of knowledge to interest provides a socially effective connection of theory with practice.

In order to show the relation of emancipatory-cognitive knowledge to interest, Habermas contends that critical self-reflection will pierce the veil of ideological illusion. Now, the terms "critical" and "critique" are essential to the argument; they are meant to distinguish a form of self-reflection allegedly linked to the development of human freedom from self-reflection in general, for instance in Husserl's phenomenology, which supposedly deceives itself about the relevance of pure theory.

At this point Habermas, following Horkheimer and Korsch, does not use such terms as "critical" and "critique" to refer to the characteristically Kantian transcendental meditation on the conditions of possibility whatsoever; rather he employs these terms to indicate a concern with emancipation and its real conditions. But a concern with self-reflection as such is different from an interest in self-reflection on the problem of human freedom, which in turn differs from an awareness of its real conditions. If Habermas desires to avoid the abstract Kantian approach to human being, he needs to respect these distinctions.

In order to make out a distinction between theory following from self-reflection in general and that which derives from critical self-reflection, Habermas must address the relation of the latter to practice. It is well known that in his ethical theory Kant was concerned, but manifestly unable, to demonstrate that happiness follows from morality since he could not establish the transition from pure practical reason to practical reason. It is arguable that since his analysis applies equally to all situations without regard to their particular conditions, it applies to none; in a word, he was unable to demonstrate the relation of his theory to practice.

Habermas, who raises this problem against Husserl and, by implication, other representatives of traditional theory, must meet it in his own thought.

To avoid the reduction of the link between critical self-reflection and knowledge to a simple truism—or a statement which is analytically true but devoid
of practical significance—he needs to show that, beyond mere theoretical
awareness, critical theory in fact practically contributes to human emancipation; but this he cannot do.

Habermas' list of five theses elucidates the relation of knowledge to interest;
but it does not shed light on the relation of critical theory to practice and,
hence, fails to establish the crucial difference in the relation of critical and noncritical forms of theory to practice. He accuses traditional theory in general,
and Husserl in particular, of a quasi-positivistic disavowal of reflection, manifested in an inability to clarify the relevance of reason to practice; but his own
analysis of the relation of critical theory and interest is hoist with the same
petard. His analysis is subject to the kind of objection he brings against Husserl
and others since he does not demonstrate the difference between the interest
supposedly intrinsic in theory in all its forms and the specifically emancipatory
interest inherent in critical theory.

Even a rapid review of the theses in question shows that only the fourth
among them directly addresses the suggested link between self-reflection,
knowledge, and interest. The first one, or the claim that the transcendental
subject is rooted in natural history, is a revised formulation of Husserl's analysis of the link, mediated in his theory by phenomenological reduction, between the transcendental plane and the life-world. The second thesis, namely
the assertion that knowledge is an instrument transcending mere self-
preservation, is only denied in the putative attempt by Nietzsche and his followers to reduce epistemology to biology. The statement in the third thesis
that different forms of interest appear in different ways is an application of
Habermas' familiar triple distinction. The last member on the list, or the view
that the unity of knowledge and interest can be established retrospectively
through a dialectical reconstruction of a suppressed dialogue, presupposes, for
instance, in such cases as ideological distortion or psychoanalytic repression,
that hidden concerns can be retrospectively revealed.

Habermas' main effort to demonstrate the relation of theory and practice
occurs in connection with his fourth thesis, or the statement that in self-
reflection knowledge and interest come together. His demonstration, which
consists of a two-step analysis of the concept of self-reflection, resembles the
German idealist association of consciousness and certainty. It is well known
that Fichte, in opposition to Kant, reintroduced a notion of intellectual intuition in order to ground consciousness in self-consciousness. In similar fashion,
Habermas appeals to an immediate intuition of the relation of knowledge and
interest in self-reflection, which he regards as theoretically certain and as the
measure of all other forms of cognition.

The argument for the link between knowledge and interest allegedly revealed with certainty in self-reflection does not speak to a connection with
human emancipation. Habermas argues for this connection through extremely brief remarks on maturity [Mündigkeit], discourse, and language. He

maintains that at least in German idealism reason is linked to the will to reason, speech necessarily aims at possible agreement, and speech presupposes maturity. Since self-reflection is formulated in speech, it follows that knowledge and interest presuppose as well the goal of emancipation.

For present purposes it is unnecessary to examine in detail this controversial argument. We can restrict ourselves to comments on the argument in general and its relation to the problem of theory and practice. On the one hand, if the argument is successful it proves too much by stultifying Habermas' effort to make out a particular role for critical theory, and hence undercutting the purpose of his familiar triple distinction. If speech is intrinsically linked to human emancipation, the fact that it is common to all kinds of theory, and to practical life as well, widens the range of phenomena linked to the attainment of maturity to all forms of verbal activity.

On the other hand, even if the argument is successful it does not prove enough. An analysis of the connection of reason with an interest in human emancipation casts no light on the relation of theory and practice. Like Kant, whose influence is clear in the remark on the inseparable connection between reason and the will to reason, [24] at this point Habermas merely asserts, but does not analyze, the relevance of reason to practice.

In summary, the initial phase of the positive analysis of the problem of theory and practice, stated in the inaugural lecture, founders on Habermas' inability to relate one to the other, that is, on his incapacity to show the practical relevance of theoretical reason. Accordingly, the first part of his constructive attempt to show that critical theory differs from its traditional variant in its ability to contribute to human emancipation fails to convince. In a later phase, in the third part of *Knowledge and Human Interests*, appropriately entitled "Critique as the Unity of Knowledge and Interest," he supplements his earlier discussion of this relation through an analysis of its development in modern German philosophy.

His discussion here both surpasses and remains on the same plane as his initial effort to analyze knowledge and interest. It surpasses his previous discussion in various ways, such as in his remarks on the relation of interest and human emancipation, and in a historical analysis of the idea of interest in German thought, including Freudian psychoanalysis. The latter leads Habermas to accept what he regards as the Freudian inversion of the traditional philosophical relation of knowledge and interest, which he further defends against Nietzsche's alleged biological reductionism. But his later discussion also shares its predecessor's inability to clarify the relation of theory to practice.

In general, the entire discussion of the concept of interest in German thought from Kant to Nietzsche and Freud can be described as a complex defense of the notion of self-reflection in Fichte against Nietzsche's effort, allegedly influenced by Hegel, to turn reason against itself on the one hand, and to argue for the relevance of critical reason on the other. A helpful feature of this double argument is a series of comments intended to clarify the concept of interest, which Habermas has previously treated as an undefined primitive term in his discussion. He now defines "interest"—in terms reminiscent of Marx's definition of human being as the being which differs from other animals in the production of its means of subsistence[25]—as the concern with the solution of the general problems posed by the reproduction and self-constitution of the human species.[26]

His definition here conflicts with his earlier description of interest in less restrictive terms and further undermines his effort to link the critical theory to human emancipation. His characterization at this point of interest in relation to the maintenance of life is in tension with his earlier, broader view of this notion, noted in the second thesis, as linked to life and to a better life.[27] In restricting interest to the production and reproduction of the species, it is unclear how interest is supposed to relate to the human emancipation which aims at the reorganization of the social context as the condition, not of living, but of living better, or living well.

Habermas develops his idea of interest against the background of its evolution in German thought beginning with Kant. He maintains that Kant has no coherent idea of interest; and he further maintains that Fichte is the first to propose a concept of an emancipatory interest intrinsic to acting reason.[28] In other words, even before Marx, by implication Fichte is the first representative of a critical theory which conjoins self-reflection with emancipatory interest. In that sense, he goes beyond Hegel who, although he follows Fichte, fails to realize that the conditions of human life surpass the connection of knowledge and interest. In effect, Habermas adopts an analysis of the relation of theory and practice he perceives in Fichte's thought as the high point of the effort to deal with this problem in German idealism.

Habermas' reading of the evolution of German philosophy from the perspective of the concept of interest is meant to discover in Fichte's thought his own view of critical theory concerned with emancipatory-cognitive interests. He points out that Fichte unifies theoretical and practical reason; identifies theory with interest; and interprets interest as emancipation, that is, as emancipation from dogmatism. Accordingly, he asserts that Fichte differs from Kant in a concern with, in Habermas' words, the independence of the ego operative in reason itself.[29] According to Habermas, Fichte for the first time makes interest constitutive of knowing and acting;[30] or, as he also says, without reference to Fichte, the conditions of instrumental and communicative action are those of the possibility of objective knowledge.[31]

In order to assess the contribution of his view of the evolution of the concept of interest to the problem of theory and practice, we do not require any further general comment on his interpretation of Fichte. We need rather to address two issues relevant to the proposed depiction of Fichte as the forerunner, within German idealism, of Habermas' understanding of critical theory: the sense in which Fichte turns away from Kant in the direction of historical materialism, and the related sense in which he can be said to surpass German idealism in order to achieve a genuine resolution of the problem of theory and practice.

The proposed description of Fichte as an early representative of critical theory rests on what is arguably an exaggeration of the difference between critical and transcendental philosophy, conjoined with a hasty assimilation of the latter to historical materialism. Fichte understands the opposition of idealism to dogmatism in a Kantian sense as that of fully critical reason opposed to belief undemonstrated by reason alone, which is not to be conflated with the ideological appearance of truth.

Since Fichte did not possess a concept of the distortion of thought by its relation to the social context, his concept of self-reflection is unrelated to lifting the ideological veil that is a prominent theme in Marx and Marxism. Emancipation of the ego in the sense Habermas identifies in Fichte's thought is unlike emancipation in the Marxian sense. More precisely, for Fichte self-reflection is not directly related to social emancipation subsequent to the achievement of an awareness of the true structure of the social context or, more generally, to an appreciation of what Habermas calls the (ideologically) frozen relations of dependence.

Perhaps because he overestimates the distance between Fichte and Kant, Habermas further overestimates Fichte's contribution to the problem of theory and practice. At this point in his development, Habermas continues to regard materialism, and its supposedly fundamental revision of the idealist concept of practice, as an improvement in kind on idealism. He states his belief here in the remark that the self-constitution of the human species cannot be expressed as the movement of self-reflection.[32]

Now, in Habermas' interpretation, Fichte's unified conception of reason is merely a proposed solution to a difficulty arising within the critical philosophy. From his perspective, Fichte does not unify theory and practice in the way in which these terms have traditionally been understood within historical materialism, that is, as basically different; he merely brings together two forms of reason which Kant differentiated and then later failed to unify. As Lukács would say, Fichte achieves a unity of theory and practice in theory, but not a unity in practice.[33]

Fichte thus remains on the terrain of German idealism and does not rise to Habermas' understanding of the plane of critical theory. In fact, in his view of the unity of theory and practice Fichte makes a qualified return to the ancient Socratic doctrine of the identity of knowing and doing, in which self-determination according to the principles of reason alone and action in conformity with such principles—which Kant distinguished in his concepts of pure practical reason and practical reason—are inseparably conjoined.

There is an obvious tension between the claim that Fichte demonstrates the unity of theory and practice, and the assertion of a difference in kind between idealism and materialism. Since Fichte is an idealist, he cannot solve a problem that allegedly can only be resolved on the post-idealist level of materialism. From Habermas' angle of vision, Fichte resembles other idealists by remaining within reason and in failing to effect the transition to practice.

Habermas makes this point in the invidious comparison of the view attributed to Fichte, that is, of an absolute ego which produces itself and its world, to Hegel's analysis of phenomenological experience.[34] There is a clear implication that Fichte does not even reach the level of Hegel's idealism, which differs in kind from materialism. But the result is a clear contradiction since either Fichte demonstrates the unity of theory and practice and he is not an idealist, or he is an idealist and he fails to provide the needed demonstration; he cannot be both.

In his remarks on the evolution of the concept of interest in German idealism, Habermas arrives at the insight, which he attributes to Fichte, that reason grasps itself as interested in self-reflection. He further clarifies the relation of reason and interest in his comments on Freud and Nietzsche. According to Habermas, idealism teaches that interest inheres in reason, but it is reason that inheres in interest;[35] he believes that Freud's study of the interest of self-preservation shows that reason depends upon it.[36] Nietzsche, on the contrary, supposedly psychologized the connection of knowledge with interest in order to deny reflection,[37] in the process availing himself of self-reflection in order to deny its possibility.[38]

From the vantage point of the notion of interest and its relation to knowledge, the comments on Freud and Nietzsche serve different purposes. The brief discussion of Nietzsche is an occasion to reject a well-known critique of reflection on the grounds of inconsistency. Habermas uses Freud to invert the relation of knowledge and interest in German idealism. Now, as concerns this relation, there is an obvious tension in the proposed inversion since Habermas' own interpretation denies the existence of an opposition between German idealism in general and Freud.

On the contrary, in terms of Habermas' reading of the principal figures of German idealism, there is an opposition between Kant and Freud since, in effect, he depicts Fichte as anticipating the latter's view of the dependency of reason on interest. He points out in his comparative analysis of Kant and Fichte, that in the latter's position reason loses its secondary character and becomes constitutive of knowing and acting; as a result interest acquires precedence over knowledge[39] and, hence, we can add, over reason. Although these remarks further clarify Habermas' comprehension of knowledge and interest, they do not contribute to the analysis of theory and practice.

In order to evaluate Habermas' contribution to the traditional theme of theory and practice we have so far examined three phases of his discussion: the first description of historical materialism in the "Literaturbericht;" his initial analysis of knowledge and interest in his inaugural lecture; and his further, historically oriented elaboration of this text.

In the "Literaturbericht" we have noted his uncritical assumption of Horkheimer's distinction between traditional and critical theory as the criterion employed to differentiate historical materialism from other forms of philosophy, especially metaphysics, or ontology. This distinction further provides the basis for his examination of knowledge and interest in the inaugural lecture. As concerns the relation of theory and practice, we have considered his argument that traditional theory cannot, and critical theory does, provide a view of relevant reason. We have further commented on his attempted clarification of knowledge and interest in remarks on German idealism, Nietzsche, and Freud.

Our examination of his contribution to the problem of theory and practice presupposes that it differs in kind from the relation of knowledge and interest. Throughout we have argued, most forcefully in a review of his constructive effort to show that the critical form of reason is relevant, that Habermas' multistage clarification of the relation of knowledge and interest does not surpass the plane of German idealism; it accordingly does not resolve the problem of theory and practice as it has traditionally been understood in historical materialism.

In effect, and despite his later professed intention to discard German idealism, which is arguably exhausted, in favor of a new paradigm, his discussion paradoxically constitutes a new contribution to this traditional problem from a closely idealist perspective. Habermas, as noted, is quick to accuse other thinkers of misunderstanding their own positions, which by implication he understands better than their authors. But at least as concerns the theme of theory and practice, it appears that Habermas misunderstands the nature of his own position, which he incorrectly regards as opposed to, and not as continuous with, German idealism.

In his writings, the claim for the break between his own position and German idealism is based on two suppositions: the oft-repeated statement of the difference in kind between materialism, including its historical form in Marx and Marxism, and idealism, which has traditionally been constitutive of historical materialism's self-interpretation; and the incompatibility of both with communicative action, which Habermas presents as a kind of *tertium quid*, basically unlike either the Hegelian view of consciousness or its rejection by Nietzsche. As might be expected, the fourth and most recent phase of his contribution to the problem of theory and practice occurs in his subsequent writings on communicative action.

Communicative action is another name for interaction. The argument for the relevance of this form of reason begins prior to his massive treatise on communicative action, in the critique of Marx's supposed inability to separate work and interaction. Obviously any claim for the significance of Marx's reduction of interaction to work presupposes the importance of interaction.

In *Knowledge and Human Interests*, there are occasional comments on communicative action, for instance in the remarks on Dilthey's view of interpersonal action as mediated by symbols which finally refer to language;[40] but there is no attempt to pursue the relevance of communicative action as a form of critical reason in the context of the discussion of knowledge and interest. At this point, Habermas is content to pursue his effort to demonstrate the relevance of critical reason, as distinguished from critical philosophy without specifically invoking his own rival theory, which he did not yet possess. A more overt, but still circumspect argument for the relevance of communicative action is implicit in his later treatise on this theme, especially in his critique of Marxian value theory.

We can restate his argument for the relevance of communicative action in terms of Habermas' view of its relation to historical materialism and to critical theory. In both cases he argues for a similar connection of his own theory to views which his own was earlier meant to prolong; in each case his theory is still meant to carry out the intrinsic intent of a position he earlier accepted but now rejects.

Through the critique of Marxian value theory, Habermas rejects historical materialism in favor of his own theory, which is intended to fulfill the goals of Marx and Marxism by other means. These goals specifically still include a concern with social relevance, earlier correlated with human emancipation through revolution, which putatively distinguishes historical materialism from traditional theory. Through the rejection of the critical theory of Horkheimer and Adorno, he gives up the original form of critical theory while maintaining a new form of its seminal distinction between traditional and critical theory; and he maintains as well his attachment to what he earlier described as an emancipatory-cognitive interest.

The familiar seminal distinction now assumes a new shape as a difference between traditional theory, as well as historical materialism and the classical form of critical theory on the one hand, and the new form of critical theory, as exemplified in communicative action, on the other. This new version of critical theory under the heading of communicative action differs from the original formulation in a crucial respect. Marx's attempt to lay bare the anatomy of capitalism is an integral part of Horkheimer's original understanding of the difference between traditional and critical theory. According to Horkheimer, in respect to contemporary society the critical theory must begin with the characterization of an economy based on exchange, as exemplified in Marxian political economy.[41]

We have already noted that Habermas follows Lukács's view of the theoretical superiority of Marx's approach to commodity analysis, but he rejects the value theory upon which it is based. His argument for the relevance of his new form of critical theory as communicative action by implication eschews a reliance either on Marx's or on any other form of economic analysis. Now, an important difference between Marx's position and German idealism has always been expressed in terms of Marx's attention to the economic dimension of reality, which the latter supposedly either ignores or does not fully grasp. Hence, the result of the revision of the concept of critical theory is to move Habermas' view ever closer to the mainline German philosophical tradition which, paradoxically, he simultaneously attempts to reject.

We can bring out this point through a contrast between the different ways in which Horkheimer and Habermas are critical thinkers. Marxists, including Horkheimer, have always linked a belief in the relevance of Marx's thought to its economic dimension. Now, a rejection of the economic approach to social reality does not in itself undermine the pretension of a theory to be critical in Horkheimer's sense. Unlike many others interested in historical materialism, Horkheimer never thought of critical theory in exclusively economic terms. But unlike Habermas, who through his critique of historical materialism seems here to reject the very idea of an economic approach to social theory, Horkheimer continued to insist on the need for critical theory to take shape within an economic understanding of capitalism.[42]

There is a further difference in the respective views of the usefulness of critical theory. Horkheimer located its supposed relevance in the task of reducing the tension between insight and social oppression, in short, in the supposed power of true consciousness to overcome the difference between what is and what ought to be. This view of critical social reflection maintains an obvious connection with Lukács's concept of revolutionary class consciousness and the Marxian idea of truth as a contrast to ideology. In contrast, Habermas associates the utility of communicative action with its presumed capacity to provide a more adequate social theory in a concept of society which is not subject to the criticisms he has earlier advanced against historical materialism, including Marx's position as well as forms of Marxism.

When Habermas suggests the relevance of communicative action—through its putative ability to carry out with other means what historical materialism intended, but failed to do—he seems mainly to have in mind the elaboration of an adequate social theory as an end in itself. Rather than insisting on human emancipation through social change, he stresses the relevance of communicative action in such areas as a capacity to understand the relation of a monetary form of economy—including the contradiction of wages and capital—to an administrative level which takes up into itself and, hence, grounds money and power;[43] a proposed need to abandon the old paradigm of goal-directed activity as fundamental to social activity in favor of a qualitatively different theory of communicative action;[44] and a new view of social theory which replaces the monism of the value theory by a complex form of dualism.[45]

For Habermas, his theory of communicative action provides the necessary basis to overcome the theoretical problems criticized in other forms of social theory in a new and better view. But an explicit consideration of the social impact of correct social theory which was central in historical materialism in Marx's writings and in all forms of Marxism, and which still retains its central role in Horkheimer's understanding of critical theory, has here receded into the background.

If this interpretation is correct, we can detect in Habermas' view of communicative action a position which basically differs from a main current of historical materialism and classical critical theory, and rethinks the relation of theory and practice in a nontraditional way. Marx and many of his followers have often regarded the problem of theory and practice in relation to the question of a social revolution. Since Habermas' understanding of communicative action aims only, or at least mainly, at an adequate social theory, it does not share Marx's concern to substitute communism for capitalism through a social revolution if necessary; in Habermas' writings, the newest form of critical theory apparently abandons the aim at fundamental social change, for which it substitutes the goal of viable social theory supposedly intrinsic to, but not attained by, historical materialism.

Now, in itself this difference does not mean that communicative action is not a critical theory since Horkheimer, for instance, was not concerned to link the critique of society to revolutionary action only, or even mainly. In fact, the problem of revolution as such is not a main theme in his thought. But Habermas apparently transgresses Horkheimer's deepest conviction that a form of philosophy which finds peace within itself, in other words, which has itself as its object, has nothing to do with critical theory.[46]

In his suggestion that the aim of communicative action is a better social theory, like Horkheimer Habermas takes society as his object, although he separates its comprehension from a basic concern with the transformation of society. It follows that what was earlier described as the aim at social emancipation through knowledge incorporating cognitive-emancipatory interests now survives only, in the theory of communicative action, in the guise of a conceptually adequate view of society.

It follows that for Habermas true theory is relevant to social emancipation since reason, or in this case the form of social reason embodied in the view of communicative action, is relevant.[47] In this way, Habermas, who objected in the inaugural essay to the traditional view of reason as relevant, comes full circle by returning to a form of the so-called traditional view, now reformulated as the tacit claim that so-called critical social reason, or a critical theory of society, is relevant.

This understanding of social reason as relevant does not break, but only strengthens, the connection, already noted, of Habermas' view of communicative action to German idealism and beyond that to the Socratic view of the inseparability of knowing and doing. As was earlier the case, so here as well Habermas understands the relation of reason and activity, or action, as two sides of the same basic phenomenon.

It is true that he no longer speaks of knowledge, interest, and self-reflection. But although his language has changed, his concern has not since he is still oriented toward a defense of unimpeded thought in terms of the Enlightenment model elaborated by Kant. This commitment is evident here above all in his suggestion, noted earlier, that not only must social theory be based on communicative action, but in an undefined sense the social context is based on it as well.

Habermas' return toward, or rather failure to break free from, the German idealist view of reason determines the relation of his concept of communicative action to the problem of theory and practice. He attempts now to minimize in various ways the differences which separate his own position from historical materialism. In his statements that he only means to free historical materialism from its historical ballast[48] and to clarify the normative basis of critical theory,[49] he suggests a direct continuity between his own thought and historical materialism in general.[50] But he is mistaken about the extent to which his own view, which is clearly inspired by years of thought about the problems of Marx and Marxism, remains within its conceptual orbit.

Certainly, as already noted, there is a clear break with respect to the problem of theory and practice. He maintains, for instance, that in his own position he follows Marx's model of a theory critical with respect to the contemporary social sciences as well as the reality they are intended to comprehend.[51] Now, it is well known that Hegel desired to surpass mere subjectivity for objectivity. This is a central theme in his criticism of Kant and Fichte. Yet as concerns the problem of theory and practice, Hegel accorded a primacy to theory, not because, as Horkheimer would say, he was a conformist in thought who regarded thinking as a self-enclosed realm;[52] he rather preferred theory to practice on practical grounds since, as he wrote in a famous letter, once formulated ideas tend to realize themselves.[53]

Marx shared Hegel's conviction that theory must be made an effective social force, although he believed that Hegel had failed in this task. While it is not clear that Marx understood Hegel's view of the efficacy of theory, it is clear that he strongly opposed it. As concerns the question of theory and practice, Marx accused Hegel in effect of attempting to resolve problems solely on the level of thought, which Hegel confused with reality. Like Hegel before him Marx sought, if not always perspicuously, to go beyond theory to practice, in order to surpass mere interpretation for real social change.

This desire is evident in various ways, for instance, in the famous, but obscure, last of the "Theses on Feuerbach," and in the turn to the proletariat as the indispensable instrument of basic social change, through a putatively Christian view of self-sacrifice similar to the Pauline concept of kenosis.[54] If we bracket the complex question of the extent to which Marx remains an idealist, we can note an at least intended opposition between his position and (earlier) idealism, especially Hegel's view, as concerns the problem of theory and practice.

With respect to this problem, Habermas' view of communicative action is basically unlike either the Marxian doctrine of social change through action, as distinguished from theory, or the Hegelian doctrine of theory as an effective force. On the contrary, Habermas clearly offers his view as a theory of social practice, which will comprehend society without changing it. He earlier maintained that historical materialism differed from traditional philosophy by refusing metaphysics in a theory of history with practical intent. But his view of communicative action abandons the supposedly no longer relevant theory of history in order to take up again the theme of capitalistic modernization through an alternative to historical materialism.[55] The fruitfulness of the theory of communicative action is not said to lie in its ability to transform the social context; rather it is held to lie in its capacity to understand the social context by stimulating various forms of research in the social sciences and in philosophy under the heading of social theory.[56]

There is an obvious evolution in the concept of critical theory in this stage of his thought. "Critical social theory" no longer means "the opposition to what is the case in terms of what ought to be"; it rather means "the rejection of dogmatic, or otherwise epistemologically insufficient, forms of social theory in favor of the most rigorous possible epistemological view," arguably exemplified in the latest form of communicative action, in order to comprehend, not reality as a whole, but the social context. In the theory of communicative action, action has lost its distinction from reason and become a theory which knows its object; from this perspective social action is a theory of society.

The elaboration of critical theory as communicative action does not suppress the distinction between traditional and critical thought, which still remains visible in the difference between theoreticians who are unaware, and those who are aware of and consciously desire to correct, social injustice; but it suppresses the distinction between traditional and critical theory. In Habermas' thought critical theory, like the traditional theory from which it earlier emerged, again relies for the justification of its claim for social utility on a presumed, but undemonstrated, relevance of reason.

From the perspective of theory and practice, we can conclude that the theory of communicative action obviously differs from historical materialism, since the former is not intended as a unified theory of the relation of theory and practice in order to change practice from the plane of theory; it is rather intended as a critical, that is, rigorous, theory of practice. Hence, Habermas' contribution is not to resolve the problem of the relation of theory and practice as understood in historical materialism, since he reinterprets it in a characteristically Kantian sense as the specification of the conditions of knowledge of the social world. On the contrary, his contribution lies in the effort to take up again the theme of the comprehension of the social context in terms of the epistemological standards introduced in the critical philosophy—and allegedly perpetuated in contemporary analytic thought—which he attempts to apply in the realm of social theory. In sum, Habermas' contribution to the problem of theory and practice is to provide a theory of social practice which adheres to rigorous epistemological standards within the sphere of social theory, and which, if reason is relevant to society, presumably remains socially relevant.

CONCLUSION
THE RELEVANCE OF REASON

An aim of this discussion of Habermas' reading of historical materialism is to study an approach to Marx and Marxism which is important in itself and for the light it sheds on his own theory of communicative action. Since the beginning of the Marxist tradition in Engels's writings, many of the most significant contributions to Marxism have emerged from the interpretation of Marx's thought. In that sense, although an original thinker, Habermas is typical of other important students of Marx who, through the effort to establish an acceptable reading of the nature and limits of Marx's position, provide new ways to understand it and advance the debate. It should further be noted that Habermas' own theory, which arose in part through his extended study of historical materialism, can usefully be understood from this perspective, that is, as an effort to go beyond the letter of Marx's thought while preserving its spirit in a new, more adequate position.

At the close of this study, it seems unnecessary to summarize it in detail. Suffice it to say that we have described Habermas' reading of Marx and Marxism as a process in four stages, leading to his own theory of communicative action, consisting of the interpretation, critique, reconstruction, and rejection of historical materialism. Although he now rejects the latter theory as a means, he continues to accept it as an end, more precisely as a goal of his own rival view. According to Habermas, the theory of communicative action is intended to function as an alternative paradigm which will better achieve the purposes of the old philosophy of history, and perhaps of the entire post-Kantian philosophical tradition.

The claim that the theory of communicative action is an alternative to historical materialism implies that they are different types of theories. The substitution of the former for the latter represents a change in theoretical paradigm, but both views share a common concern with the relation of theory and practice. This theme is a central thread which traverses Habermas' reading of historical materialism from beginning to end and which is further ingredient in his self-described nascent theory of communicative action. Despite his ultimate rejection of Marx's position, in Habermas' writings concerning historical materialism he is persistently concerned with the relation of theory and practice, in particular with an analysis of the nature and conditions of the relevance of reason.

Habermas' merit in this regard is two-fold. At the present time, more than a hundred years after his death, Marx's theory has already been studied from a wide variety of perspectives in an immense and quickly expanding literature. An important contribution of Habermas' approach to historical materialism from the vantage point of the critical philosophy is to suggest an end to generations of special pleading for a compassionate position by applying to it rigorous standards of theory.

It is possible that this kind of approach is not unprecedented, since at this late date even the most industrious student can no longer master the available literature on Marx; but it is certainly salutary. In this way historical materialism, which has often been shunned by more orthodox philosophy, is shown to be worthy of careful attention and even of philosophical respect. In a word, the same standards of intellectual rigor which are applied elsewhere in philosophy can and must be utilized in the discussion of social theory.

The rigor that inspires Habermas' approach to Marx and Marxism suggests an appropriate approach to his reading of historical materialism. The burgeoning debate on Habermas' thought is replete with uncritical accounts of his supposedly critical theory. But if it is correct that his contribution in part lies in the application of critical, quasi-Kantian standards to historical materialism and social theory in general, it would indeed be remiss to fail to apply similar standards to his own thought. A claim for rigor always deserves a fair, but never an indulgent, hearing; the latter is only an implicit concession that the claim in question cannot be sustained.

Habermas' other contribution is to redirect attention to a theme which, more than twenty-five centuries after the beginning of the philosophical quest, has lost none of its importance. With some notable exceptions (e.g. Sartre, Merleau-Ponty), representatives of so-called traditional philosophy have mainly been unconcerned with historical materialism, and representatives of Marxism have often argued for a difference in kind between their views and philosophy as such. As a result, it has not been sufficiently understood that the Marxist concern with the relation of theory and practice is not novel as such; for this theme is nearly as old as philosophy itself.

Two inferences follow from this observation. First, the Marxist self-comprehension as *sui generis* and beyond philosophy, which goes back to Engels, cannot be correct. Since it takes up a central philosophical question, Marxism does not merely leave philosophy behind. It rather considers anew and from a fresh perspective one of the main themes of the philosophical tradition. It further follows that even from an orthodox philosophical perspective Marxism deserves attention as one of the main contemporary efforts to reflect on this problem.

In calling attention to the relation of theory and practice, there is no intention to drive a wedge between philosophy and the history of philosophy. The question of theory and practice is not merely of antiquarian interest as a venerable theme lost in the origins of the philosophical tradition, to which Marxism unwittingly recurs. It is widely present elsewhere in philosophical thought, particularly in German idealism, whose major representatives are deeply concerned with the relation of theory, especially philosophical theory, to the social context. We can further note that this apparently abstract problem is socially relevant since it addresses the link that can be said to exist between social reality and thought in general.

This question is of particular interest as a permanent, indeed peculiarly important aspect of the philosophical task. If philosophy is to defend its traditional claim to be the highest form of knowledge which reflects even on itself, then it can do no less than to raise the question of the relevance of reason in general, especially that form which it proposes. Since as philosophers we need to submit all claims to reasoned examination, then one of our central preoccupations should be to examine the relation between philosophy and life.

Obviously, this is not a novel claim. Throughout the philosophical tradition it has been widely understood that an important part of the search for wisdom concerns the relevance of that search beyond itself. The history of philosophy is replete with different answers to the question of the relation of theory and practice in general, especially the social interest of philosophical practice. At present, this theme is particularly relevant for two reasons. First, as a continuing consequence of the emancipation of the natural sciences following Galileo, there is a steadily increasing tendency to mistrust, or to reject as incompetent, a philosophical approach. An important part of this mistrust is the conviction that natural science is more relevant, or indeed alone relevant, to the social context.

Second, ever since the beginning of the tradition there has been a healthy skepticism about aspects of philosophy, for instance the possibility of metaphysics or, more recently, the possibility of epistemology. The contemporary outbreak of philosophical doubt about philosophy as such, for instance in the wake of the supposed failure of foundationalism, is a less welcome development. For in the assimilation of philosophy in general to one of its aspects, that is, the epistemological problem which it allegedly fails to resolve, philosophy as such is said to fail when judged by its own claims. Hence, the interest in the question of the relevance of reason is not diminished, but only reinforced by the evolution of contemporary society.

Habermas' reading of historical materialism from the vantage point of theory and practice raises questions concerning his analysis of this theme and the problem as such. So far we have examined the manner in which his view of relevant reason emerges from his consideration of Marx and Marxism. Now we need to examine the view that has emerged. It will further be useful to reflect briefly on the underlying question of the relation of theory and practice, which is too often presupposed without being subjected to the scrutiny routinely accorded to the various analyses of this relation.

Habermas intends his theory of communicative action as a view of social practice. In the previous discussion, we have commented on the ties which bind Habermas' position in general, including the filiation of his own analysis of the problem of theory and practice, to the historical tradition. His understanding of social practice is obviously related in different ways to other positions, including those of Marx, the classical form of critical theory, and Kant. As concerns Marx Habermas maintains that theory can be socially relevant and respect the canons of rigorous thought which he believes reach a highwater mark in the critical philosophy. With respect to Kant he holds that rigorous thought, as Kant himself believed, is socially relevant. In opposition to the classical form of critical theory he proposes a new formulation which mainly or wholly dispenses with the economic analysis basic to historical materialism; but he shares the concern which already animated Horkheimer's thought to preserve a difference between traditional, putatively socially irrelevant, and socially relevant critical theory.

In the present context, there can be no pretense of evaluating Habermas' theory of communicative action as such, which is not the task of this book. We must further leave to one side assertions that communicative action is relevant for the theory of argumentation or for the interpretation of Mead and Weber, in order to concentrate on it as a beginning point for social theory, that is, as a supposed alternative to historical materialism. In this respect, questions arise concerning the internal consistency of Habermas' view of theory and practice in the evolution of his position; the success of his effort to bring together within a single theory insights inspired by such disparate thinkers as Marx and Kant; and the sense in which a theory of this type can be described as socially relevant.

Habermas' understanding of the nature of historical materialism evolves from an initial, enthusiastic interpretative phase to a final critical rejection of the theory. The problem of the internal consistency of his view of theory and practice can be stated in terms of the extremes of his reading of historical materialism in relation to its alleged intent: at one extreme, his early view of Marxism as an empirically falsifiable philosophy of history with practical intent, and at the other, the view of social practice he later formulates, intended to replace it.

We have Habermas' word that his theory of communicative action is in part intended to achieve the goals supposedly intrinsic to historical materialism by other means. Now, the latter is and has always been recognized as a theory intended to lead to a social revolution in which communism will replace capitalism through an unspecified series of events. The result is a clear dilemma, which we can describe in terms of alternative, but exclusive, possibilities.

One possibility is that Habermas has now abandoned his earlier reading of historical materialism as a theory of revolution in favor of its interpretation as a theory of practice. This alternative is admittedly incompatible with his initial comprehension of historical materialism; but it has the advantage of enabling him to maintain his claim that his own theory in a sense realizes the goals of Marx's. The second possibility, incompatible with the first, is that in his later thought Habermas maintains his original comprehension—which we can now paraphrase more fully as both a theory of practice and of revolutionary action—while restricting his claim to carry out the aims of historical materialism only to the former dimension. This latter interpretation allows for a consistent reading of historical materialism although it requires a clear limitation of the extent to which communicative action can even claim to achieve the goal of Marx and Marxism.

Each possibility has its advantages and limits. In the former case, the price of a claim to achieve the goal of historical materialism in his own view is to reinterpret the former in a manner that is nonstandard and arguably rejects a main aspect of Marx's thought. In the latter case, Habermas has tacitly revised his often stated, but unnuanced assertion that he intends to attain the aims of historical materialism by other means as the price of maintaining his original comprehension of the latter theory.

We can state the resultant dilemma as follows: Either his own theory is inconsistent with respect to Marx's supposed intention, which it does not fulfill; or it is consistent with a part of the intention only and hence can only partially sustain the claimed intention to carry out the aims of historical materialism by other means. In each case, Habermas' theory is inadequate to the claims he makes about its relation to historical materialism. In a word, a theory of social practice is not, and should not be confused with, a theory mainly intended to change social practice.

The problem of the internal consistency of Habermas' view of the relation of theory and practice is related to the success of his effort to combine within a single theory insights borrowed from thinkers as disparate as Marx and Kant. This question arises on two levels: as concerns the compossibility of what are finally different views of the nature of theory, even in Habermas' own interpretation of the history of philosophy; and in relation to his earlier, limited defense of the Frankfurt School distinction as concerns relevance between so-called critical and traditional forms of theory.

In his theory of communicative action Habermas proposes a position which is obviously intended to combine the social relevance of Marx's thought with the epistemological rigor of the critical philosophy. The problem is the real possibility of a view intended to be both epistemologically rigorous and socially relevant. In the history of philosophy, in general we can discern different views of the relevance of reason. On the one hand, there are those, such as Plato, Kant, Husserl, and even Whitehead, who hold that reason as such is socially relevant, which in turn implies that the most rigorous form of reason is rigorously relevant. On the other hand, there are those, such as Aristotle, Hegel, and Marx, who are concerned to limit, or even to reject, some claims for the relevance of reason.

It is difficult to adjudicate this dispute since it is difficult to show that a given form of reason, even of the most abstruse type, cannot, under proper conditions, be or be regarded as socially useful in a broad sense, i.e., for men and women in general. Now, this should not be taken to mean that reason as such is socially relevant; it only means that many, perhaps even all of its forms are potentially so under appropriate conditions.

On the other hand, Aristotle and his followers are clearly correct that for the most part the aim at disinterested reason characteristic of much of philosophy and certain other disciplines renders this kind of theory of little intrinsic interest for the social context. For a consequence of the search for invariant truth has often meant that the existential conditions of human being become irrelevant. It follows that even if on occasion a form of thought that deliberately abstracts from contingent factors can be seen as socially useful, this is not often the case.

As concerns Habermas' analysis, it is unnecessary to decide whether reason as such is relevant, or only certain forms of reason. If one accepts Kant's view that reason is relevant without further qualification, and further holds that after the critical philosophy epistemology declines, it is unclear why it would be necessary to attempt to bring together Marx and Kant. From Habermas' angle of vision, it should suffice to adopt a rigorously epistemological perspective, confident that the result of a revision of the critical philosophy would be socially relevant. From his quasi-Kantian perspective, it seems irrelevant to combine epistemologically rigorous thought with socially relevant thought; for by definition the former and the latter dimensions are inseparable. Rather than embarking on the perilous course of creating a fragile synthesis of Marx with Kant, it would be easier and hence preferable to provide a contemporary, appropriately updated version of the critical philosophy.

As concerns the relevance of reason, this same point can be sharpened in terms of Habermas' joint allegiance to Kant and to critical social theory. In his influential examination of the relation of knowledge and interest, which he has never renounced, in effect Habermas argues that traditional theories fail to justify their claims to the interest of reason, but that reason as such is interested. The Kantian inspiration of this argument is clear. In Kantian language, we can say that Habermas regards claims for the relevance of reason as dogmatic, since they are merely asserted without the demonstration of their possibility. He further follows Kant's conviction that all forms of reason are intrinsically interested.

Simultaneously, Habermas attempts to maintain his interest in critical social theory, which is not to be confused with the critical philosophy. In his initial discussion of knowledge and interest, he accepts the distinction between traditional and critical theory, which precisely rejects the Kantian transcendental philosophy as socially irrelevant. We further know that as late as his recent analysis of modernity, Habermas attempted to disjoin critical theory, which he continued to defend in modified form, from historical materialism, which he now rejects. In sum his thought combines a quasi-Kantian concern with rigorous argument and the relevance of reason with a continued interest in critical social theory, supposedly liberated from its original link to historical materialism.

Now, Habermas' quasi-Kantian claim for the relation of reason and interest creates a difficult situation for the defenders of critical theory. If all forms of reason are interested, then it is difficult to choose between traditional and critical theory merely in terms of relevance without introducing further distinctions. Since the original distinction between types of theory was precisely meant to differentiate among socially useful and socially useless forms of thought, critical theory as such is threatened by this line of argument.

On the other hand, if we deny Habermas' claim that reason as such is relevant and revert to the original distinction between traditional and critical theory, there are other difficulties. Other than the simple claim, critical theory does not demonstrate its assertion that, unlike so-called traditional theory, it alone is socially relevant. In fact, Habermas seems to make this point in indirect fashion through his attempted refutation of historical materialism. For if the theory cannot reach its intrinsic goal, and critical theory is a form of neo-Marxism, then the latter cannot justify its constitutive claim for the social relevance of a nontraditional form of reason.

This examination of the internal consistency of Habermas' discussion of theory and practice is related to his reading of the history of philosophy. In our review of Habermas' reading of historical materialism, we have been constantly aware of the historical roots which underlie the development of his quasi-Kantian approach to Marx and Marxism. From this angle of vision, we can distinguish two phases in his discussion: an earlier, more overtly epistemological moment, directed against Marx's alleged failure to pose the epistemological question of the possibility of his theory, which presupposes a close relation of social theory and epistemology; and a later, less overtly epistemological moment, in which Habermas rejects the supposedly intrinsic monism of Marx's theory as well as the theory itself in favor of a dualistic perspective. The latter is intended to respect his own distinction between work and interaction in the form of wholly unconstrained communication.

Now, it is clear that the two phases of Habermas' discussion are not unrelated. Their connection lies in a strongly Kantian point of view which subtends both the earlier critique of Marx's position for a failure to take the transcendental turn and the later critique obviously intended to recover the notion of a transcendental subject. The incompatibility of the Kantian and Marxian views of subjectivity is obvious against the background of the philosophical tradition. The Cartesian cogito presents a thematic analysis of the ahistorical subject widely presupposed in earlier thought, which survives as late as Husserl, and which is specifically restated in the Kantian view of the transcendental unity of apperception as the highest principle of all philosophy. It is this idea of subjectivity which is specifically threatened by Hegel's insistence on the social side of human being, and is further threatened in Marx's thought.

In his later turn away from epistemology Habermas does not reject the Kantian perspective; he merely rejects his own earlier effort to couple social theory with the general problem of epistemology. He is, then, consistent with respect to his generally Kantian approach in his objection to Marx's incapacity to differentiate work and interaction; this is the same problem which later resurfaces under the heading of a monism that purportedly undercuts the possibility of the unfettered communication of what is clearly a transcendental subject. But the effort to resurrect a form of transcendental subjectivity clearly runs against Habermas' expressed desire to cut his ties to the old *Bewußtseins-*

philosophie. For in his resurrection of the idea of an absolute subject he restates the concern with absolute subjectivity which is a staple of the modern philosophical tradition, especially German idealism, in the views of Fichte, Schelling, and Hegel.

If Habermas' critique of Marx were immanent, then the angles of vision represented by Kantian critical philosophy and Marxian social criticism would need to be compatible. As concerns the relation of theory and practice, there seems to be a clear difference which precisely illustrates the supposed distinction between traditional and critical theory. As a consequence of the widespread conviction that Marx's position emerges out of Hegel's, there is an equally frequent tendency to regard Marx's critique of the inutility of philosophy mainly in relation to so-called absolute idealism.

Now, although Marx in fact addresses his most vigorous criticism of the social dysfunctionality of prior philosophy to Hegel, it is not certain that he understood, or fully understood, the latter's position. There is reason to believe that in important ways Marx misunderstood the extent to which Hegel remained committed, early and late, to a belief in the merely limited social relevance of philosophical reason. It is perhaps not often enough noted that on the question of theory and practice Marx's disagreement is less with his illustrious predecessor, who was closer to Marx's view than its author realized, than with the founder of the critical philosophy who believed in the unlimited relevance of reason as such.

In interesting ways Habermas helps to enlarge the philosophical frame of reference for the comprehension of Marx's thought by surpassing the usual effort to consider it wholly or even mainly in relation to Hegel. Beyond the specific questions raised by his reading of particular theories, his effort to bring Marx into contact with philosophers other than Hegel, especially Kant and Fichte, is certainly useful. The problem is that he does not perceive the limited compatibility of a Kantian perspective with Marx's thought.

A Kantian angle of vision may be desirable and even advantageous with respect to Marx's. But as concerns the relation of theory and practice, it is incompatible with, and hence merely external to, Marx's theory, which embodies a different theoretical paradigm. In fact in another context, Habermas showed his awareness of this incompatibility in his recognition of the basic differences between communicative action, which is in part obviously inspired by the critical philosophy, and historical materialism. It is, then, inconsistent to criticize Marx for not proposing a different kind of theory than the one he offers.

The question of the compatibility of quasi-Kantian criticism with Marxian theory is related to the further, deeper problem of the social relevance of the theory of communicative action. At the beginning of his treatise, Habermas enumerates a series of domains which he intends his theory to address. Other than to specify the objects of the theory, he does not dwell on its relation to practice. He rather characterizes his view in different ways, as a theory of social practice, a rigorous social theory which refuses dogmatic or otherwise deficient modes of argumentation, and a way to understand the social context intended to stimulate further interdisciplinary research under the heading of social theory.

These various descriptions of the theory of communicative action share an insistence on a form of social theory intended to provide a rigorous approach to social practice, or knowledge of the social context, susceptible of further development. What is missing, however, is a demonstration of the relevance of this form of reason. Instead, we are offered a social theory which is arguably a source of social knowledge. Now, social knowledge, in turn, is relevant if knowledge is relevant. But it remains to be shown that reason is relevant or, in other words, if and how theory that 'grasps' or otherwise understands the social context is relevant to it.

This point can be broadened. Following the example of critical social theory, Habermas accuses so-called traditional theory of failing to consider its claim for social relevance. But even if he is correct that earlier thinkers are sometimes insufficiently concerned to demonstrate the relation of their theories to social practice, he is himself guilty of the same error. For at best his theory of communicative action is relevant if social knowledge is socially relevant. What we require, then—and what is apparently lacking in Habermas' discussion and in his own theory of communicative action—is an analysis of social relevance.

In order to understand the relation of theory and practice, an analysis of the concept of the relevance of reason is indispensable. At the close of this discussion of Habermas' reading of historical materialism, it will be sufficient to note that he offers a theory which is meant to be relevant, but he does not propose an analysis of the relevance of reason which is supposed by his and any other theory intended to relate to the social context. This is not the place to develop a general theory of the relevance of reason. But it will at least be useful to anticipate some of its main lines through two remarks.

First, we can note that the question of the relevance of reason is a form of the ancient problem which Marxism approaches as the relation of theory and practice. In part perhaps because he initially accepts the intrinsically dichotomous perspective of so-called critical theory, Habermas poses the problem in terms of incompatible alternatives which are relevant or irrelevant to social practice. In this way, he only follows Marx who, in his distinction between theories that understand and theories that change social reality, implicitly construed the genus theory in terms of relevant and irrelevant subspecies.

Now, this kind of dichotomous approach to the relation of theory and practice is simplistic, as can be seen through a remark on the concept of relevance. Theories cannot correctly be classified as either relevant or irrelevant only, since relevance is a matter of degree. Insofar as all theories embody an end of some kind, they are therefore relevant in that respect. It is further perilous to claim that a certain kind of theory is irrelevant as such. Theories which at present may not seem relevant, such as certain types of so-called pure research, may later become so in ways difficult and sometimes not possible to anticipate. Marx's original claim for the irrelevance of theories that merely provide interpretation only has meaning with respect to his own precise goal, that is, social revolution; it and its dichotomous descendants are unacceptable as a way to classify forms of theory in general.

All forms of theory are at least potentially relevant, even if some forms of reason are more socially useful than others. For reason in general, which by definition embodies the aims of human beings, is at least potentially socially relevant. It follows that the problem is not the relevance of reason as such, which is intrinsically relevant as Kant held and Marx denied.

Marx was clearly mistaken since he was not concerned with relevance in the widest sense; he was rather concerned with a specific kind of relevance, exemplified by a theory intended to promote the replacement of capitalism by communism. His conclusion that comprehension is irrelevant or that it fails to change the social context does not follow from an argument and does not in fact hold. It is more insightful to maintain that an understanding of the social context, such as that which Marx and his followers attempt to offer in their views, is precisely relevant to social progress.

Second, there is the related, more difficult question of how theory is relevant to social practice. Now, Habermas is wrong to believe that prior thinkers merely assumed a relation, but did not address this issue. As noted, starting with Plato a long list of important and unimportant members of the philosophical tradition have examined this problem. They include such figures as Aristotle and Aquinas, the Stoics and Boethius, Hume and Whitehead, Hegel and Husserl, Sartre and Heidegger, etc.

In order to respond to the question of how theory is relevant to social practice, it will be useful to differentiate forms of relevance and relevance as such. Now, it is at least interesting to note that the concept of relevance has not often been studied in detail. Suffice it to say that if we assume that human beings are capable of action motivated by conscious choice, then the obvious relevance of social knowledge is to make possible action intended to bring about desirable consequences. Theories are relevant to social practice since knowledge provides the social comprehension which is an indispensable guide to possible action in the social context. In that sense, knowing and acting are inseparably conjoined since rational action depends upon socially relevant reason. The relevance of reason lies in its relation to action of whatever kind, whether in the pursuit of further knowledge or in those other forms of action which are more directly intended to realize the aims of human beings in the modification and perfection of the social context. Theory relates to practice through the relevance of reason.

NOTES

Introduction

I gratefully acknowledge William L. McBride's careful comments on an earlier draft of this manuscript.

1. With the exception of an early, now outdated book on Habermas and Marxism, written from a more 'orthodox' perspective, this theme has been much neglected in the secondary literature. See Julius Sensat, *Habermas and Marxism: An Appraisal* (Beverly Hills and London: Sage, 1979). More recent items that bear on this theme include F. Cerutti, "Habermas e Marx," in *Paradigmi* (Bari), I, pp. 479–510, and H. Brunkhorst, "Paradigmadenkern und Theoriedynamik der kritischen Theorie der Gesellschaft," in *Soziale Welt*, XXXIV, 1983. See also Rick Roderick, *Habermas and the Foundations of Critical Theory* (New York: Macmillan, 1986).

2. Geuss, for instance, makes the unwarranted assumption that the very possibility of critical theory, as a form of Marxism, can be evaluated when it is understood as a critique of ideology. See Raymond Geuss, *The Idea of a Critical Theory: Habermas and the Frankfurt School* (Cambridge: Cambridge University Press, 1981), pp. 2–3, 94.

3. Ingram, for instance, points out that in his recent writings Habermas rejects his own earlier identification of critical social theory as the critique of ideology [Ideologiekritik]. See David Ingram, *Habermas and the Dialectic of Reason* (New Haven: Yale University Press, 1987), pp. 172–177. It is, however, less clear that Habermas has now moved to an esthetic view of reason from a holistic perspective, as Ingram believes. See ibid., pp. 180–186.

4. An example among many is provided by Ingram's recent, but misleading, claim that in his theory of communicative action Habermas returns to Marx. See ibid., p. 173. This statement, which is partly correct as concerns the problem of reification, which problem is however mediated through Lukács's early Marxism, errs in ignoring Habermas' critique of the Marxian value theory. This critique, which leads Habermas to reject historical materialism as an even potentially viable theory, moves him away from rather than toward Marx.

5. See *Zur Logik der Sozialwissenschaften. Materialien* (Frankfurt a.M.: Suhrkamp, 1973).

6. See *Theorie des kommunikativen Handelns* (Frankfurt a.M.: Suhrkamp, 1981), 2 volumes, translated as *The Theory of Communicative Action* (Boston: Beacon Press, 1984), 2 volumes.

7. He has further indicated in various places that, even though he now rejects Marx's position, he continues to utilize it as a model. For instance in his recent response to critics, he stresses that although his own view may produce the static impression of a linear model, in fact he had in mind the nonlinear model of Marx's analysis of the development of capitalist modes of production. See his "Entgegnung," in Axel Honneth and Hans Joas, eds., *Beiträge zu Jürgen Habermas' "Theorie des kommunikativen Handelns"* (Frankfurt a.M.: Suhrkamp, 1986), p. 389.

8. For this kind of claim, see the introduction to the recent *Beiträge* (p. 7), where the editors write: "Die Theorien von Weber, Mead, Durkheim und Parsons sowie— allerdings mehr im Hintergrund—der Marxismus stellen das Bezugssystem dar,

179

innerhalb dessen die gesellschaftstheoretischen Grundedanken zugleich gerechtfertigt und argumentativ auf die Probe gestellt werden."

9. It is worth noting here that Habermas' assimilation of historical materialism to the philosophy of consciousness (Bewußtseinsphilosophie) in his recent book *The Philosophical Discourse on Modernity*, while it denies the basic Marxist tenet of the separation of historical materialism and traditional philosophy—which Habermas had also accepted until that point—does not affect his commitment to Marxist goals. See *Der philosophische Diskurs der Moderne. Zwölf Vorlesungen* (Frankfurt a.M.: Suhrkamp, 1985), translated as *The Philosophical Discourse of Modernity: Twelve Lectures* (Cambridge, MA: MIT Press, 1987).

10. It is not without reason that he has recently characterized the discussion of his work in Anglo-Saxon circles, in comparison to the German language debate, as "zwangsloser." See *Beiträge*, p. 327.

11. See René Görtzen, *Jürgen Habermas. Eine Bibliographie seiner Schriften und der Sekundarliteratur, 1952–1981* (Frankfurt a.M.: Suhrkamp, 1982). For a partial updating, which covers only those titles concerned with his recent study of communicative action, see *Beiträge*, pp. 406–416.

12. The acknowledged classic study of his early thought is Thomas McCarthy, *The Critical Theory of Jürgen Habermas* (Cambridge, MA: MIT Press, 1978).

13. For a good, recent study of his later thought, see Ingram, *Habermas and the Dialectic of Reason*.

14. See, e.g., Garbis Kortian, *Métacritique* (Cambridge: Cambridge University Press, 1980).

15. See, e.g., Michael Theunissen, *Gesellschaft und Geschichte. Zur Kritik der kritischen Theorie* (Berlin: de Gruyter, 1969) and Geuss, *The Idea of a Critical Theory*.

16. See Richard J. Bernstein, ed., *Habermas and Modernity* (Cambridge, MA: MIT Press, 1985).

17. See Peter Dews, ed., *Habermas: Autonomy and Solidarity. Interviews* (London: New Left Books, 1986), p. 94.

18. See *Rekonstruktion des historischen Materialismus*, p. 9, *Beiträge*, p. 395, and *Habermas: Autonomy and Solidarity*, p. 94. Habermas attributes insight into the possibility of going beyond a historical approach to Marx to Adorno's 'electrifying' influence on him.

I. Theory Reconstruction and Theory Replacement

1. See the title essay in his book, *Technik und Wissenschaft als 'Ideologie'* (Frankfurt a.M.: Suhrkamp, 1974), pp. 48–103. See also, in the same book, the essays on "Technischer Fortschritt und soziale Lebenswelt," pp. 104–119, and "Verwissenschaftliche Politik und öffentliche Meinung," pp. 120–145.

2. See *Zur Logik der Sozialwissenschaften*.

3. See, for instance, his book on the logic of the social sciences, passim, where the discussion ranges widely over the views of many authors, including Chomsky, McIntyre, Hempel, Lorenzen, Albert, Popper, etc.

4. For instance, in an important essay in which Habermas maintains that Marxism is critique, he writes: "With its position "between" philosophy and positive science only a formal designation of Marxist theory has been established. Nothing has been ascertained thereby about its distinctive status from the perspective of the philosophy of science." *Theory and Practice*, p. 212.

5. For Kant's distinction between *cognitio ex principiis* and *cognitio ex datiis*, see the *Critique of Pure Reason*, B 864.

6. For a clear example of the inability of even the best Kantians to take a historical approach to the philosophical tradition, see Emil Lask, *Fichtes Idealismus und die*

Geschichte, in *Emil Lask. Gesammelte Schriften*, Eugen Herriegel, ed. (Tübingen: J.C.B. Mohr [Paul Siebeck], 1923), I.

7. See *Critique of Pure Reason*, B xvi.

8. See *Critique of Pure Reason*, B xix.

9. Husserl, for instance, clearly argues that we need to begin again from the beginning since although much has been tried, nothing of permanent value has been accomplished. See his *Philosophie als strenge Wissenschaft* (Frankfurt a.M.: Vittorio Klostermann, 1965).

10. A typical example is Quine's *boutade*, as reported by Richard Rorty, concerning the difference between those interested in the history of philosophy and those interested in philosophy. See Richard Rorty, *Consequences of Pragmatism* (Minneapolis: University of Minnesota Press), p. 211.

11. The locus classicus of this view is the famous comment in the preface to the *Philosophy of Right* (Oxford: Oxford University Press, 1967), T.M. Knox, trans., p. 11, where Hegel writes in part: "Whatever happens, every individual is a child of his time; so philosophy too is its own time apprehended in thoughts. It is just as absurd to fancy that a philosophy can transcend its contemporary world as it is to fancy that an individual can overleap his own age, jump over Rhodes."

12. See Karl Popper, *Conjectures and Refutations: The Growth of Scientific Knowledge* (New York and Evanston: Harper and Row, 1965), especially the title essay and passim. See also *The Logic of Scientific Discovery* (New York and Evanston: Harper and Row, 1968).

13. See Thomas S. Kuhn, *The Structure of Scientific Revolutions* (Chicago: The University of Chicago Press, 1970). For a discussion of the ambiguity of the term "paradigm," see ibid., p. 175.

14. For his views, see, for instance, Wolfgang Stegmüller, *Rationale Rekonstruktion von Wissenschaft und ihrem Wandel* (Stuttgart: Reklam, 1979). For a brief overview of the entire discussion, see Rüdiger Bubner, *Modern German Philosophy* (Cambridge: Cambridge University Press, 1981), Eric Matthews, trans., pp. 128–142.

15. See "Literaturbericht zur philosophischen Diskussion um Marx und den Marxismus," in *Theorie und Praxis*, pp. 387–463.

16. See "Einleitung: Historischer Materialismus und die Entwicklung normativer Strukturen," in *Rekonstruction des historischen Materialismus*. This essay appears in translation under the title "Historical Materialism and the Development of Normative Structures" in the volume called *Communication and the Evolution of Society* (Boston: Beacon Press, 1979).

17. *Communication and the Evolution of Society*, p. 98.

18. Ibid., p. 95.

19. The best general discussions of Marxism with which I am familiar are Leszek Kolakowski, *Main Currents of Marxism* (Oxford: Oxford University Press, 1978), P.S. Falla, trans., 3 volumes; and Predrag Vranicki, *Geschichte des Marxismus* (Frankfurt: Suhrkamp, 1972), Stanislava Rummel and Vjekoslava Wiedmann, trans., 2 volumes.

20. See *Critique of Pure Reason*, B 370.

21. Kolakowski, for instance, has called attention to a series of differences in the views of Marx and Engels. See his *Main Currents of Marxism*, I, chapter XVI, esp. pp. 399–407. Michel Henry has defined Marxism in a controversial manner as the series of misunderstandings concerning Marx's thought. See his *Marx: A Philosophy of Human Reality* (Bloomington and London: Indiana University Press, 1983), Kathleen McLaughlin, trans., p. 1.

22. See Shlomo Avineri, *The Social and Political Thought of Karl Marx* (Cambridge: Cambridge University Press, 1970), p. 65.

23. According to George L. Kline, the term "historical materialism" was first

introduced by Engels in 1892 in the English translation of *Socialism, Utopian and Scientific*. He further points out that the term "dialectical materialism" originally appeared in Joseph Dietzgen's article, "Streifzüge eines Sozialisten in das Gebiet der Erkenntnistheorie," initially published in 1887, and only reappeared four years later in Georgi Plechanov's well-known article, "Zu Hegels sechzigstem Todestag," published in 1891. For an excellent discussion, see George L. Kline, "The Myth of Marx's Materialism," in Helmut Dahm, Thomas J. Blakeley, and George L. Kline, eds., *Philosophical Sovietology: The Pursuit of a Science* (Dordrecht: D. Reidel, 1988), pp. 158–203.

24. See the text attributed to him, "Dialectical and Historical Materialism," in *Ten Classics of Marxism* (New York: International Publishers, 1940).

25. See Oswald Spengler, *Der Untergang des Abendlandes*, 2 vols., 1918, 1922.

26. Hegel develops this idea in various places, including *Vernunft in die Geschichte* and the third part of the *Enzyklopädie der philosophischen Wissenschaften*, entitled "Philosophie des Geistes."

27. See Tom Rockmore, "Idealist Hermeneutics and the Hermeneutics of Idealism," in *Idealistic Studies*, vol. 12, no. 2 (May 1982), pp. 91–102.

28. See *Critique of Pure Reason*, B xliv. This idea was further developed by Fichte. See his study, "Über Geist und Buchstabe in der Philosophie," in *Fichtes Werke*, I.H. Fichte, ed. (Berlin: Walter de Gruyter, 1971), VIII, pp. 270–301.

29. See *Critique of Pure Reason*, B xliv.

30. See *The Theory of Communicative Action*, II, chapter VIII, part 2: "Marx and the Thesis of Inner Colonisation," pp. 489–547.

31. See *The Philosophical Discourse of Modernity*, especially "Excursus on the Obsolescence of the Production Paradigm," pp. 75–83.

32. For Heidegger's description of the attempt to renew metaphysics as a *gigantomachia peri tes ousias*, see *Being and Time* (New York and Evanston: Harper and Row, 1962), p. 2.

33. For a discussion of the nature and limits of the Hegelian approach to the interpretation of German idealism, see Tom Rockmore, "Hegel, l'homme agissant et la philosophie allemande moderne," in *Archives de philosophie*, vol. 44, no. 1 (January/March 1981), pp. 3–19.

34. This view is in part the basis of the traditional Marxist claim, which goes back to Engels, that Marxism cannot be and in fact is not a philosophy. For a typical example of the Young Hegelian view that philosophy comes to an end in Hegel's system, see Heinrich Heine, *Zur Geschichte der Religion und Philosophie in Deutschland*, in *Werke und Briefe*, ed. Hans Kaufmann (Berlin: Aufbau Verlag, 1961), vol. 5, p. 303: "Unsere philosophische Revolution ist beendigt. Hegel hat ihren großen Kreis geschlossen." For an echo of this same view in the later discussion, see Rudolf Haym, *Hegel und seine Zeit* (1857; reprint Darmstadt: Wissenschaftliche Buchgesellschaft, 1974), p. 5: "Jenes Pathos und jene Überzeugtheit der Hegelianer vom Jahre 1830 muß man sich vergegenwärtigen, welche im vollen, bitteren Ernste die Frage ventilirten, was wohl den ferneren Inhalt der Weltgeschichte bilden werde, nachdem doch in der Hegel'schen Philosophie der Weltgeist an sein Ziel, an das Wissen seiner selbst hindurchgedrungen sei."

35. See Karl Löwith, *From Hegel to Nietzsche* (Garden City: Doubleday, 1967), David E. Green, trans.

36. See Richard J. Bernstein, *Praxis and Action* (Philadelphia: University of Pennsylvania, 1971).

37. See *Critique of Pure Reason*, B xix.

38. See ibid., B xii–xiii.

39. See ibid., B xxxviii.

40. See *The Philosophical Discourse of Modernity*, pp. 309–311.

41. Ibid., p. 309.
42. See ibid., p. 296.
43. See *Die neue Unübersichtlichkeit*, p. 59.
44. See *The Philosophical Discourse of Modernity*, p. 300.
45. See ibid., p. 316.
46. See ibid., pp. 316–321.

II. Philosophical Anthropology or Theory of History?

1. For a now outdated list of his writings and the discussion surrounding them, see René Görtzen, ed., *Jürgen Habermas: Eine Bibliographie seiner Schriften und der Sekundarliteratur, 1952–1981.*

2. For a description by an intellectual historian, see Martin Jay, *The Dialectical Imagination: A History of the Frankfurt School and the Institute of Social Research, 1923–1950* (Boston: Little Brown, 1973).

3. See Albrecht Wellmer, *Critical Theory of Society* (New York: Herder and Herder, 1971).

4. The only book currently available, in fact an attempt to defend Marxism against Habermas, has been outdated by later writings. See Julius Sensat, *Habermas and Marxism. An Appraisal*. See also Rick Roderick, *Habermas and the Foundations of Critical Theory*.

5. See *Autonomy and Solidarity*, p. 94.

6. See, for instance, his criticism of Marx's supposed lack of criteria to differentiate traditional forms of life from the objectification, or reification, [Verdinglichung] of post-traditional life-worlds, in *The Theory of Communicative Action*, II, p. 340.

7. See *Technik und Wissenschaft als 'Ideologie.'*

8. We can include among his books in English translation that are more than incidentally concerned with historical materialism: *Theory and Practice, Knowledge and Human Interests, Communication and the Evolution of Society, The Theory of Communicative Action*, and *The Philosophical Discourse of Modernity*.

9. Since the term will appear frequently below, it might be useful to comment on it. A literal translation of the German term "Literaturbericht" would be 'report on the literature.' This suggests that Habermas' lengthy discussion is what in English one might call a book report, or a book review. Now, in part that is the case, although it is also a misleading comparison. In any case, we need to avoid the idea that Habermas here offers a giant book report, since the term seems less than scholarly. In a way, this is partly a book review, but what this means requires a comment. In comparison to Anglo-Saxon or even French scholarship, book reviews in German academic circles tend to be less interpretative and more oriented toward relatively nonjudgmental, objective presentation of the main points of the work under study in summary form. Habermas' review of the literature manifests the German tendency toward objective summary of the work under discussion, which is here combined with much critical commentary. Accordingly, in Habermas' discussion the world "Literaturbericht" has the dual senses of an objective presentation and an evaluation of the currently available secondary discussion, in this case the discussion concerning Marx and Marxism.

10. For an excellent example of the anthropological approach to the reading of Marx's theory, see Michel Henry, *Marx: A Philosophy of Human Reality* (Bloomington and London: Indiana University Press, 1983).

11. For the so-called humanist approach to Marx, see Jean-Paul Sartre, *Search for a Method* (New York: Vintage, 1968).

12. See Louis Althusser, *For Marx*, Ben Brewster, trans. (New York: Vintage, 1970).

13. For an understanding of historical materialism that excludes a reading of it as philosophy of any kind, see the article entitled "Historical Materialism" in *A Dictionary*

of Marxist Thought, Tom Bottomore et al., eds. (Cambridge, MA: Harvard University Press, 1983), pp. 206–210.

14. For a fine response to Althusser and other so-called 'Marxist' readings of Marx, which is also a major interpretation of the position, see Michel Henry, *Marx: A Philosophy of Human Reality*.

15. Among the commentators on Marx, Henry has gone as far as anyone in showing the compatibility of a theory of the subject with a derivative understanding of political economy and history. This is especially clear in the French version of his Marx study, which contains a more extended study of Marxian political economy. See his *Marx* (Paris: Éditions Gallimard, 1976), 2 volumes, esp. vol. 2: *Une philosophie de l'économie*.

16. See *Autonomy and Solidarity*, p. 152.

17. See *Hegels Ontologie und die Grundzüge einer Theorie der Geschichtlichkeit* (Frankfurt a.M.: Vittorio Klostermann, 1932).

18. Heidegger develops this theme in his critique of Sartre. See his "Letter on Humanism," in *Martin Heidegger: Basic Writings*, David Farrell Krell, ed. (New York: Harper and Row, 1977), pp. 189–242.

19. According to Habermas, Marcuse was the first "Heideggerean Marxist [Heideggermarxist]." See *Theorie und Praxis*, p. 463, f.n. 129.

20. For instance, in *Knowledge and Human Interests* he associates it with a possible "transcendental-logical misunderstanding." See *Knowledge and Human Interests*, p. 28.

21. See, e.g., Erich Fromm, *Marx's Concept of Man* (New York: Frederick Ungar, 1969). See also Erich Fromm, ed., *Socialist Humanism: An International Symposium* (Garden City: Doubleday Anchor, 1966).

22. See "The Foundations of Historical Materialism," in Herbert Marcuse, *Studies in Critical Philosophy* (Boston: Beacon Press, 1972), pp. 3–48. For another contemporaneous reaction, see H. de Man, "Neu entdeckte Marx," in *Der Kampf*, 1932, nos. 5 and 6.

23. According to Habermas, in virtue of its concern with the relation of theory and practice Marxism presents itself as a political reality and as a theory which wants to transform reality in a fundamental way. See *Theorie und Praxis*, pp. 389–390.

24. For the classical statement of this understanding of philosophy, see Aristotle, *Metaphysics*, Bk. I, ch. 2, passim.

25. For this view, see Karl Marx and Friedrich Engels, *The German Ideology*, Part One (New York: International Publishers, 1970), esp. preface, p. 37 and "Feuerbach: Opposition of the Materialist and Idealist Outlook; A. Idealism and Materialism: The Illusions of German Ideology," pp. 41–48.

26. For a recent effort to develop an analysis of political philosophy as 'originary', clearly influenced by Habermas and, beyond him, Marx, see Dick Howard, *From Marx to Kant* (Albany: State University of New York Press, 1985).

27. The relevance of reason is a main theme in Habermas' corpus. He provides a systematic analysis of some of the issues in his lecture, "Knowledge and Human Interests: A General Perspective," in *Knowledge and Human Interests*, pp., 301–317.

28. See *Theorie und Praxis*, p. 402.

29. This theme is especially prominent in the important essay "Between Philosophy and Science: Marxism as Critique," in *Theory and Practice*.

30. See Karl Korsch, *Marxismus und Philosophie* (Frankfurt a.M. and Vienna: Europäische Verlangsanstalt and Europa Verlag, 1961), p. 139.

31. See *Theorie und Praxis*, pp. 422–428.

32. It is important to distinguish between the epistemological concept of the ground, which becomes clear in German idealism in Fichte's rejection of what has recently come to be known as epistemological foundationalism, and the ontological concept of the ground in earlier German thought, especially in Böhme. For the problem of epistemological antifoundationalism in general in German idealism, see Tom

Rockmore's *Hegel's Circular Epistemology* (Bloomington: Indiana University Press, 1986). For the ontological sense of the concept of ground in Schelling and earlier in Böhme, see Robert F. Brown, *The Later Philosophy of Schelling: The Influence of Böhme on the Works of 1809–1815* (Lewisburg: Bucknell University Press, 1977).

33. See Jean-Paul Sartre, *Search for a Method* (New York: Vintage, 1968), p. 179. For further discussion, Tom Rockmore, "Sartre and the 'Philosophy of Our Time',," in *British Journal of Phenomenology*, vol. 9, no. 2 (May 1978), pp. 92–101. For some recent remarks in which Habermas rejects the idea of an ultimate ground, see his "Entgegnung," in *Beiträge zu Jürgen Habermas' "Theorie des kommunikativen Handelns,"* pp. 350–352.

34. Although this aspect of Habermas' relation to historical materialism is only implicit here, it later becomes explicit, particularly in *The Theory of Communicative Action* and *The Philosophical Discourse of Modernity*.

35. *See The Transcendence of the Ego: An Existentialist Theory of Consciousness* (New York: Farrar, Straus and Giroux, 1957), p. 105.

36. See Maurice Merleau-Ponty, *Les Aventures de la dialectique* (Paris: Gallimard, 1955), esp. chapter 5, "Sartre et l'ultra-bolchévisme," pp. 131–272.

37. *Theorie und Praxis*, p. 424.

38. See ibid., p. 427.

39. For an early exploration of the relation between Husserlian phenomenology and Marxism by a student of Merleau-Ponty, see Tran Duc Thao, *Phénoménologie et marxisme* (Paris: Minh-Tan, 1951).

40. On this point, see his important essay, "The Primacy of Perception and Its Philosophical Consequences," in Maurice Merleau-Ponty, *The Primacy of Perception* (Evanston: Northwestern University Press, 1964), pp. 12–42, especially p. 13.

41. This is the single theme of *Being and Time* and of all of Heidegger's later writings. For a statement of Heidegger's approach to this problem, see *Being and Time*, John Macquarrie and Edward Robinson, trans. (New York and Evanston: Harper and Row, 1962), especially the introduction, pp. 21–64.

42. Habermas' tendency to transcend the overly narrow, but widespread approach to Marx through exclusive study of the latter's relation to Hegel is an important feature of his approach. For a later development of this tendency, see especially *Knowledge and Human Interests*, chapters 1–3.

43. See Georg Lukács, *History and Class Consciousness: Studies in Marxist Dialectics*, Rodney Livingstone, trans. (Cambridge, MA: MIT Press, 1972), especially "Reification and the Consciousness of the Proletariat," pp. 83–222.

44. For a Marxist effort to work out a social ontology in which the concept of work is central, see Georg Lukács, *Zur Ontologie des gesellschaftlichen Seins*, passim, especially the chapter entitled "Die Arbeit," published separately as *Ontologie-Arbeit* (Neuwied and Darmstadt: Luchterhand, 1973).

45. For a discussion of Lukács's neo-Kantian form of Marxism, see our paper "Lukács on the History of Philosophy," in Tom Rockmore, ed., *Lukács Today* (Dordrecht and Boston: Reidel, 1988).

III. The Transitional Period

1. See "Between Philosophy and Science: Marxism as Critique," in *Theory and Practice*, pp. 195–252.

2. See "Knowledge and Human Interests: A General Perspective," in *Knowledge and Human Interests*, pp. 301–317.

3. See "Labor and Interaction: Remarks on Hegel's Jena Philosophy of Mind," in *Theory and Practice*, pp. 142–169.

4. See Karl Popper, "The Demarcation between Science and Metaphysics," in *Con-*

jectures and Refutations. Habermas has recently taken inordinate pains, in an embarrassed and unconvincing discussion, to deny that his own notion of fallibilism is related to Popper's view in a more than grammatical manner. See his "Entgegnung," in *Beiträge zu Jürgen Habermas' "Theorie des kommunikativen Handelns,"* pp. 350–353.

5. For instance, in his well-known "Speech at the Graveside of Karl Marx," Engels credited his friend with two fundamental discoveries, each of which is basically economic: the priority of the economic base over the superstructure, and the discovery of the theory of surplus value. See Robert C. Tucker, ed., *The Marx-Engels Reader* (New York: Norton, 1978), p. 681.

6. In a later work, Korsch abandoned his earlier emphasis on critique and argued that Marxism has a two-fold content, based on the materialist conception of history and political economy, both points Habermas stresses here. See Karl Korsch, *Karl Marx* (London and New York: Chapman and Hall/Wiley and Son, 1938).

7. See *Theory and Practice*, p. 212.

8. See ibid., p. 219.

9. For his critique of this theory, in terms of which he thinks that he can rationally reject historical materialism in favor of another approach, see *The Theory of Communicative Action*, II, chapter 8, part 2: "Marx and the Thesis of Inner Colonisation," pp. 332–372, esp. pp. 338–343.

10. See *Theory and Practice*, pp. 203–204.

11. This argument, which is developed in *The Theory of Communicative Action*, II, will be analyzed in detail below.

12. See *Theory and Practice*, p. 228.

13. See ibid., p. 234.

14. The articles and their publication dates are: "Schelling über Hegel" (December 1841), "Schelling und die Offenbarung. Kritik des neuesten Reaktionsversuchs gegen die freie Philosophie" (March 1842), "Schelling, der Philosoph in Christo, oder die Verklärung der Weltweisheit zur Gottesweisheit" (May 1842).

15. See *Theory and Practice*, p. 236.

16. See Karl Mannheim, *Ideology and Utopia: An Introduction to the Sociology of Knowledge*, Louis Wirth and Edward Shils, trans. (New York: Harcourt, Brace and World, n.d.).

17. See *Theory and Practice*, p. 236.

18. Ibid., p. 250.

19. Lukács makes this point very clearly in his analysis of proletarian class consciousness. See "Class Consciousness," in *History and Class Consciousness*, pp. 46–82.

20. See *Theory and Practice*, p. 248.

21. See ibid., p. 249.

22. See ibid., p. 251.

23. See the essays included in *Rekonstruktion des historischen Materialismus* and available in translation in *Communication and the Evolution of Society*.

24. See the *Critique of Pure Reason*, B 867.

25. On the 'authorized' Husserlian reaction to the neo-Kantian critique of phenomenology, see Eugen Fink, "Die phänomenologische Philosophie Edmund Husserls in der gegenwärtigen Kritik," in *Kant-Studien*, vol. 38, 1933, pp. 319–383.

26. For the classic study of the relation of Husserl to Kant, see Iso Kern, *Husserl und Kant* (The Hague: Nijhoff, 1964).

27. *Knowledge and Human Interests*, p. 301.

28. For Husserls' view of this concept, see paragraph 14: "Precursory characterization of objectivism and transcendentalism," in *The Crisis of European Sciences and Transcendental Phenomenology*, David Carr, trans. (Evanston: Northwestern University Press, 1970).

29. See Max Horkheimer, "Traditional and Critical Theory," in Matthew J.

O'Connell, ed., *Critical Theory: Selected Essays* (New York: Herder and Herder, 1972), pp. 188–243.

30. See ibid., p. 242.

31. See "Moral Development and Ego Identity," in *Communication and the Evolution of Society*, pp. 95–129.

32. The translator's suggestion of "autonomy and responsibility" for "Mündigkeit" is obviously an interpretation of the meaning of the term, as distinguished from a translation of it. See *Knowledge and Human Interests*, p. 314. For the original text, see *Technik und Wissenschaft als 'Ideologie,'* p. 163. The German term, which means "an eine bestimmte Rechtshandlungen erforderliche Reife, Volljährigkeit, Großjährigkeit," can be better rendered as "maturity" or "adulthood." Kant offers an influential analysis of maturity in his essay, "Beantwortung der Frage: Was ist Aufklärung?," in *Ausgewählte kleine Schriften* (Hamburg: Felix Meiner, 1969), pp. 1–9.

33. See, e.g., *Nicomachean Ethics*, I, 7, 1079b 20–21.

34. See Kant, *Ausgewählte kleine Schriften*, p. 1.

35. For his effort to work out a consensus theory of truth, see his article "Wahrheitstheorien," in H. Fahrenbach, ed., *Wirklichkeit und Reflexion. Festschrift für Walter Schulz* (Pfullingen: Neske, 1973), pp. 211–265.

36. Plato alludes to this issue in the beginning of the *Republic* where he raises the problem of persuading those who will not listen. See *Republic* 327 C.

37. See *Knowledge and Human Interests*, p. 314.

38. This is one of the guiding assumptions of the discussion in *Knowledge and Human Interests*.

39. See *Theory and Practice*, pp. 147–148.

40. See *Fichtes Werke*, I, pp. 188–190.

41. See *Theory and Practice*, p. 159.

42. See ibid., p. 161.

43. Ibid., pp. 168–169.

44. See ibid., p. 169.

45. See ibid., p. 163.

46. Habermas quotes this passage without giving its source in the *Paris Manuscripts*. See T. B. Bottomore, ed. and trans., *Karl Marx: Early Writings* (Toronto: McGraw-Hill, 1964), p. 202.

47. See ibid., pp. 203–204.

48. See *Theory and Practice*, pp. 163, 164.

49. See ibid., p. 167.

50. See ibid., p. 169.

51. He examines this theme in more detail elsewhere, especially in "Towards a Reconstruction of Historical Materialism," in *Communication and the Evolution of Society*.

52. This theme is further examined in *Knowledge and Human Interests*.

IV. Knowledge and Interest Again

1. The title in translation speaks of "human interests," which is an interpretation of the German word "Interesse" to reflect Habermas' view that knowledge is socially relevant. The original resemblance between the titles of the book (*Knowledge and Human Interests* is the rendering of *Erkenntnis und Interesse*) and the lecture ("Knowledge and Human Interests. A General Perspective" is the translation of "Erkenntnis und Interesse") is not quite preserved in a loose translation of both.

2. See the relevant essays collected under the title *Rekonstruktion des historischen Materialismus* and, in translation, in the volume *Communication and the Evolution of Society*.

3. See *Knowledge and Human Interests*, p. vii.

4. See ibid., p. vii. The suggestion that Marx is also guilty of positivism has been explored by Albrecht Wellmer. See *Critical Theory of Society*, John Cumming, trans. (New York: Herder and Herder, 1971).

5. See *Knowledge and Human Interests*, p. vii.

6. He elaborates this reading of Nietzsche in *The Philosophical Discourse of Modernity*.

7. See *Knowledge and Human Interests*, pp. 3–5.

8. This point is later abandoned by Habermas in his rejection of the German philosophical tradition in general. See *The Philosophical Discourse of Modernity*.

9. The rendering of "Aufhebung" as "abolition" in the translation is a serious mistranslation of this standard Hegelian term.

10. *Knowledge and Human Interests*, p. 9.

11. See ibid., p. 20.

12. For this argument, see our book *Hegel's Circular Epistemology*.

13. The term "philosophy of identity" [Identitätsphilosophie] is often and routinely applied, especially in German-language discussions of philosophy, to designate Schelling's and Hegel's views. Schelling developed a concept of identity in his early writings, especially in his *System of Transcendental Idealism*, which influenced Hegel's own nascent philosophy. Since a major aim of Hegel's entire position was to demonstrate the identity of thought and being, or subject and object, it has become customary to describe his view as a "philosophy of identity," a term which is sometimes, but arguably incorrectly, employed as a synonym for "idealism."

14. See, e.g., the *Encyclopedia of the Philosophical Sciences*, paragraph 1, where Hegel reasserts this traditional view. His claim is not that philosophy substitutes itself for science, but rather that science depends upon philosophy to justify its claims for knowledge.

15. Although Lukács originally argued that Marx in fact proved the unity of subject and object, which Hegel only asserted, he later came to regard this view as an idealist misreading of Marx. See *History and Class Consciousness*, p. xxviii.

16. If we take this warning seriously, it must count against his later concern to substitute a revised form of the concept of the life-world for the concept of social practice in *The Theory of Communicative Action*.

17. See *Knowledge and Human Interests*, p. 29. But this break here with the perspective of philosophical anthropology apparently conflicts with the statement several pages later, where Habermas asserts that before Darwin Marx was already familiar with the instrumental interpretation, on the basis of an anthropological cognition, of transcendental philosophy. See *Knowledge and Human Interests*, p. 41.

18. From this angle of vision one could argue that his discussion of Peirce in chapter 5 of his book is an extension of historical materialism.

19. This argument, which is omnipresent in Marxism, is made forcefully by Lukács. See "Reification and the Consciousness of the Proletariat" in *History and Class Consciousness*.

20. For his most detailed critique of the labor theory of value, see *The Theory of Communicative Action*.

21. This is a main argument of the central essay of Lukács's most important work. See "Reification and the Consciousness of the Proletariat," esp. part 3, "The Antinomies of Bourgeois Thought," in *History and Class Consciousness*, pp. 110–148.

22. See "Class Consciousness" in *History and Class Consciousness*, pp. 46–82.

23. See *Knowledge and Human Interests*, p. 52. For a later restatement of the same point, see p. 281.

24. See *Knowledge and Human Interests*, p. 57. The translator's use of the term "could" seems too weak here. The original passage reads in part as follows: "Marx hätte sich dieses Modells bedienen . . . können." *Erkenntnis und Interesse*, p. 78.

25. See *Knowledge and Human Interests*, p. 58.
26. See ibid., p. 59.
27. See ibid., p. 62.
28. See ibid., p. 63. The translation of "Aufhebung" as "elimination" is an interpretation, not a direct rendering, which hides the meaning of this Hegelian term.
29. For Lukács's well-known comments on Engels's erroneous understanding of the thing-in-itself, see *History and Class Consciousness*, pp. 131–133.
30. See *Knowledge and Human Interests*, pp. 191, 197, 198.
31. See, e.g., Spinoza, *Ethics*, III, proposition 4, and IV, proposition 20, scholium.
32. See *Hegel's Phenomenology of Spirit*, chapter 6, part B, section 3, "Absolute Freedom and Terror," pp. 355–363.
33. The reference both in the translation and in the original to the Weischedel edition of the *Kant Werke* (Darmstadt: Wissenschaftliche Buchgesellschaft, 1975), mistakenly substitutes volume 6 for volume 4, which contains this text.
34. See *Knowledge and Human Interests*, p. 205.
35. See the reference above to the understanding of philosophy as a *conceptus cosmicus*, or *Weltbegriff*, in the *Critique of Pure Reason*, A 840/B 868.
36. See especially the discussion of the fourth antinomy in the *Critique of Pure Reason* and the introductions to the two editions of the *Critique of Judgment*. For a brief discussion of these passages, see Tom Rockmore, *Fichte, Marx and the German Philosophical Tradition* (Carbondale: Southern Illinois University Press, 1980), pp. 135–136.
37. See, e.g., *Fichtes Werke*, I, 244.
38. For some obvious examples from his early writings, see his "Zurückforderung der Denkfreiheit" and "Beitrag zur Berichtigung der Urtheile des Publicums über die französische Revolution," both from 1793, in *Fichtes Werke*, VI.
39. See *Fichtes Werke*, I, pp. 433–434.
40. See e.g., Herbert Marcuse, *Eros and Civilization* (Boston: Beacon Press, 1956).
41. The translator renders this term as "civilization." Freud indicates in another passage, which Habermas also quotes (see *Knowledge and Human Interests*, p. 277), that he does not distinguish between civilization and culture. But it is important to note that he uses both terms in a broad sense which encompasses what for Marxists would fall under the twin headings of superstructure and base.
42. He continues to maintain this view in later writings. See, e.g., *The Theory of Communicative Action*, II, p. 386.
43. See J.G. Herder, *Verstand und Erfahrung. Eine Metakritik zur Kritik der reinen Vernunft*, in *Herders sämtliche Werke*, B.L. Suphan, ed. (Berlin: Weidmann, 1877– 1913), vol. 21. See also *J.B. Hamann, Metakritik über den Purismus der reinen Vernunft*, 1788, reprinted in F. Roth, ed., *Hamann's Schriften* (Berlin: G. Reimer, 1821–1843), vol. 7.

V. The Reconstruction of Historical Materialism

1. According to Habermas, who is less than precise in this regard, the essays printed in the volume are further developments [Ausarbeitungen], apparently revisions of earlier papers, which were written within the last two or three years (see *Zur Rekonstruktion des kommunikativen Handelns*, p. 1). Since the book appeared in 1976, this would place them in the time frame of 1973–1974 until 1976. In fact, the earliest essays, e.g. chapter 2, "Die Rolle der Philosophie im Marxismus" and chapter 10, "Was heißt Krise? Legitimationsprobleme im Spätkapitalismus" date from 1973. For more bibliographical information on the various texts, whose origins are not always clearly identified in this volume, see *Jürgen Habermas: Eine Bibliographe seiner Schriften und der Sekundärliteratur 1952–1981*.
2. See *Communication and Evolution of Society*, pp. 95–96.
3. See ibid., p. 126.

4. See *The German Ideology*, Part I, in *The Marx-Engels Reader*, pp. 151 ff.

5. See *The Theory of Communicative Action*, II, pp. 342–343.

6. Habermas does not undertake this task here. For his later effort to develop a discourse theory of ethics, strongly influenced by K. O. Apel's attempt to revive ethical foundationalism, see his essays "Diskursethik—Notizen zu einem Begründungsprogramm" and "Moralbewußtsein und kommunikatives Handeln," in *Moralbewußtsein und kommunikatives Handeln* (Frankfurt a.M.: Suhrkamp, 1983).

7. See *Communication and the Evolution of Society*, p. 98.

8. See *Rekonstruktion des historischen Materialismus*, p. 9.

9. See *Speech Acts* (London: Cambridge University Press, 1969). The influence of Searle on Habermas' view of communicative action becomes clearer in *The Theory of Communicative Action*. See also his "Entgegnung," esp. Part 2. "Probleme der Beudeutungs- und Handlungstheorie," in *Beiträge zu Jürgen Habermas' "Theorie des kommunikativen Handelns,"* pp. 353–377.

10. See *Communication and Evolution of Society*, p. 98. He has continued to defend variations of this view in later writings. For instance, he has recently repeated his suggestion that social pathology can be understood as distorted communication. See his "Entgegnung," in *Beiträge zu Jürgen Habermas' "Theorie des kommunikativen Handelns,"* p. 342.

11. See *Communication and the Evolution of Society*, p. 117.

12. See Gajo Petrovic, "Philosophie und Sozialismus wieder-Ausnahme einer Diskussion," *Praxis*, nos. 1–2, 1974, pp. 53–69.

13. Habermas himself emphasizes the connection to social psychology in this book in the lengthy discussion of the developmental studies of ego identity carried out by Lawrence Kohlberg. See the essay entitled "Moral Development and Ego Identity" in *Communication and the Evolution of Society*.

14. See *Zur Rekonstruktion des historischen Materialismus*, p. 50.

15. See ibid., p. 50.

16. See ibid., p. 51.

17. Habermas here follows Lukács's well-known view that Hegel's thought is characterized by the concept of totality, or the effort to think the whole. For present purposes, since we have emphasized the Kantian element in Habermas' approach to historical materialism, it is useful to point out that Kant regarded reason, as distinguished from understanding, as a synthetic faculty.

18. Habermas refers to philosophy here as a "Statthalter" (*Zur Rekonstruktion des historischen Materialismus*, p. 57), in the sense of 'there where its place is,' from the German "Statt," which is synonymous with the terms "Stätte" and "Platz," related to the idea of a placeholder, or in German a *Platzhalter*. For a further development of this view of philosophy, see his essay "Die Philosophie als Platzhalter und Interpret," in *Moralbewußtsein und kommunikatives Handeln*, pp. 9–28.

19. It was prepared in order to begin a panel discussion in a session of the Internationale Hegel-Gesellschaft, a leading society of Hegel scholars, which met in 1975 in Stuttgart, West Germany. It is not clear what is to be gained by failing to note the occasional nature of this and other essays in the volume, which is not indicated in the English translation. This omission is especially mystifying since Habermas himself states in the Einleitung to the original German volume that he has not attempted to remove the signs of the occasional status of these essays. See *Zur Rekonstruktion des Historischen Materialismus*, p. 1.

20. See Lawrence Krader, ed. and trans., *The Ethnological Notebooks of Karl Marx* (Assen: Van Gorcum, 1974).

21. See *Communication and the Evolution of Society*, p. 130.

22. See Joseph Stalin, "Dialectical and Historical Materialism," in *Ten Classics of Marxism*.

23. For the relevant passage, see *The Marx-Engels Reader*, p. 75.

24. For this text, see ibid., p. 145.

25. See *Communication and the Evolution of Society*, p. 137.

26. See ibid., p. 140.

27. For an extended argument which rests on Marx's supposed later rejection of the notion of species being as the basic insight for a theory of psychology, see Lucien Sève, *Man In Marxist Theory and the Psychology of Personality* (Atlantic Highlands: Humanities Press, 1978), John McGreal, trans.

28. See *Communication and the Evolution of Society*, p. 142.

29. See ibid., p. 143.

30. See ibid., p. 146.

31. See ibid., p. 148.

32. See ibid., p. 152.

33. See ibid., p. 153.

34. See ibid., p. 160.

35. See ibid., p. 166.

VI. The Rejection of Historical Materialism

1. See our review in *Archives de philosophie*, vol. 46, no. 4, October–December 1983, pp. 668–673. For a detailed, recent study, see Ingram, *Habermas and the Dialectic of Reason*.

2. For discussion of this book, see *Beiträge zu Jürgen Habermas' "Theorie des kommunikativen Handelns."*

3. See *Zur Logik der Sozialwissenschaften*, first published in 1967.

4. For a more recent statement of the same claim to a provisional status for his theory of communicative action, see Habermas "Entgegnung," in *Beiträge zu Jürgen Habermas' "Theorie des kommunikativen Handelns,"* p. 327.

5. This is a dominant theme in *History and Class Consciousness*.

6. See *Habermas: Autonomy and Solidarity*, p. 152.

7. See ibid., pp. 103ff. For a more detailed discussion, which offers an intricate self-interpretation of various facets of the theory of communicative action and an equally complex response to various critics, see Habermas' "Entgegnung," in *Beiträge zu Jürgen Habermas' "Theorie des kommunikativen Handelns,"* pp. 327–405.

8. *The Theory of Communicative Action*, II, pp. 342–343.

9. Ibid., II, p. 367.

10. Ibid., II, pp. 355–356.

11. Lukács argues this view as early as *History and Class Consciousness*, and makes it the basis of his discussion in *The Young Hegel*.

12. For a discussion of Sartre's Marxist phase, see our "Sartre and the 'Philosophy of Our Time'," in *British Journal of Phenomenology and Phenomenological Psychology*, vol. 9, no. 2 (May 1978), pp. 92–101.

13. See F. Engels, "Umrisse zu einer Kritik der Nationalökonomie," in *Marx-Engels Werke* (Berlin: Dietz, 1970), pp. 499–524.

14. See Maurice Merleau-Ponty, *Les Aventures de la dialectique*, chapter 2, "Le Marxisme 'occidental'."

15. See ibid., chapter 1, "La Crise de l'entendement."

16. See ibid., p. 44.

17. See *The Theory of Communicative Action*, II, p. 313.

18. See ibid., II, p. 332.

19. Ibid., II, pp. 333–334.

20. See ibid., II, p. 334.

21. See ibid., II, pp. 338–339.

22. See ibid., II, p. 336.
23. See ibid., II, p. 336.
24. Ibid., II, pp. 338–339.
25. Habermas agrees by implication with Lukács's later realization, which he formulated as the claim that the economic interpretation of social reality is incompatible with the Hegelian concept of totality. See the preface to the second edition, in *History and Class Consciousness*, p. xx.
26. *The Theory of Communicative Action*, II, p. 340.
27. In his early writings, Marx uses such terms as "Entfremdung" or "Entäusserung" and "Vergegenständlichung" to refer respectively to "alienation" and "objectification." For Lukács's admission that he had earlier conflated the two terms of this distinction, see *History and Class Consciousness*, pp. xxiii–xxiv. Since the German terms "Reifikation" and "Verdinglichung" conceal the distinction in question but have no exact equivalent in the English language, it is difficult to know how they should be rendered into English.
28. It has been noted that for Lukács it is precisely this error that attracted many of his students to his work. See Nicolas Tertulian, *Georges Lukács. Etapes de sa pensée esthétique* (Paris: Le Sycamore, 1980).
29. *The Theory of Communicative Action*, II, pp. 342–343.
30. Ibid., II, p. 342.
31. Ibid., II, pp. 342–343.
32. In German the title reads "Exkurs zum Veralten des Produktionsparadigmas." See *Der philosophische Diskurs der Moderne*, pp. 95–103.
33. *The Philosophical Discourse of Modernity*, p. 75.
34. Ibid., p. 76.
35. Ibid., p. 82.
36. Ibid., p. 82.
37. See *Kleine politische Schriften*, IV, p. 527.
38. See ibid., IV, p. 516.
39. See "Reification and the Consciousness of the Proletariat," in *History and Class Consciousness*.
40. See "What is Orthodox Marxism?," in *History and Class Consciousness*.

VII. The Concept of Ideology and the Crisis Theory

1. For a very brief effort at this kind of evaluation, see Kolakowski's remarks on Habermas, in *Main Currents of Marxism*, III, pp. 387–394.
2. See *Habermas: Autonomy and Solidarity*, pp. 151–152.
3. See *Knowledge and Human Interests*, p. 47.
4. See ibid., p. 63.
5. See *History and Class Consciousness*, p. 83.
6. For a recent study of this concept, see Jorge Larrain, *Marxism and Ideology* (Atlantic Highlands: Humanities Press, 1983).
7. See Karl Korsch, *Marxismus und Revolution*, edited and introduced by Erich Gerlach (Frankfurt and Vienna: Europäische Verlagsanstalt and Europa Verlag, 1966), p. 139.
8. This is a central theme in *History and Class Consciousness*. See especially the essays "Class Consciousness" and "Reification and the Consciousness of the Proletariat."
9. See *Theory and Practice*, pp. 236–237.
10. See ibid., pp. 237–238.
11. See *Communication and the Evolution of Society*, p. 143.
12. For instance, in the preface to the *Fundamental Principles of the Metaphysics of Mor-*

als, he revives the distinction in ancient Greek philosophy, identified with Aristotle, of three basic philosophical sciences: physics, ethics, and logic.

13. See, for example, Fichte's *Grundlage der gesamten Wissenschaftslehre* and Hegel's *Wissenschaft der Logik*.

14. This is a central theme in Husserl's thought from his initial phenomenological breakthrough until his final writings. See especially his programmatic treatise, *Philosophie als strenge Wissenschaft*.

15. See, e.g., the *Encyclopedia of the Unified Sciences*.

16. See, e.g., Louis Althusser, *For Marx*, Ben Brewster, trans. (New York: Vintage Books, 1969).

17. The theory of atomic facts depends on a version of the copy theory of knowledge, similar to the Marxist view. See Ludwig Wittgenstein, *Tractatus Logico-Philosophicus*, D.F. Pears and B.F. McGuiness, trans. (London: Routledge and Kegan Paul, 1961).

18. See Karl Marx, *Grundrisse: Foundations of the Critique of Political Economy*, Martin Nicolaus, trans. (Middlesex/Baltimore/Victoria: Penguin, 1973), introduction, part 3: "The Method of Political Economy," pp. 100–108.

19. See, e.g., Klaus Hartmann, *Die Marxsche Theorie. Eine philosophische Untersuchung zu den Hauptschriften* (Berlin: Walter de Gruyter, 1970), pp. 387–393.

20. See *Legitimation Crisis*, Thomas McCarthy, trans. (Boston: Beacon Press, 1975), p. 2, where he writes: "But I do not wish to add to the history of Marxian dogmatics yet another elucidation of his crisis theory. My aim is rather to introduce systematically a social-scientifically useful concept of crisis."

21. *Theory and Practice*, p. 219.

22. Popper, for instance, on whom Habermas seems in part to rely in his introduction of a fallibilistic interpretation of historical materialism, employs the criterion of empirical falsifiability to differentiate philosophy, which is not falsifiable, from science, which is. See his account of the so-called demarcation problem under the heading of "The Demarcation Between Science and Metaphysics," in *Conjectures and Refutations*, pp. 253–292.

23. See, for instance, Louis Althusser and Etienne Balibar, *Lire le Capital* (Paris: Maspéro, 1968), 2 vols.

24. See the preface to *A Critique of Political Economy*, in McLellan, p. 389, where, in a description of his own research, he writes: ". . . the anatomy of civil society is to be sought in political economy."

25. See the first preface to *Capital*, in McLellan, p. 416, where he writes: "In this work I have to examine the capitalist mode of production, and the conditions of production and exchange corresponding to that mode."

26. *Theory and Practice*, p. 222.

27. A rare slip by the translator at this crucial point distorts Habermas' meaning by incorrectly making the crisis theory depend on the notion of ideology, and not conversely. See, for a comparison of the translation and the original, *Theory and Practice*, p. 22, and *Theorie und Praxis*, p. 252.

28. See the article entitled "Economic Crises" in *A Dictionary of Marxist Thought*, pp. 138–143.

29. See Eduard Bernstein, *Evolutionary Socialism* (New York: Schocken Books), 1978.

30. *Theory and Practice*, p. 226.

31. In another context, Bertram Wolfe has observed that Marx argued for the tendency of wages to fall, but ignored contrary empirical evidence. See *Marxism: One Hundred Years in the Life of a Doctrine* (n.p.: Delta, 1967), p. 323, where he writes: "Significantly, though his study of British statistics goes up to 1866, his study of public health reports up to 1865, of the reports of the factory inspectors up to 1866, and every

other such datum is as late as he can make it, Marx has not one word to say on the movement of wages in England after 1850! Indeed, there is no serious study of the movement of real wages at all."

32. Marx makes this point repeatedly. See *Capital: A Critique of Political Economy*, Samuel Moore and Edward Aveling, trans. (New York: International Publishers, 1967), I, p. 39, where he writes: "We see then that that which determines the magnitude of the value of any article is the amount of labour time socially necessary, or the labour-time socially necessary for its production." See also ibid., pp. 40, 71, 80–81.

33. *Theory and Practice*, p. 228.

34. See ibid., p. 231.

35. On the problem of crises of realization, see Klaus Hartmann, *Die Marxsche Theorie. Eine philosophische Untersuchung zu den Hauptschriften,* passim, especially pp. 353–357, and pp. 432–439. Hartmann helpfully distinguishes two Marxian concepts of realization (ibid., p. 355).

36. See *Theory and Practice*, pp. 234–235.

VIII. The Labor Theory of Value and Historical Materialism

1. For a summary of Böhm-Bawerk's critique of Marx's labor theory of value, see Kolakowski, *Main Currents of Marxism*, II, pp. 290–294. For Kolakowski's restatement of similar criticisms, see *Main Currents of Marxism*, I, pp. 325–334.

2. See Rudolf Hilferding, *Böhm-Bawerk's Criticism of Marx*, P. Sweezy, ed. (New York and London: Augustus Kelly and Merlin, 1975).

3. See M.G. Howard and J.E. King, *The Political Economy of Marx* (New York: Longman, 1975), chapter 5. "The Labor Theory of Value," pp. 128–180, esp. p. 166.

4. See Robert L. Heilbroner, *Marxism: For and Against* (New York and London: Norton, 1980), pp. 99–101.

5. See *Theory and Practice*, p. 232.

6. See Capital, I, chapters 6 and 19. For a discussion of this distinction, see "Labor Power," in *A Dictionary of Marxist Thought*, pp. 265–267.

7. According to Kolakowski, who perhaps follows Popper here, Marx's value theory is not a scientific hypothesis in a normal sense since it is not falsifiable. See *Main Currents of Marxism*, I, p. 329.

8. *The Theory of Communicative Action*, II, pp. 333–334.

9. See *The Crisis of European Sciences and Transcendental Phenomenology: An Introduction to Phenomenological Philosophy*, David Carr, trans. (Evanston: Northwestern University Press, 1970), part III A: "The Way into Phenomenological Transcendental Philosophy by Inquiring back from the Pregiven Life-World," paragraphs 28–55, pp. 103–189. For a short discussion of this concept in Husserl's thought, see Herbert Spiegelberg, *The Phenomenological Movement. A Historical Introduction* (The Hague: Martinus Nijhoff, 1982), pp. 144–147. For a series of essays on this theme, see Elisabeth Ströker, *Lebenswelt und Wissenschaft in der Philosophie Edmund Husserls* (Frankfurt a.M.: Vittorio Klostermann, 1979).

10. See David Carr, *Phenomenology and the Problem of History* (Evanston: Northwestern University Press, 1970).

11. See *The Theory of Communicative Action*, II, e.g., pp. 130–131, 138–139, 141, etc.

12. Lukács provides a famous statement on the importance of Marx's theory of the commodity in *History and Class Consciousness*. He writes (p. 83, Lukács's emphasis): "For at this stage in the history of mankind there is no problem that does not ultimately lead back to that question and there is no solution that could not be found in the solution to the riddle of commodity-*structure*."

13. See *Theory of Communicative Action*, II, p. 336.

14. See ibid., II, p. 336.

15. See ibid., II, p. 336.
16. See Julian Huxley, *Soviet och Vetenskapen* (Malmö: Gleerups, 1951).
17. See *The Theory of Communicative Action*, II, pp. 338–339.
18. See V.I. Lénine, *Cahiers sur la dialectique de Hegel*, Henri Lefebvre and Norbert Guterman, trans. (Paris: Gallimard, 1967), p. 241.
19. See *History and Class Consciousness*, passim, especially "What is Orthodox Marxism?," pp. 8, 10, 12, 15, 17, etc.
20. See *The Theory of Communicative Action*, II, pp. 340–341.
21. See Charles Taylor, *Hegel* (Cambridge: Cambridge University Press, 1977), chapter 1, "Aims of a New Epoch," pp. 3–51.
22. For a summary of, and a response to, this argument, see Istvan Mészáros, *Marx's Theory of Alienation* (London: Merlin Books, 1970), chapter 8, "The Controversy about Marx," pp. 217–253, esp. 217–227.
23. See Mészáros, *Marx's Theory of Alienation*, p. 227, and Kolakowski, *Main Currents of Marxism*, I, pp. 261–267.
24. *The Theory of Communicative Action*, II, p. 342.
25. Ibid., II, pp. 342–343.
26. On this point, see Tom Rockmore, *Fichte, Marx and German Philosophy* (Carbondale and London: Southern Illinois University Press, 1980).
27. See, e.g., his early observation that, unlike the Middle Ages, modern man has freed himself from his surroundings. In "Die Kategorien- und Bedeutungslehre des Duns Scotus" in *Martin Heidegger. Frühe Schriften* (Frankfurt: Vittorio Klostermann, 1972), p. 141, he writes: "Es fehlt dem Mittelalter, was gerade einen Wesenszug des modernen Geistes ausmacht: die Befreiung des Subjekts von der Gebundenheit an die Umgebung, die Befestigung im eigenen Leben."
28. On this point, see the discussion of social categories in the general introduction to the *Grundrisse*, part 3: "The Method of Political Economy."
29. See *The Theory of Communicative Action*, II, pp. 342–343.
30. See Kuhn, *The Structure of Scientific Revolutions*.

IX. Theory, Practice, and the Relevance of Reason

1. For a very different, recent analysis of Habermas' recent writing, which sees him, not as moving away from, but rather as returning to Marx, through a new theory of rationality from an esthetic perspective, see Ingram, *Habermas and the Dialectic of Reason*, chapter 11, "The Theory-Practice Problem Revisited." Ingram underplays the Kantian element in Habermas' view of reason. He further fails to appreciate the significance for Habermas' theory of communicative rationality of the critique of Marx since he does not appear to notice the rejection of historical materialism as a result of Habermas' critique of the Marxian value theory.
2. Many discussions touch on this theme but there are few extended treatments of it. See Nicholas Lobkowicz, *Theory and Practice: History of a Concept from Aristotle to Marx* (Notre Dame and London: Notre Dame University Press, 1967).
3. For a good account of the Marxist discussion of praxis in the historical context, see Gajo Petrovic, "Praxis," in *A Dictionary of Marxist Thought*, pp. 384–389.
4. For different analyses of the relation between the idea of the state and political reality, see *Republic*, e.g., bk. III, 414, bk. V, 471, 473; and bk. VII, 540.
5. See *Metaphysics*, I, 2, 982b 26–28.
6. See *Nicomachean Ethics*, I, 3, 1094b 13–15. For an interpretation of the difference between Plato and Aristotle which turns on the disagreement about the precision of ethical knowledge, see Werner Jaeger, *Aristotle: Fundamentals of the History of his Development*, Richard Robinson, trans. (Oxford: Oxford University Press, 1962).
7. *Critique of Pure Reason*, B 867.

8. For an analysis that reconciles these two Hegelian views of the role of reason, see Tom Rockmore, "Hegel und die gesellschaftliche Funktion der Vernunft," *Zur Architektonik der Vernunft. Festschrift für Manfred Buhr* (Berlin: Akademie Verlag, 1987), pp. 205–219.

9. See, e.g., Mihailo Markovic, "Praxis als Grundkategorie der Erkenntnis-theorie," in his book *Dialektik der Praxis* (Frankfurt: Suhrkamp, 1968), pp. 17–41. For an earlier argument that practice is the leading concept in Marx's position, see G. Gentile, *La filosofia della prassi*, 1899, reprinted as *La filosofia di Marx* (Florence: Einaudi, 1974).

10. This is a key concept in the effort to carry further the insights of Marx's position. Lukács, for instance, regards it as the central notion of his own early work on Marxism (see *History and Class Consciousness*, p. xviii), and his last, unfinished study of social being (see *Zur Ontologie des gesellschaftlichen Seins*) can fairly be regarded as new Marxist theory of practice.

11. See Tom Rockmore, "Marxian Praxis," *Philosophy and Social Criticism*, vol. 5, no. 1, January 1978, pp. 3–15.

12. See the second of the "Theses on Feuerbach," in *The Marx-Engels Reader*, p. 144.

13. See *Ludwig Feuerbach and the Outcome of Classical German Philosophy*, p. 22. See also the introduction to the first English edition of *Socialism: Utopian and Scientific*, where he links his notion of the experimental determination of the truth of theory to such disparate ideas as action, the view that the proof of the pudding is in the eating, and Goethe's *Faust*, in *Ten Classics of Marxism*, pp. 15–16.

14. For Lukács's initial critique of Engels's view of practice, see *History and Class Consciousness*, pp. 131–133. For his later comment on this critique, see *History and Class Consciousness*, pp. xix-xx.

15. "Traditional and Critical Theory," in *Critical Theory*, p. 221.

16. For the classical statement of this view, see Heinrich Heine, *Religion and Philosophy in Germany* (Albany: State University of New York Press, 1986), especially part 3, "From Kant to Hegel."

17. See J.G. Droysen, *Grundriß der Historik*, R. Hübner, ed. (Darmstadt, 1974), paragraph 14, p. 330, cited in Herbert Schnädelbach, Eric Matthews, trans., *Philosophy in Germany 1831–1933* (Cambridge: Cambridge University Press, 1984), p. 119.

18. See "Knowledge and Human Interests: A General Perspective," part 4, in *Knowledge and Human Interests*, p. 308.

19. See ibid., p. 308.

20. See Max Horkheimer, "Traditional and Critical Theory," in *Critical Theory*, p. 242.

21. See ibid., p. 242.

22. See *Knowledge and Human Interests*, p. 310.

23. See Kant, "Of the Interest Attaching to the Idea of Morality," in *Fundamental Principles of the Metaphysics of Morals*, pp. 65–70, esp. p. 66.

24. Kant's notion of moral autonomy, for instance, is directed toward a wholly rational and, hence, objective determination of the will by reason. This idea is widespread in his ethical thought. For example, in a passage taken almost at random from this text (p. 30), he writes: "Since the deduction of actions from principles requires reason, the will is nothing but practical reason." Habermas curiously attributes the idea of the identity of reason with the will to reason to Hegel. See *Knowledge and Human Interests*, p. 197.

25. See *The German Ideology*, Part I, in *The Marx-Engels Reader*, p. 150.

26. See *Knowledge and Human Interests*, p. 196.

27. See ibid., p. 313.

28. See ibid., p. 198.

29. See ibid., p. 209.

30. See ibid., p. 210.
31. See ibid., p. 211.
32. See ibid., p. 210.
33. For this view, see "Reification and the Consciousness of the Proletariat," part II: "The Antinomies of Bourgeois Thought," in *History and Class Consciousness*, pp. 110–148.
34. See *Knowledge and Human Interests*, p. 210.
35. See ibid., p. 287.
36. See ibid., p. 289.
37. See ibid., p. 290.
38. See ibid., pp. 298, 299.
39. See ibid., p. 210.
40. See, e.g., ibid., p. 157.
41. See *Critical Theory*, p. 225.
42. This point is based on the apparent logic of Habermas' argument at this point. It is not, however, clear whether he consciously desires to reject the economic approach to social theory as such or whether he merely wants to diminish its importance in order to preserve the possibility of unrepressed communication. For a recent effort to clarify the nature and implications of his dualistic approach, see his "Entgegnung," especially "III. Probleme des zweistufen Konzepts der Gesellschaft: System und Lebenswelt," in *Beiträge zu Jürgen Habermas' "Theorie des kommunikativen Handelns"*, pp. 377–396.
43. See *The Theory of Communicative Action*, II, p. 342.
44. See ibid., II, pp. 342–343.
45. See ibid., II, p. 343.
46. See *Critical Theory*, p. 252.
47. Other thinkers linked to the Frankfurt School have also suggested the traditional view of the relevance of reason to human emancipation. See, for instance, Karl Heinz Haag, who writes, at the close of a recent work on metaphysics, *Der Fortschritt in der Philosophie* (Frankfurt a.M.: Suhrkamp, 1983), p. 201: "Auf ihn, den negativen Schritt ins Metaphysische, kann ein Denken, das kritisch sein möchte, nicht verzichten. [. . .] Dies zu demonstrieren, war das leitende Interesse der Untersuchung über den Fortschritt in der Philosophie. Sie wurde niedergeschrieben in der Überzeugung, daß einzig Aufklärung des Gewesenen eine Zukunft ermöglichen kann, in der freiere Menschen leben."
48. See *The Theory of Communicative Action*, II, p. 383.
49. See ibid., pp. 396–397.
50. More recently, he has implicitly denied this connection in his direct statement, which apparently encompasses Marx, Marxism, and critical social theory, that the philosophy of praxis cannot be reconstructed in satisfactory manner. In his recent "Entgegnung," he writes (*Beiträge*, p. 377): " . . . das leckgeschlagene Schiff der Praxisphilosophie dürfte sich auch mit Ersatzteilen aus dem Trockendock von symbolischem Interaktionismus und Sozialphänomenologie nicht wieder flott machen lassen."
51. See *The Theory of Communicative Action*, II, pp. 374–375.
52. See *Theory and Practice*, p. 243.
53. See Hegel's well-known letter of October 8, 1808 to Niethammer, in J. Hoffmeister, ed., *Briefe von und an Hegel* (Hamburg: Meiner Verlag, 1952–1959), I, p. 253: "Die theoretische Arbeit, überzeuge ich mich täglich mehr, bringt mehr zustande in der Welt als die praktische; ist erst das Reich der Vorstellung revolutioniert, so hält die Wirklichkeit nicht aus."
54. See Michel Henry, *Marx* (Paris: Gallimard, 1976), II, pp. 445.
55. See *The Theory of Communicative Action*, II, pp. 396–397.
56. See ibid., II, p. 383.

INDEX

action: and reason, 165; communicative—*see* theory of communicative action; instrumental, 47, 48, 57, 60, 83, 87, 159, 160; strategic, 47, 87
administration, 141
Adorno, T., 18, 29, 31, 94, 100, 134, 151, 164
alienation, 19, 23, 84, 93, 97, 98, 99, 102, 103, 122, 132, 138, 139, 140, 143
Althusser, L., 118, 129
analytic philosophy of science. *See* philosophy
anthropology, 83
Aquinas, T., 178
Aristotle, 12, 23, 24, 43, 129, 148, 150, 153, 155, 156, 157, 173, 178
art, 80

base, economic (substructure), 100, 115, 119, 120
Bataille, G., 13
Bell, D., 79
Berger, P., 109
Bernstein, E., 124
Bernstein, R., 13
Bewußtseinsphilosophie. See philosophy of consciousness
biology, 158
Boethius, 178
Böhm-Bawerk, E., 129
Böhme, J., 26
Brunkhorst, H., 136

capital, 76, 101, 123, 126, 128, 136, 142, 165
capitalism, 36, 72, 77, 80, 83, 87, 102, 104, 116, 120, 122, 123, 124, 125, 127, 132, 135, 141, 143, 144, 145, 149, 164, 165, 166, 172, 178
class consciousness, 29, 30, 37, 97, 99, 165
cogito, 26, 175
commodity, 129, 132, 139; and commodity analysis, 113, 114, 136, 163; fetishism, 114
communication, 46, 91, 141, 142; distorted, 66; non-repressive, 44; theory—*see* theory of communicative action
communicative action, theory of. *See* interaction
communism, 166, 172, 178
Comte, A., 61
conatus, 62
conceptus cosmicus, Kant's, 39, 149
consensus, 43, 87
crisis complex, 120

critical philosophy. *See* philosophy
critical theory of society, vii, x, 18, 22, 39, 40, 41, 42, 94, 95, 100, 107, 108, 151, 152, 153, 154, 155, 156, 158, 159, 160, 162, 165, 166, 167, 169, 170, 174, 175, 177; and traditional theory, criticism, 51, 153, 162, 164, 169, 173, 174, 175, 176
criticism, 88
critique, 28, 34, 35, 37, 38, 50, 58, 59, 61, 69, 78, 81, 83, 86, 93, 104, 111, 113, 114, 116, 120, 121, 124, 128, 130, 133, 157, 166, 176
critique of ideology. *See* ideology
culture, 75

Derrida, J., 13
Descartes, R., 142, 150; "Discourses on Method," 151
Dewey, J., 54
Dialectic of the Enlightenment, 94
dialectical materialism. *See* materialism
dialogue, 43, 44, 45, 48, 49, 153, 154
Dilthey, W., 40, 61, 155, 163
dogmatism, 64, 159
Droysen, J. G., 155
dualism, 165

economic crisis, theory of. *See* theory
economics. *See* political economy
Eder, K., 87
emancipation, human, 58, 64, 109, 150, 152, 155, 156, 157, 158, 159, 160, 161, 164, 165, 166
emancipatory interest. *See* interest
empirically falsifiable philosophy of history, 72
energeia, Aristotle's theory of, 141
Engels, F., 6, 7, 9, 10, 12, 21, 23, 29, 34, 36, 61, 77, 80, 83, 99, 117, 118, 121, 147, 149, 150, 169, 170
Enlightenment, 43, 63, 166
epistemology. *See* theory of knowledge
ethics, communicative, 109
existentialism, 5, 22, 28, 71, 78, 92, 99
expressivism, 135

fallibilism, 33
false consciousness, 79, 101, 115
Feuerbach, L., 83
Fichte, J. G., 9, 46, 50, 55, 56, 57, 58, 59, 61, 62, 63, 64, 65, 68, 117, 141, 158, 159, 160, 161, 162, 167, 176; "First and Second Intro-

practice [Praxis]. *See* philosophy
pre-Socratics, 8
profit, 124, 125, 127, 130, 131; law of the falling rate of, 124, 125, 126, 130
proletariat, 30, 107, 167
psychoanalysis, Freudian, 65, 66, 67, 153, 156, 159

rationality, 94, 95, 96
rationalization, 100, 103, 108
reason, 43, 61, 62, 63, 64, 66, 68, 82, 107, 108, 149, 152, 158, 159, 161, 162, 166, 173, 174, 176, 177; critique of, 94, 95, 96; practical, 28, 43, 52, 63, 64, 81, 156, 161; relevance of, xi, xii, 40, 153, 158, 159, 169, 171, 174, 177, 178
reflection, 57, 62, 67, 81, 92, 108, 114, 117, 156, 158, 162; reflection theory of knowledge, 118
reification [Reifikation]. *See* alienation
religion, 80, 81
revolution, 57, 102, 116, 164, 172
Ricardo, D., 129

Saint-Simon, P. H., 58
Sartre, J.-P., 5, 20, 25, 26, 30, 53, 72, 75, 77, 88, 92, 98, 108, 170, 178; *Being and Nothingness,* 27; *Critique of Dialectical Reason,* 25, 98; "Marxism and Revolution," 26, 98; *Search for a Method,* 97; "Transcendence of the Ego," 26
Schelling, F. W. J., 9, 26, 36, 37, 176
Schutz [Schütz], A., 101, 133
science, 1, 33, 38, 40, 41, 42, 44, 45, 50, 51, 52, 57, 60, 61, 62, 66, 67, 68, 69, 70, 74, 75, 77, 78, 80, 81, 117, 121, 136, 144, 148, 151, 152, 155; classification as empirical-analytic science, 40, 41; classification as historical-hermeneutic science, 40, 41, 44, 67; cultural—*see* social science; natural science, 7, 33, 40, 58, 62, 67, 73, 75, 114, 121, 171; of man, 60, 114, 117; social, 2, 7, 30, 40, 57, 62, 72, 75, 79, 92, 121, 166
scientism, 67, 79, 81, 117, 118
Searle, J., 75
self-reflection, theory of, 42, 51, 52, 55, 62, 64, 65, 68, 74, 79, 81, 82, 156, 157, 158, 159, 160, 161, 162, 166
Smith, A., 129
social labor. *See* work
social theory. *See* theory
socialism, democratic, 124, 127, 131, 155
Socrates, 43, 44
species being, 83
speech act theory. *See* theory
Spengler, O., 10
Spinoza, B., 62
Stahl, 14
Stalin, J., 84, 89, 136
Stegmüller, W., 4

Stoics, 178
structuralism, 88
structure of modern philosophy. *See* philosophy
subject philosophy (philosophy of consciousness). *See* philosophy
superstructure, 74, 75, 76, 119; and base, relation of, 37, 75, 101, 105, 106, 128, 135, 137, 144, 145, 146; theorem [Überbautheorem], 86, 101, 106, 112, 113, 115, 117, 119, 128
surplus value, theory of. *See* theory
system, 94, 100, 102, 137, 144; administrative, 105

Taylor, C., 137
technology, 80, 155
theory, 45; action, 94; and practice, xi, 24, 29, 30, 39, 42, 45, 64, 113, 147, 148, 149, 150, 151, 152, 153, 154, 157, 158, 159, 160, 161, 162, 163, 165, 166, 167, 169, 170, 171, 172, 175, 176, 277, 278; of communication, 5, 85; of communicative action, vii, viii, xi, 14, 16, 24, 26, 32, 37, 48, 49, 58, 59, 60, 72, 86, 87, 89, 91, 92, 93, 95, 97, 100, 105, 108, 109, 110, 114, 116, 123, 133, 141, 147, 160, 165, 166, 167, 168, 169, 172, 173, 176, 177; crisis, 34, 35, 36, 76, 110, 113, 118, 120, 121, 122, 123, 124, 125, 126, 127, 128, 130, 131, 133; of realization, 126, 130, 131; of the evolution of society, 25; of history (old), 33, 84; of knowledge (epistemology), 41, 50, 51, 52, 54, 55, 56, 61, 67, 68, 70, 78, 92, 93, 116, 117, 118, 142, 152, 158, 171, 174, 175; of revolution, 83, 166; of surplus value, labor theory, 34, 35, 36, 58, 74, 91, 99, 100, 101, 103, 105, 110, 112, 113, 114, 115, 121, 122, 123, 124, 125, 127, 128, 129, 130, 131, 132, 133, 134, 135, 136, 137, 138, 139, 140, 141, 143, 144, 146, 147, 163; of theory reconstruction, x, 1, 2, 3, 4, 5, 6, 8, 10, 12, 13, 19, 39, 44, 50, 72, 73, 81, 83, 85, 87, 89, 95, 97, 99, 105, 111, 114, 125, 131, 132, 135, 146; of theory replacement, 1, 2, 3, 4, 13, 15, 16, 17, 98; rejection of Marxist view of, 19, 110; renaissance of, 5, 6, 8, 9, 10, 12; restoration of, 5, 6, 8, 9; social, xi, 34, 45, 48, 50, 52, 60, 73, 76, 78, 93, 94, 95, 103, 104, 107, 112, 134, 135, 136, 141, 142, 144, 148, 155, 166, 167, 169, 170, 172, 174, 175, 176, 177; speech act, 76, 77
theory and practice. *See* theory
theory of reconstruction. *See* theory
thing-in-itself, 11, 145, 150
thought and being, relation of, 3, 118
Torricelli, E., 14
totality, concept of, 138
transcendental unity of apperception, 55, 175

Ursprungsphilosophie. See foundationalism